BACH PERSPECTIVES

VOLUME II

J. S. Bach and His Sons

BACH PERSPECTIVES

VOLUME II

J. S. Bach and His Sons

Edited by
Mary Oleskiewicz

UNIVERSITY OF ILLINOIS PRESS
Urbana, Chicago, and Springfield

Library of Congress Control Number: 2017952814
ISBN 978-0-252-04148-8 (hardcover)
ISBN 978-0-252-05008-4 (e-book)

CONTENTS

PREFACE

This volume of *Bach Perspectives* presents five essays that investigate topics surrounding Johann Sebastian Bach and his five most musically gifted sons arising from two marriages. The diverse subjects treated here are approached by each author with distinctive and, in a few cases, alternative or interdisciplinary methodologies. Several broad topics recur throughout the volume, including organology, performance practice, the (un)reliability of anecdotal evidence, and recent musical discoveries that provide new perspectives on older themes.

Robert Marshall, whose essay opens the volume, takes on a deeply psychological perspective by examining how Wilhelm Friedemann, Carl Philipp Emanuel, Johann Gottfried Bernhard, Johann Christoph Friedrich, and the youngest, Johann Christian—who, in "killing Sebastian," went even further than the rest of his siblings by rejecting his father's very religion—personally dealt with Sebastian's imposing legacy and succeeded in creating a style of their own. Marshall questions previous literature's failure to address (or, rather, its propensity to ignore) certain, sometimes troubling, aspects of Sebastian's relationships with his sons.

My essay investigates the Bach family's connections to historical keyboard instruments and musical venues at the Prussian court. It continues an avenue of inquiry previously begun in two essays by John Koster and myself in an earlier volume of *Bach Perspectives*.[1] Whereas Koster explored the keyboard culture surrounding Sebastian Bach more generally, I had considered specific musical implications of Gottfried Silbermann pianos at Frederick's court. The present essay identifies the location, size, and characteristics of the many palace music rooms where Bach and his sons would have performed for the king and members of the immediate royal family and provides details of each of the keyboard instruments these rooms contained. By examining surviving, lost, and recently rediscovered instruments and previously overlooked documents, I have been able to solve long-standing puzzles concerning the placement and number of Silbermann pianos, Shudi harpsichords, and other keyboards at court; to connect several compositions by members of the Bach family to specific rooms and instruments; and to correct a variety of misunderstandings in previous literature.

---

1. John Koster, "The Harpsichord Culture in Bach's Environs," in *Bach Perspectives 4: The Music of J. S. Bach: Analysis and Interpretation*, ed. David Schulenberg (Lincoln: University of Nebraska Press, 1999), 57–77; and Mary Oleskiewicz, "The Trio in Bach's Musical Offering: A Salute to Frederick's Tastes and Quantz's Flutes?," in ibid., 79–110.

In the next chapter, David Schulenberg argues that Emanuel Bach's most significant contribution to European music is the large and diverse body of keyboard music he composed for harpsichord, fortepiano, organ, and his favorite instrument, the clavichord. Schulenberg shows that the hundreds of works Emanuel wrote over his long life continually introduced new idioms into the repertoire, and, like Beethoven after him, Emanuel also "pushed the envelope" of what the currently available instruments could do. Although these innovative works could not all have been conceived for a single type of instrument, Emanuel rarely assigned a particular variety of keyboard to a given composition. Schulenberg thus draws important connections between the organological features of the instruments of the time and specific works of the composer.

Evan Cortens's essay takes a detailed view of Emanuel Bach's singers, vocal performance materials, and pay records in Hamburg. Cortens concludes that, as in most other parts of Germany of the time, one singer per part was the norm for Emanuel's performances of liturgical music after 1767.

Finally, Christine Blanken's essay continues research into Breitkopf publishing firm, the subject of another early volume of *Bach Perspectives*.[2] Her surprising discovery of a "forgotten box" containing unknown musical manuscripts by several members of the Bach family demonstrates once again that sometimes what we are looking for might lie right under our noses and that persistence pays off. Her examination here of a number of previously unknown musical manuscripts from the Breitkopf archive, including works by Sebastian Bach, Wilhelm Friedemann, Carl Philipp Emanuel, and Johann Christian, expands upon her previous work on this topic and demonstrates how much there is still to learn about eighteenth-century musical transmission, performance practice, and concert life in Bach's Leipzig.

Mary Oleskiewicz, editor, Boston, October 2016

2. *Bach Perspectives 2: J. S. Bach, the Breitkopfs, and Eighteenth-Century Music Trade*, ed. George B. Stauffer (Lincoln: University of Nebraska Press, 1996).

ABBREVIATIONS

A-BNba	Beethoven-Haus, Forschungszentrum Beethoven-Archiv.
A-Wgm	Gesellschaft der Musikfreunde in Wien, Archiv.
BDOK	*Bach Dokumente*. Edited by Andreas Glöckner, Anselm Hartinger, Karen Lehmann, Michael Maul, Werner Neumann, Hans-Joachim Schulze, and Christoph Wolff. 7 vols. Kassel: Bärenreiter; Leipzig: VEB Deutscher Verlag für Musik, 1953–2008.
BG	*Bach-Gesellschaft Ausgabe*. Johann Sebastian Bach's complete works. Edited by the Bach-Gesellschaft. 47 vols. Leipzig: Breitkopf & Härtel, 1851–99, 1926.
BJ	*Bach-Jahrbuch*.
BPH	Brandenburg-Preußisches Hausarchiv.
BR-JCFB	*Bach Repertorium*, vol. 4. *Johann Christoph Friedrich: Thematisch-systematisches Verzeichnis der musikalischen Werke*. Edited by Ulrich Leisinger. Stuttgart: Carus-Verlag, 2013.
BR-WFB	Bach Repertorium, vol. 2. *Wilhelm Friedemann Bach: Thematisch-systematisches Verzeichnis der musikalischen Werke*. Edited by Peter Wollny. Stuttgart: Carus-Verlag, 2012.
BWV	[Bach-Werke-Verzeichnis] *Thematisch-systematisches Verzeichnis der musikalischen Werke von Johann Sebastian Bach (Bach-Werke-Verzeichnis)*. Revised edition. Edited by Wolfgang Schmieder. Wiesbaden: Breitkopf & Härtel, 1990.
CPEB:B	Ernst Suchalla, ed. *Carl Philipp Emanuel Bach: Briefe und Dokumente: Kritische Gesamtausgabe*, 2 vols. Göttingen: Vandenhoek & Ruprecht, 1994.
CPEB:CW	*Carl Philipp Emanuel Bach: The Complete Works*. Los Altos, CA: Packard Humanities Institute, 2005–.
D-B	Staatsbibliothek zu Berlin / Preußischer Kulturbesitz and its predecessor institutions.
D-Bsa	Staatsbibliothek zu Berlin, Collection of the Berlin Sing-Akademie.
D-Hs	Staats- und Universitätsbibliothek Hamburg Carl von Ossietzky, Musiksammlung.
D-Hsa	Hamburg Senatsarchiv, now located within the Hamburg Staatsarchiv (D-Ha).
D-LEm	Leipziger Stadtbibliothek—Musikbibliothek, Leipzig.
D-LEsta	Sächsisches Staatsarchiv—Staatsarchiv Leipzig.

Fk   Martin Falck. *Wilhelm Friedemann Bach: Sein Leben und seine Werke, mit thematischem Verzeichnis seiner Kompositionen und zwei Bildern.* Leipzig: C. F. Kahnt, 1913.

GraunWV   [Graun-Werke-Verzeichnis] Christoph Henzel. *Graun-Werkverzeichnis (GraunWV): Verzeichnis der Werke der Brüder Johann Gottlieb und Carl Heinrich Graun.* 2 vols. Beeskow: Ortus Musikverlag, 2006.

GStA PK   Geheimes Staatsarchiv Preußischer Kulturbesitz.

H   Eugene E. Helm. *Thematic Catalogue of the Works of Carl Philipp Emanuel Bach.* New Haven, CT: Yale University Press, 1989.

HWV   [Händel-Werke-Verzeichnis] Bernd Baselt, ed. *Händel-Handbuch: Thematisch-systematisches Verzeichnis der musikalischen Werke von Georg Friedrich Händel*, Händel-Handbuch of the Hallische Händel-Ausgabe, 4 vols. Kassel: Bärenreiter, 1978–86.

KB   Kritischer Bericht (critical report) of the NBA.

NBA   [Neue Bach-Ausgabe] *Johann Sebastian Bach: Neue Ausgabe sämtlicher Werke.* Edited by the Johann-Sebastian-Bach-Institut, Göttingen, and the Bach-Archiv, Leipzig. Kassel: Bärenreiter; Leipzig: Deutscher Verlag für Musik, 1954–2010.

NBR   *The New Bach Reader: A Life of Johann Sebastian Bach in Letters and Documents.* Edited by Hans T. David and Arthur Mendel. Revised and enlarged by Christoph Wolff. New York: W. W. Norton, 1998.

PL-Kj   Biblioteka Jagiellońska, Krakow.

QV   [Quantz-Verzeichnis.] Horst Augsbach. *Thematisch-systematisches Werkverzeichnis (QV).* Stuttgart: Carus, 1997.

RISM   *Répertoire International des Sources Musicales* (International Inventory of Musical Sources). Kassel: Bärenreiter; Munich: G. Henle, 1960–.

SPSG   Stiftung Preußische Schlösser und Gärten.

S-Skma   Statens Musiksamlingar, Kungliga Musikaliska Akademiens Biblioteket, Stockholm.

US-NHub   Beinecke Rare Book and Manuscript Library, New Haven, CT.

Warb   Ernest Warburton, ed. *The Collected Works of Johann Christian Bach, 1735–1782*, vol. 48, pt. 1, thematic catalog. New York: Garland, 1999.

Wq   Alfred Wotquenne. *Thematisches Verzeichnis der Werke von Carl Philipp Emanuel Bach.* 2nd edition. Leipzig: Breitkopf & Härtel, 1905.

Father and Sons

Confronting a Uniquely Daunting Paternal Legacy

Robert L. Marshall

FOR RICHARD KRAMER

In his provocative essay "Carl Philipp Emanuel Bach and the Aesthetics of Patricide," Richard Kramer remarks that "everywhere, Emanuel felt the need to speak of his father. In his music, he fails to do so. The patrimony is not acknowledged there."[1] Kramer demonstrates this in a perceptive analysis of one of Emanuel's challenging keyboard compositions, the Sonata in C Major, Wq 65/47 (1775).

Coping with their patrimony could not have been a picnic for the male offspring of Johann Sebastian Bach. The towering shadow cast by J. S. Bach on the lives, careers, and ambitions of all five of his sons was undoubtedly overwhelming.[2] Kramer's comment invites us to ponder the various tactics and strategies these uniquely privileged—and uniquely challenged—offspring developed to come to terms with that intimidating legacy. He has also offered an intriguing way to assess and understand the meaning of the careers of the Bach sons, namely, by determining the degree to which—and the manner in which—they succeeded in emerging from their father's shadow. Much

---

1. Richard Kramer, "Carl Philipp Emanuel Bach and the Aesthetics of Patricide," in *Historical Musicology: Sources, Methods, Interpretations*, ed. Stephen A. Crist and Roberta Montemorra Marvin (Rochester, NY: University of Rochester Press, 2004), 121–42 (esp. 128), reprinted in Kramer, *Unfinished Music* (New York: Oxford University Press, 2008), 25–46 (esp. 37).

2. This essay will consider, in turn, Wilhelm Friedemann (1710–84), Carl Philipp Emanuel (1714–88), Johann Gottfried Bernhard (1715–39), Johann Christoph Friedrich (1732–95), and Johann Christian (1735–82). Johann Christoph Friedrich and, especially, Johann Gottfried Bernhard have often been ignored in discussions of the Bach sons—a practice, as we shall see, that had already begun in the eighteenth century.

I am indebted to Mary Oleskiewicz for her valuable suggestions during the preparation of this essay. The translations from historic J. S. Bach sources, unless otherwise noted, are those published in *The New Bach Reader: A Life of Johann Sebastian Bach in Letters and Documents*, ed. Hans T. David and Arthur Mendel, revised and enlarged by Christoph Wolff (New York: W. W. Norton, 1998), cited throughout as NBR.

of what follows will be conjectural, but very little is not conjectural in historical or biographical writing concerned with comprehending the meaning of events centuries old. On the other hand, much of it will be a matter of reasonably "connecting the dots," that is, the documented facts, that we may have become overly reluctant to connect or account for in rather obvious ways.

Bach and His Sons

According to at least one eighteenth-century author, there was an abundance of mutual disdain between Johann Sebastian Bach and his musical sons. Carl Friedrich Cramer (1752–1807), the editor of the important *Magazin der Musik*, personally knew both Philipp Emanuel and Friedemann.[3] In his autobiography, written in 1792–93, Cramer mentions that "the old Sebastian had three sons. He was satisfied only with Friedemann, the great organist. Even about Carl Philipp Emanuel he said (unjustly!): ''Tis Berlin blue! It fades easily!'—Regarding the London Chrétien, [Sebastian] Bach was wont to cite the verse by Gellert: 'The boy is sure to thrive owing to his stupidity!' In fact, among the three Bach sons this one had the greatest success.—I have these opinions from Friedemann himself."[4] Cramer goes on to report that Sebastian "rejoiced over his son Friedemann with whom the organ died out, so to speak. 'This is my beloved son,' he used to say, 'who pleases me well.'"[5] This is clearly a paraphrase of Luke 3:22, which describes the heavenly voice that was heard at the baptism of Jesus: "Thou art my beloved Son; in thee I am well pleased" (King James version). What should be made of the fact that Johann Sebastian Bach here cites the Bible in such a way that he compares himself to God the Father and Friedemann to Jesus? Is this blasphemy, or is it self-deprecating, ironic humor?

All these remarks are rather flattering to Friedemann, so it is no surprise to learn that he, and not Emanuel, was Cramer's source for these self-serving comments. But there is a problem with many, if not all, of these quotations from Cramer: Wilhelm Friedemann Bach, as we shall see shortly, was a liar!

Wilhelm Friedemann Bach (1710–1784)

The great mystery in the life of Friedemann—Sebastian's oldest son and allegedly his favorite—is this: Why did he fail so miserably? As David Schulenberg remarks at the

---

3. Carl Friedrich Cramer, *Magazin der Musik* (Hamburg: Musicalische Niederlage, 1783–89).

4. Carl Friedrich Cramer, *Menschliches Leben: Gerechtigkeit und Gleichheit*, no. 8 (achtes Stück) (Altona: Kavenschen Buchhandlung, 1792), 159n, cited in BDOK 3:518, no. 973. English translation in NBR, 413, modified by the present author. In a private communication, Hans-Joachim Schulze has kindly provided me with additional bibliographical information pertaining to this source.

5. Cramer, *Menschliches Leben*, no. 13 (dreizehntes Stück) (Altona: Kavenschen Buchhandlung, 1793), 755, cited in BDOK 3:519, no. 973.

beginning of his indispensable study of Friedemann's music, he was "a brilliant disappointment or underachiever"; "he enjoyed early success but, *for unknown reasons*, quit a respectable position as organist during his middle years."[6] Schulenberg has no hesitation in dismissing the "unfortunate . . . facile but largely groundless psychologizing" that "continues to color present-day views of the composer and his music," insisting that "psychological speculation can lead *only* to *doubtful* presumptions and hypotheses."[7] Are *plausible* presumptions and hypotheses so unimaginable that they should not even be sought? Must repeated observations of, say, manifestly self-destructive behavior be merely inventoried, with no further attempts at understanding?

As is well known, Friedemann's life poses an array of intriguing questions. Here are a few of them: Why, in 1762, did he turn down a magnificent job offered to him on the proverbial silver platter, namely, that of *Kapellmeister* in Darmstadt? Why did he throw away his job in Halle just two years thereafter at a time when he had no other job prospects, only to linger there unemployed for another seven years? Why, in the late 1770s, did he destroy his chances in Berlin by clumsily intriguing against Johann Philipp Kirnberger (1721–83) at court?[8] Kirnberger, a devoted student and champion of Johann Sebastian Bach's, had been eager to help Friedemann in his dire circumstances. Is it unreasonable to see in Friedemann's conspiring against a fellow student of his father's and attempting to replace him in the favor of Princess Anna Amalia as some form of sibling rivalry? According to Kirnberger, even Philipp Emanuel—at least around 1779—distanced himself from Friedemann: "And his brother in Hamburg also will have nothing to do with him."[9]

Kirnberger was one of the great collectors and preservers of Sebastian Bach's musical legacy and did more than almost anyone else, next to Philipp Emanuel, to promulgate Johann Sebastian Bach's aesthetic and compositional principles and teaching method. Friedemann, on the other hand, was one of the great squanderers and losers of his father's musical legacy. Actually, within fewer than ten years of Sebastian's death, his favorite son had begun selling off the master's music manuscripts. This activity had started not, as is commonly thought, in the mid-1770s, when he was thoroughly des-

6. David Schulenberg, *The Music of Wilhelm Friedemann Bach* (Rochester, NY: University of Rochester Press, 2010), 3, x (emphasis added).

7. Ibid., 3, 5 (emphasis added).

8. For Friedemann's intrigue against Kirnberger, see Martin Falck, *Wilhelm Friedemann Bach: Sein Leben und seine Werke, mit thematischem Verzeichnis seiner Kompositionen* (Leipzig: C. F. Kahnt Nachfolger, 1913), 52–53.

9. "Und sein Herr Bruder in Hamburg will auch von ihm nichts wissen." Martin Geck, *Die Bach-Söhne* (Hamburg: Rowohlt Taschenbuch Verlag, 2003), 25, citing Carl Hermann Bitter, *Carl Philipp Emanuel und Wilhelm Friedemann Bach und deren Brüder* (Berlin: Wilhelm Müller, 1868; reprint, Leipzig: Zentralantiquariat der Deutschen Demokratischen Republik, 1973), 2:323.

perate and indigent, but well before, during his Halle years, admittedly also a period of great financial difficulty.[10]

Long before that, in 1733, Sebastian had helped Friedemann—arguably, to an unseemly degree—get his first job as organist at the Sophienkirche in Dresden. Sebastian ghost-wrote the job application in his son's name (two applications, actually) and even forged Friedemann's signature on them.[11] Could not Friedemann, at the age of twenty-three, compose his own job application letters? It is also almost certain that at his audition Friedemann played one of his father's masterpieces: the great G Major Prelude and Fugue, BWV 541.[12] Whether this fact was made known to the audition committee or whether Friedemann played BWV 541 in addition to, or instead of, compositions of his own is unknown.

It is known that Friedemann falsely claimed to have authored his father's organ transcription of Vivaldi's Concerto in D Minor, BWV 596. The claim is written on his father's autograph manuscript, a document penned when Friedemann was around five years old.[13] Martin Geck suggests that we must not judge Friedemann too harshly for this, remarking that collaborative work among Bach family members was common. Geck advises us rather "to leave the whole matter in semi-darkness."[14] This, surely, is an example of what could be called "Friedemann apologetics." Recent scholarship has attempted to rehabilitate Wilhelm Friedemann Bach's reputation by dismissing not only nineteenth-century fictionalized depictions of his life and character (epitomized by unfounded claims that he was an alcoholic) but even eighteenth-century and contemporary accounts as romanticized fantasies and exaggerations. The pendulum of the undeniably necessary corrective when considering Friedemann's life and character

10. See Peter Wollny, "Studies in the Music of Wilhelm Friedemann Bach: Sources and Style" (Ph.D. diss., Harvard University, 1993), 18–19, regarding Friedemann's sale of J. S. Bach autographs of chorale cantatas between 1759 and 1762 to Johann Georg Nacke, presumably owing to the hardships of the Seven Years' War.

11. The documents are transcribed in BDOK 1:71–74, nos. 25–26.

12. J. S. Bach's autograph of the work, written on the same paper used for the letters of application he penned in Friedemann's name for the Dresden position, was in Friedemann's possession. See Hans-Joachim Schulze, *Studien zur Bach-Überlieferung im 18. Jahrhundert* (Leipzig: Peters, 1984), 17.

13. The manuscript is preserved as D-B, Mus. ms. Bach P 330. At the top of the first page of the score, following the work heading (in J. S. Bach's hand), Friedemann wrote: "di W. F. Bach / manu mei Patris / descript" (by W. F. Bach, written in the hand of my father). See NBA IV/8, *Kritischer Bericht* (Karl Heller), 23. The manuscript dates from J. S. Bach's later Weimar period, ca. 1714–17. See Georg von Dadelsen, *Beiträge zur Chronologie der Werke Johann Sebastian Bachs*, Tübinger Bach-Studien, 4/5 (Trossingen: Hohner-Verlag, 1958), 79; and Schulze, *Studien*, 157–61.

14. "lässt man die ganze Angelegenheit besser in jenem Halbdunkel." Geck, *Die Bach-Söhne*, 26.

has, perhaps, in the present emphatically nonjudgmental age, swung too far in the opposite direction.

A remarkable document dating from the mid-1730s helps illuminate the relationship between Sebastian and Friedemann. In it we literally observe Bach and his son collaboratively, or perhaps competitively, working out problems in double and triple counterpoint, augmentation, diminution, inversion, and so on. With some embarrassment we witness Friedemann struggling with—and Sebastian completing with effortless insouciance—these tricky exercises in sixteenth-century style (Example 1). It seems that Sebastian "treated" Friedemann to this diversion (rather than, say, taking out a deck of cards) when the elder Bach went to Dresden for a visit around 1736 or so.[15] We can imagine how enjoyable Friedemann might (or might not) have found this friendly contest of musical wits. Was Sebastian at all aware of Friedemann's certain humiliation, or was he simply clueless?

The Darmstadt episode alluded to earlier is quite perplexing. In 1746, after thirteen years in Dresden, Friedemann resigned his position in order to take a better one: that of organist and director of church music at the Liebfrauenkirche in Halle. In 1762, following the death of the Darmstadt court's long-serving *Kapellmeister*, Christoph Graupner, Friedemann received a firm offer to replace him. Apparently, as was the case in Halle, the Darmstadt position, too, was offered to Friedemann on the basis of no known audition. This position was better than the respectable Halle job Friedemann had been occupying, increasingly unhappily, since 1746. It was so desirable, in fact, that in 1723 Graupner had turned down the Leipzig Thomas Cantorate in order to remain in Darmstadt. Graupner had been persuaded to stay by a counteroffer from his patron, Count Ernst Ludwig, that he evidently couldn't resist.[16] Only thereafter was the Leipzig position offered to, and of course accepted by, J. S. Bach.

Friedemann dragged out the negotiations with Darmstadt for so long that the offer was eventually withdrawn. (This did not prevent him, however, from describing himself some years later, in 1767, as "the recently appointed *Kapellmeister* to the landgrave of Hesse-Darmstadt."[17] A doctrinaire Freudian—if any still exist—might suggest that Friedemann let the job slip through his fingers because he could not allow himself to exceed his father. It is as if Friedemann had been determined to commit career suicide,

15. Peter Wollny, "Ein Quellenfund in Kiew: Unbekannte Kontrapunktstudien von Johann Sebastian und Wilhelm Friedemann Bach," in *Bach in Leipzig—Bach und Leipzig: Konferenzbericht Leipzig 2000*, ed. Ulrich Leisinger (Hildesheim: Georg Olms Verlag, 2000), 275–87.

16. The details are provided by Bernhard Friedrich Richter, "Die Wahl Joh. Seb. Bachs zum Kantor der Thomasschule i[m] J[ahr] 1723," BJ 2 (1905): 48–67 (esp. 54–55).

17. "Dem Landgrafen zu Hessen-Darmstadt ohnlängst berufener Capell Meister." Falck, *Wilhelm Friedemann Bach*, 44.

Ex. 1a. W. F. Bach, exercise in counterpoint (Dresden, ca. 1736–39).

Ex. 1b. J. S. Bach, exercise in counterpoint (Dresden, ca. 1736–39).

thus dashing his father's high expectations of him. But is such self-inflicted failure on the part of a formidably talented child not merely a self-destructive act but also an act of spite, or retribution, against a parent for some perceived wrong or injury?

The Darmstadt incident, in any event, marked the turning point in Friedemann's fortunes. Two years later, in 1764, he suddenly resigned his job in Halle. No precipitating cause or dispute is known. Friedemann evidently had inherited his father's temper and temperament but not his survival instinct. Friedemann apparently stayed on in Halle with no official or visible employment other than taking on private pupils. Perhaps, as has been surmised, he may, like the legendary Flying Dutchman, have journeyed for some seven years as a traveling virtuoso to places like Vienna, Russia, and the Baltic states, until, in 1770 or 1771, he showed up in Braunschweig as a freelance organist.[18]

In the end, Friedemann entered upon a wandering life, supporting himself by selling his wife's property, giving organ recitals, teaching, and selling (or trying to sell or at least rent out) his father's music manuscripts. In doing the latter, was he perhaps symbolically erasing his father's legacy (or at least casting off his own personal connection with it) while at the same time attempting to insure that Sebastian—his formidable father—materially continued to support him?

It is not easy to avoid entertaining Freudian notions when pondering Wilhelm Friedemann Bach. Martin Geck, who, as we have seen, was something of an apologist for Friedemann, concludes his discussion of Friedemann's tragic existence by introducing a famous Freudian term: Geck wonders whether perhaps "the father may have cast his eyes all too insistently on [Friedemann]—not only during [the father's] lifetime

18. Peter Wollny, "'. . . welche dem größten Concerte gleichen': The Polonaises of Wilhelm Friedemann Bach," in *The Keyboard in Baroque Europe*, ed. Christopher Hogwood (Cambridge: Cambridge University Press, 2003), 169–83 (esp. 176–79).

but also, in the sense of a superego [*Über-ich*]—even after his death."[19] An overzealous superego does not seem to have been Friedemann Bach's main problem.

Even David Schulenberg, an outspoken skeptic about Freudian approaches to biography, almost succumbs to the temptation when he addresses the Plümicke episode. The dramatist Carl Martin Plümicke (1749–1833) wrote in his memoir-cum-history, *Entwurf einer Theatergeschichte von Berlin* (1781), that he had "undertaken in the years 1778 and 1779 for Herr (Wilhelm Friedemann) Bach, who is famous for his great musical genius, the preparation of a serious opera (after [Jean-François] Marmontel): *Lausus und Lydie*. . . . But it remained unfinished owing to the illness of the composer and until now has not been printed."[20] In the appendix of his monograph, Martin Falck cataloged the opera as the last numbered item (number 106) in his catalog of Friedemann's works.[21]

It is easy to imagine that Wilhelm Friedemann, in Berlin and in increasingly desperate straits at just that time (owing to the Anna Amalia–Kirnberger fiasco, which unfolded between February 1778 and 1779), would have been more than receptive to Plümicke's evident initiative, had he not been indisposed by "sickly circumstances" ("kränkliche Umstände," in a word, by illness).[22]

Whether the initiative originated with Plümicke or with Friedemann himself, there is yet another reason to think that the opera's plot would have had special appeal and meaning for Wilhelm Friedemann. Ultimately deriving from Virgil's *Aeneid*, the original story recounted the rivalry between the virtuous Laurus and his tyrannical father for the love of Lydia. It ends with Laurus sacrificing his life defending his malevolent father. In Marmontel's version, however, son and father were reconciled before the end.

Discussing this episode, Schulenberg, like Geck in a different context, introduces a famous Freudian term, but only to dismiss the notion. He writes: "It is not necessary to imagine that some latent Oedipal urge impelled Friedemann to this subject. Still, without making any anachronistic or simplistically Freudian assumption, it is *reasonable to suppose* [emphasis added] that the relationship between Friedemann and his father

---

19. "Der Vater mag seine Augen allzu beharrlich auf ihn gerichtet haben—nicht nur zu Lebzeiten, sondern im Sinne eines Über-Ichs auch über seinen Tod hinaus." Geck, *Die Bach-Söhne*, 31.

20. "Für den durch sein großes musikalisches Genie berühmten Herrn (Wilhelm Friedemann) Bach unternahm er . . . in den Jahren 1778 und 1779 die Verfertigung einer ernsthaften Oper (nach Marmontel) Lausus und Lydie . . . doch ist selbige, weil die Komposition kränklicher Umstände des Komponisten wegen unbeendigt verblieben, bis jetzt noch ungedruckt." Carl Martin Plümicke, *Entwurf einer Theatergeschichte von Berlin* (Berlin: Friedrich Nicolai, 1781), 338, cited in Falck, *Wilhelm Friedemann Bach*, 55–56.

21. Falck, *Wilhelm Friedemann Bach*, appendix, 31.

22. For details on the fiasco with Anna Amalia and Kirnberger, see ibid., 52–53.

was the source of profound tensions; these might have been expressed by his taking an interest in Marmontel's story."[23] Before proceeding any further, it is necessary to point out that Schulenberg has overinterpreted Plümicke's text by construing it to claim that the impetus for the opera had come not from the librettist but from Friedemann. Schulenberg writes: "Evidently in 1778, four years after coming to Berlin, Friedemann had 'engaged' [*unternahm*] the playwright and historian Carl Martin Plümicke to prepare for him a libretto based on Marmontel's moral tale," and so on.[24] The original text is obscure on this point, since *unternahm* means "undertook" (not "engaged"), while the pronoun "he" (*er*) is a self-reference to Plümicke, not to Friedemann Bach. The rest is inference. In any event, I wish to expand on Schulenberg's *reasonable supposition* by exploring what may have drawn Wilhelm Friedemann Bach to this particular story and not some other treatment of the archetypal conflict between father and son.

We can begin by noting that Friedemann's mother, like Sebastian's in his time, died (in July 1720) when the boy was not yet ten years old. Perhaps the death was even more traumatic in Friedemann's case than in Sebastian's, since Friedemann's father was not there to share the boy's grief or provide comfort when the tragedy struck. Johann Sebastian Bach was away at the time, having accompanied his patron, Prince Leopold, to Karlsbad, and he only learned about the death and burial of his wife, Maria Barbara, when he returned home to Köthen. Is it unreasonable to suppose that Sebastian's absence may have further exacerbated the boy's sense of abandonment during those painful days?

Barely one and a half years later, in December 1721, Johann Sebastian took a new wife: the twenty-year-old court singer Anna Magdalena Wilcke (1701–60), a woman sixteen years Sebastian's junior and just nine years Friedemann's elder. Thereafter, except for the year spent in nearby Merseburg taking violin instruction from Johann Gottlieb Graun (1726–27), Bach's oldest son would continue to live in the household with his father and young stepmother for another twelve years, that is, throughout his adolescence and early adulthood. By the time the twenty-three-year-old had finally left home for Dresden in 1733, Anna Magdalena was herself only thirty-two. (By then, incidentally, she had given birth to nine children, with a tenth on the way.) Rather than (or in addition to) resisting a latent Oedipal urge directed against his father, can Friedemann have been battling with stressful guilt-inducing feelings directed toward his stepmother? To repeat a familiar refrain: we shall never know.

Finally, what, if anything, should be made of the fact that Friedemann waited until he was forty-one years old (and Johann Sebastian had very recently been safely laid to rest) to marry? His wedding took place on February 25, 1751, barely seven months

23. Schulenberg, *The Music of Wilhelm Friedemann Bach*, 264.

24. Ibid., 263.

after his father's burial. His bride, the daughter of his landlord in Halle, was a woman he had known for some five years, since his arrival in 1746.[25]

Carl Philipp Emanuel Bach (1714–1788)

In his analysis of Emanuel's C Major Sonata, Richard Kramer seems to imply that under the surface there is evidence of defiance and subversion directed at the heart of Johann Sebastian Bach's aesthetic legacy. Like Kramer, we can describe this posited rejection of the artistic ethos that Bach had presumably imparted to his sons as "aesthetic patricide," or, more flippantly, "killing Sebastian." Exactly what were the aesthetic premises of Bach the Father that Emanuel was repudiating? Before addressing that question directly, it will be helpful to provide some further context.

Whether or not Philipp Emanuel had set out to commit *aesthetic* patricide, he certainly made no effort to "bury" his father, that is, to consign him to oblivion, to expunge his shadow and his memory as completely as possible. In Emanuel's case, quite the contrary obtains: he made every effort to keep J. S. Bach's memory and his legacy alive. One need only mention Emanuel's role in the publication of Sebastian's four-part chorales and *The Art of Fugue*; Emanuel's coauthorship of an obituary for his father; his informative letters to Johann Nikolaus Forkel (1749–1818), Sebastian Bach's first biographer; and, above all, his systematic collection and preservation of his share of Sebastian's musical legacy, not to mention his public performances of his father's church music.

On a relatively trivial level, Emanuel Bach may have been asserting his professional independence from his father by failing to follow in his "footsteps" when it came to mastering the organ, especially its pedals, the skill that was perhaps the principal source of Sebastian's towering reputation throughout the eighteenth century. In 1733 Emanuel unsuccessfully applied for the organist post at the Wenzelskirche in Naumburg. Twenty years later, in 1753, he was again unable to obtain an organist post, this time in Zittau. Finally, in September 1772, it was no doubt with embarrassment bordering on humiliation that the Bach son had to find a surrogate—a dilettante, at that—to demonstrate the glories of the Hamburg organs to the visiting Charles Burney. As recounted by David Yearsley,

> When Burney came to Hamburg and marveled at its organs in 1772, . . . this second son of J. S. Bach did not—could not!—demonstrate any of the city's organs for his visitor. . . . Burney writes . . . "M. Bach has so long neglected organ-playing, that he says he has lost the use of the pedals, which are thought so essential throughout Germany, that no one can pass for a player worth hearing, who is unable to use them." . . . One should not underestimate the irony and indignity of a Bach son finding himself

---

25. Karl Geiringer, *The Bach Family: Seven Generations of Genius* (London: Allen & Unwin, 1954), 310.

in arguably the greatest organ city in Europe and not feeling himself able to do jus-
tice to its organs. . . . [Emanuel] was surrounded by an embarrassment of riches yet
plagued by an embarrassing lack of ability to enjoy them. As the ardent admirer of
C. P. E. Bach, the poet Matthias Claudius put it soon after Bach's arrival in Hamburg
. . . "Bach does not play the organ at all and must endure an array of criticisms."[26]

Yearsley goes on to suggest that "such feelings of inadequacy at the ultimate Bachian
instrument must also color the 'Comparison of Bach and Handel,' a document almost
certainly [sic] written by C. P. E. Bach in response to Charles Burney's account of the
Handel commemorations of 1784 which praised Handel above Bach."[27]

Turning to the infinitely more substantial aesthetic issues at play in trying to understand the relationship between Sebastian and Emanuel Bach, it is important to
remember, first of all, that the strongest motivation driving a younger artist to follow
a different direction from the older generation is surely that of basic self-assertion.
It is a matter of psychic survival; but it also seems, at least in the Western tradition,
something like a natural law of artistic history. Carl Philipp Emanuel Bach certainly
did not reject the implicit artistic credo informing his father's works, those being a
commitment to uncompromising high-quality craftsmanship and the avoidance of
the slick, the easy, the conventional, and the audience pleasing. A consequence almost
automatically flowing from that largely unspoken commitment was a definite, if not
necessarily articulated, embrace of originality. But this leads to a paradox, namely, the
more Emanuel or any of Bach's sons cultivated originality and individuality, the more
they subscribed to and emulated, rather than rejected, a fundamental aesthetic premise
of their father.

Consider in this connection a remark by Karl Friedrich Zelter (1758–1832), a
musician, one-time director of the Berlin Sing-Akademie, and, most famously, a close
friend of Goethe's, that is notated in the margin of his copy of Forkel's biography of
J. S. Bach: "Seb[astian]. Bach was an original, because he was unlike anyone else. If
[Forkel's] assessment is correct [i.e., his comment that "Friedemann approached the
nearest to his father in the originality of all his thoughts"], then the son who came
closest to him necessarily must have been the less original, i.e., the unoriginal one;
and this is how we see Friedemann, without intending to diminish his achievement."[28]

26. David Yearsley, *Bach's Feet: The Organ Pedals in European Culture* (Cambridge: Cambridge University Press, 2012), 173–74.

27. Ibid., 174. The "Comparison" is published in NBR, 400–408, no. 396. David Schulenberg har-
bors doubts about Emanuel's authorship of the essay. See Schulenberg, *The Music of Carl Philipp
Emanuel Bach* (Rochester, NY: University of Rochester Press, 2014), 267, and his online discussion:
http://4hlxx40786q10sp7b1b814j8c0.wpengine.netdna-cdn.com/david-schulenberg/files/2014/03
/cpeb_supplement_2_02.pdf.

28. Quoted in Wollny, "Studies in the Music," 6.

Zelter was surely right: to the extent that Friedemann and Emanuel cultivated originality and individuality, they were, to the same extent, proclaiming themselves their father's acolytes.

There can be little question that much of Emanuel's music, and certainly much of his keyboard music, altogether embodies the Sebastianian principles of originality, expressivity, and seriousness. In one respect, however, Emanuel most decidedly and perhaps defiantly took a stylistic path that, at the very least, would have puzzled Sebastian, namely, Emanuel's frequent refusal—arguably his trademark—to subscribe to the cardinal Sebastianian aesthetic principle of unity. Philipp Emanuel explicitly acknowledges this when he writes in his autobiography almost as an afterthought (i.e., after presenting his catalog of works) the following: "Since I have never cared for excessive uniformity [*Einförmigkeit*] in composition and in taste, since I have heard so much and such diverse good music, and since I have always believed that one should accept whatever is good, wherever it might be and even if it only occurs in small doses in a piece, this all, together with my God-given natural talent, has led to the diversity [*Verschiedenheit*] in my works that others have observed."[29] In this explicit, publicly announced repudiation of *Einförmigkeit* (uniformity, or perhaps monotony), can it be that Emanuel was programmatically distancing himself from that compelling sense of logical consistency, unity, and coherence that is the hallmark of his father's music in order to embrace and advocate something very different indeed?

There seems to be a contradiction, incidentally, between Philipp Emanuel's urbane and sophisticated personality and the unbridled, erratic, seemingly irrational style that informs so much of his instrumental music. It is as if, in his instrumental music (especially his keyboard fantasies), he were wearing a mask, one of the *empfindsam* (sensitive), ostentatious, proto-Romantic nonconformist. Instead of inexorable unity there is the spontaneous and unpredictable: the sudden, striking contrast. The explicit purpose was to move the heart, to express the composer's feelings (i.e., his *Empfindungen*), and to awaken those of the listener: "to set the heart in motion."[30] Sebastian Bach, however, claimed far more modestly only that his keyboard music was written to "refresh the spirit" ("zur Gemüths-Ergötzung verfertiget"). Emanuel Bach, of course, shared his new expressionistic—or is it an exhibitionistic?—outlook (what music historians have variously dubbed, depending on the nature of the sentiments being expressed, the *Sturm und Drang* or *Empfindsamkeit* movement) not only with his brothers but

---

29. *Carl Burney's . . . Tagebuch seiner Musikalischen Reisen* (Hamburg: Bode, 1773), 3:198–209 (esp. 208). My translation. See also William S. Newman, "Emanuel Bach's Autobiography," *Musical Quarterly* 51 (1965): 363–72 (esp. 371), for an alternative translation of this passage.

30. "das Herz in Bewegung setzen." From a conversation reported by the Hamburg poet Matthias Claudius (1740–1815) in a letter written in 1768. See Hans-Günter Ottenberg, *Carl Philipp Emanuel Bach*, trans. Philip J. Whitmore (Oxford: Oxford University Press, 1987), 159.

with his entire generation, at least in the German-speaking world. This was their new governing aesthetic principle, representing, vis-à-vis Johann Sebastian Bach and his generation (in Kramer's formulation), "the aesthetics of patricide." No one practiced it more imaginatively or radically or compellingly than Carl Philipp Emanuel Bach.

In the most literal sense, it is clear that Philipp Emanuel Bach, far more than his father, was the "learned musician": an intellectual, a correspondent of Diderot's, and a friend of Lessing's. He demonstrated his learning most spectacularly with a lasting contribution, what is arguably his greatest achievement, to a field his father never entered: the writing of a scholarly treatise. If Sebastian had ever seriously contemplated doing such a thing—and he had been compiling materials at least since the early 1740s, possibly for a projected textbook, or instruction manual, on traditional counterpoint—he clearly never brought it to completion, as had his son.[31] Emanuel's treatise can be regarded as a monument to his father, founded as it is, to a considerable degree, on Sebastian's methods. But it also proclaims the advent of a new style grounded in a new aesthetic. The work, in short, is a testament to both and, as such, reflects perhaps both explicit allegiance and implicit rebellion.

Emanuel's impressive circle of acquaintances in Hamburg, along with his extensive correspondence, reveal that he was adept at making friends. Johann Sebastian and Friedemann Bach, however, were far more adept at making enemies. Not that Emanuel invariably pleased. While Princess Anna Amalia, King Frederick's sister, was one of Emanuel's greatest patrons, bestowing on him the title of "honorary *Kapellmeister*" (*Kapellmeister von Haus aus*) after he had left Berlin for Hamburg,[32] Frederick II himself (at least according to Zelter) "had a personal dislike of [*eine persönliche Abneigung gegen*] Emanuel Bach and for that reason did not appreciate this great artist according to his just deserts."[33]

Zelter reported this information in his biography of Karl Friedrich Fasch, who was no doubt the source for the assertion. Fasch was surely a credible source; he had joined the Prussian court in 1756 as a harpsichordist, thus becoming an immediate colleague of Emanuel Bach's, and remained at the court until his death in 1800. He was also, apparently, Emanuel's good friend. In August 1758, during the Seven Years'

31. See Walter Werbeck, "Bach und der Kontrapunkt: Neue Manuskript-Funde," BJ 89 (2003): 67–95; and Christoph Wolff, "Johann Sebastian Bachs Regeln für den fünfstimmigen Satz," BJ 90 (2004): 87–99.

32. Geck, *Die Bach-Söhne*, 43.

33. Bitter, *Carl Philipp Emanuel*, 1:182, citing Karl Friedrich Zelter, *Karl Friedrich Christian Fasch* (Berlin: J. F. Unger, 1801), 46. However, Mary Oleskiewicz has argued against the veracity of Zelter's statement and the view that Bach was unappreciated by the king in "Like Father, Like Son? Emanuel Bach and the Writing of Biography," in *Music and Its Questions: Essays in Honor of Peter Williams*, ed. Thomas Donahue (Richmond, VA: Organ Historical Society Press, 2007), 253–79.

War, Emanuel Bach and Fasch, along with their families, took refuge in Zerbst with the latter's father, *Kapellmeister* Johann Friedrich Fasch, to escape the threatened Russian invasion of Berlin. They remained in Zerbst until early December. On the other end of the thread, K. F. Fasch's relationship to Zelter was just as close. In 1791 Fasch founded the Berlin Sing-Akademie; Zelter, his student, not only was a member of the group but became its director after Fasch's death.

In 1755, two years after the publication of the treatise, Emanuel failed to step into his father's shoes as *Thomaskantor*, that is, director of church music for the city of Leipzig. Later, Philipp Emanuel did, of course, manage to fill his godfather Georg Philipp Telemann's shoes when Emanuel inherited Telemann's position as director of church music for the city of Hamburg. (This time, one of Emanuel's rivals for the position, incidentally, was his half-brother Johann Christoph Friedrich.)

One can say that in a nontrivial sense Emanuel had two fathers: his natural father and his godfather. He was evidently very fond of Telemann and had a warm, filial relationship with him.[34] Conversely, he had no mother. His true mother, Maria Barbara Bach (1684–1720), died when he was six. Despite longstanding claims to the contrary, there is no reason to think that Emanuel neglected his widowed stepmother, Anna Magdalena. In addition to whatever help he may have provided, she also had other resources: among them potential income from serving as the sales representative in Leipzig for publications of works by her late husband and her stepson, Emanuel. Emanuel also contributed from 1772 on, well after Anna Magdalena's death in 1760, to the financial support of his surviving sister and half-sisters. At that time his economic circumstances in Hamburg were much better than they had been in Berlin during the time of his stepmother's widowhood and that of the Seven Years' War.[35]

In the particular case of Emanuel, the impulse toward filial piety seems to have been considerably stronger (perhaps even suspiciously so) than any conventional, generational, rebellious impulse. Emanuel was surely far too intelligent and too intellectually

---

34. For an insightful discussion of the cordial relationship between Emanuel Bach and Telemann, see Ellen Exner, "The Godfather: Georg Philipp Telemann, Carl Philipp Emanuel Bach, and the Family Business," *Bach: Journal of the Riemenschneider Bach Institute* 48.1 (2016): 1–20.

35. After Sebastian's death, his widow survived on stipends provided by a number of Leipzig institutions, among them the municipal government and the university. In June 1751 an advertisement in the Leipzig newspapers announced a subscription for *Die Kunst der Fuge* and indicated that copies could be procured in Leipzig from "Frau Wittbe Bachin." The announcement was presumably drafted by Emanuel Bach. The resulting commercial activity, if any, would have enhanced Anna Magdalena's income. See Maria Hübner, *Anna Magdalena Bach: Ein Leben in Dokumenten und Bildern* (Leipzig: Evangelische Verlagsanstalt, 2004), 84, 96 (containing quote), 108. On Anna Magdalena's finances see also Eberhard Spree, "Die verwitwete Frau Capellmeisterin Bach: Studie über die Verteilung des Nachlasses von Johann Sebastian Bach" (Ph. D. dissertation, Hochschule für Musik Carl Maria von Weber, Dresden, 2017).

honest not to have realized that his father was the greater composer. This must have been more than a little deflating and must have generated some inevitable sense of resentment. But he was manifestly talented and resourceful enough to establish his own musical identity and to enjoy a successful career with, if anything, more worldly acclaim and prestige than his father had ever enjoyed during his lifetime. Perhaps Emanuel's extraordinary commitment to the preservation and cultivation of his late father's musical legacy was to some significant degree an act of compensation (and expiation) for his having undeservedly (as he might have thought) surpassed his father in gathering up the coin of worldly success.

Admittedly, that may be putting it too strongly. One hint as to how Emanuel Bach may have measured himself against his father is provided by the gala concert he produced in Hamburg in April 1786, just two years before his death. The program, one of the earliest historical concerts, far from burying Sebastian's music, dramatically "resurrected" it by including the complete Credo from the *B Minor Mass*. This was without question an act of profound filial veneration and perhaps marks the beginning of a serious posthumous revival of Sebastian's church music altogether, well before Mendelssohn's revival of the *St. Matthew Passion*. Also on the program were two numbers from Handel's *Messiah*: the aria "Ich weiß, daß mein Erlöser lebt" (I know that my Redeemer liveth) and the "Halleluia" chorus. But the concert concluded with two works of Emanuel's: his *Magnificat*, Wq 215, composed in 1749 (and almost certainly performed in Leipzig before the death of his father, presumably in his presence); and the grand double-chorus work, *Heilig*, Wq 217, the composition Emanuel was convinced would be his swan song and would serve "the purpose that I may not be forgotten too soon after my death."[36] May we infer from Emanuel's readiness to place his compositions before the public, along with the greatest masterpieces of G. F. Handel and J. S. Bach, that he was altogether confident that his work would comfortably hold its own in their company? And was he perhaps just as confident, too, that he fully belonged in the same pantheon as these venerable masters?

* * *

It is altogether appropriate, and not just for the sake of completeness, to include at this juncture discussion of two musical sons of Sebastian who have understandably always played minor roles in the Bach family saga.

---

36. C. P. E. Bach to J. G. I. Breitkopf, September 16, 1778, in *The Letters of C. P. E. Bach*, trans. and ed. Stephen L. Clark (Oxford: Clarendon Press, 1997), 125.

Johann Gottfried Bernhard Bach (1715–1739)

Emanuel's younger brother Johann Gottfried Bernhard was born to Maria Barbara in 1715. In many respects his fate parallels that of Friedemann, but worse. A source of endless pain, embarrassment, and heartbreak to his father, Bernhard allegedly died of "fever" at age twenty-four in May 1739, shortly after matriculating at the University of Jena the previous January and after having botched organist positions at both Mühlhausen and Sangerhausen. These two jobs, by the way (and certainly not coincidentally), were ones that Sebastian had held, or almost held: his later personal connections with the two towns were almost certainly instrumental in securing both organ positions for his son.[37] Bernhard's behavior in Sangerhausen elicited from Johann Sebastian the most personal and poignant confession he ever set down on paper. On May 24, 1738, just a year before his son's untimely, perhaps suspicious, death, Sebastian wrote a letter to the Sangerhausen town councilor Johann Friedrich Klemm (1706–67) in response to the news that Bernhard had disappeared from his post and had left unpaid debts behind. The letter reads, in part:

> With what pain and sorrow . . . I frame this reply. . . . Upon my (alas! misguided) son I have not laid eyes since last year. . . . [A]t that time I duly paid not only his board but also the Mühlhausen draft [i.e., debt] (which presumably brought about his departure at that time) but also [*sic*] left a few ducats behind to settle a few bills, in the hope that he would now embark upon a new mode of life. But now I must learn again, with greatest consternation, that he once more borrowed here and there and did not change his way of living in the slightest, but on the contrary has even absented himself and not given me to date any inkling as to his whereabouts.
>
> What shall I say or do further? Since no admonition or even any loving care and *assistance* will suffice any more [*sic*], I must bear my cross in patience and leave my unruly son to God's Mercy alone. . . . I am fully confident that you will not impute the evil conduct of my child to me. . . . I most obediently request Your Honor to have the goodness to obtain precise information as to his whereabouts . . . so that one last effort may be made to see whether with God's help his impenitent heart can be won over and brought to a recognition of his mistakes.[38]

As in the case of Friedemann, Sebastian seems, at the least, to have played too large and dominating a role in Bernhard's professional life. The consequences were disastrous,

37. Bach had served as organist of the Blasiuskirche in Mühlhausen from June 1707 to June or July 1708. In 1702, as a seventeen-year-old, he had successfully auditioned for the organist position at the Jacobikirche in Sangerhausen. The reigning duke overruled the selection committee, however, and decreed that the appointment must go to a native son. The incident is known only from Sebastian Bach's own testimony contained in a letter dated November 18, 1736, to Johann Friedrich Klemm, in which he recommended his son Johann Gottfried Bernhard for that same post.

38. NBR, 200, no. 203; the German original cited in BDOK 1:107, no. 42.

and it is hard not to wonder whether Bernhard's manifestly self-destructive behavior was in part an act of spite and punishment directed at what he had perceived as an outsized, overbearing father.

Johann Christoph Friedrich Bach (1732–1795)

In his autobiography cited earlier, Cramer altogether dismissed Johann Christoph Friedrich (the "Bückeburg") Bach, when he wrote about Sebastian: "He had three sons: Christian Bach, Carl Philipp Emanuel Bach, and Friedemann Bach. (The fourth in Bückeburg I don't count among them, since he does not really belong to the [true] 'Bachs'!)"[39] Friedemann himself, however, considered Friedrich to be the "best keyboard player [den stärksten Spieler]" of the four brothers because he "could play his father's keyboard compositions most proficiently [am fertigsten]."[40]

Johann Christoph Friedrich Bach was apparently a congenial individual with solid but limited talents. Thanks no doubt in no small part to his father's letter of recommendation sent to Count Wilhelm von Schaumburg-Lippe in December 1749 some seven months before his death, Friedrich was fortunate to find a congenial prince in whose service he spent his entire career.[41] Born in 1732, the same year as Joseph Haydn, Friedrich led a "Haydnesque" existence, arguably the ideal eighteenth-century musician's life. He thus succeeded, more than any of his brothers, in realizing his father's fond fantasy, namely, what Sebastian had found for a while and had hoped to have found forever in Köthen and with Prince Leopold.[42] Friedrich's position at Bückeburg seems to have been a fairly close copy of Sebastian's position at Köthen. And just as Sebastian had considered leaving it to become organist at the Jacobikirche in Hamburg when economic conditions in Köthen had begun to deteriorate, Friedrich too at one point during the hard times of the Seven Years' War applied for and was offered an appointment as organist in Altona (now part of Hamburg but at the time a Danish town). In the end, however, Friedrich remained in Bückeburg.[43]

39. Cramer, *Menschliches Leben*, no. 13 (dreizehntes Stück), 753; BDOK 3:519, no. 973. Translation mine; this passage does not appear in NBR. See also note 4.

40. Johann Nikolaus Forkel, *Über Johann Sebastian Bachs Leben, Kunst und Kunstwerke* (Leipzig: Hoffmeister und Kühnel, 1802), 44; an English translation appears in NBR, 458.

41. The letter is dated "den 27ten. 1obr." As transcribed in BDOK 1:123, no. 54, the month meant is December, not October, as rendered in NBR, 241, no. 267.

42. See J. S. Bach's famous letter of October 28, 1730, to his childhood friend Georg Erdmann: "There I had a gracious Prince, who both loved and knew music, and in his service I intended to spend the rest of my life" (NBR, 151, no. 152, original in BDOK 1:67, no. 23).

43. Geck, *Die Bach-Söhne*, 87.

Around ten years later Friedrich applied unsuccessfully for the Hamburg position that went instead to his brother Carl Philipp Emanuel. In 1778, after passing through Hamburg to pay a call on Philipp Emanuel, Friedrich visited his brother Christian in London for several months, leaving his eldest son, Wilhelm Friedrich Ernst, to study there for some three years with the youngest son of Sebastian.

Unlike the grim and vindictive Friedemann, the altogether realistic and unpretentious Friedrich was able not only to acknowledge and appreciate but even to celebrate the success of his brothers Emanuel and, especially, Johann Christian, just as he could recognize the talent of Mozart. He demonstrated his appreciation of the latter by putting on a performance of *Die Entführung aus dem Serail* at the Bückeburg court.[44]

Johann Christoph Friedrich Bach lived in Sebastian's household until he left for Bückeburg just before his eighteenth birthday in June 1750, shortly before his father's death in July. Thus, unlike his younger brother Christian, he did not go off to live with his older brother Emanuel. He plays no discernible role in any primal Oedipal scenario.

Johann Christian Bach (1735–1782)

The same could be said of Johann Christian Bach. According to a rumor apparently begun by the British Bach champion Samuel Wesley (1766–1837), Johann Christian referred to his father as "the old wig."[45] Whether or not the youngest son of J. S. Bach ever actually said that, it seems clear that Christian, the greatest master of the "gentle affections" (the *affetti amorosi*) who in his music largely rejected excessive complexity in favor of accessibility and amiability, was (at least from the Sebastianian perspective) the greatest radical and the true aesthetic patricide.

Christian not only "killed" Johann Sebastian aesthetically, he effectively "buried" him quite completely by obliterating virtually all traces of him not only in Christian's music but in his life. It was, however, an act of silent annihilation, not vociferous rebellion. Only Christian managed to escape his father's orbit completely, with death as his greatest ally. The other brothers followed in their father's footsteps, serving as musicians at court or municipal directors of church music. Indeed, Friedemann and Emanuel, like their father, pursued both these career paths. But Christian succeeded in separating himself totally from Johann Sebastian Bach geographically, culturally, and, in terms of music, stylistically and aesthetically.

There are few if any traces of Sebastian's stylistic influence in Christian's music, not even in his polyphonic church music, which, written in Italy under the aegis of Padre Martini, is modeled on the *stile antico*. We find virtually none of the "luxuriant"

---

44. Geiringer, *The Bach Family*, 384.

45. Terry, *John Christian Bach*, 142.

late baroque counterpoint (to use Manfred Bukofzer's apt term) of what could be called the "*stile Sebastiano*."[46] Christian does, however, make an overt reference to the opening theme of the first movement of his father's Sonata in G Minor for Viola da Gamba and Obbligato Harpsichord, BWV 1029—transposed to C major—in his early song "Mezendore," Warb H1 (Example 2), and to the opening of the Partita in B-flat Major, BWV 825, from the *Klavierübung I* in his violin sonata of the same key, op. 10, no. 1, of 1773, Warb B2 (Example 3).[47] Otherwise, for all intents and purposes, Johann Christian Bach evidently came not at all to praise his father, let alone to venerate him; he came to bury him, that is, ignore him completely, pure and simple.

After Sebastian's death, Christian spent his late teen years with Emanuel in Berlin, where he undoubtedly took the opportunity to experience Italian opera. According to Ernst Ludwig Gerber, "Various female Italian singers, whose acquaintance he had made [in Berlin], awakened in [Christian] the desire to see Italy."[48] Whether he did so with his brother's approval and encouragement is by no means certain. Indeed, it is not altogether clear what Emanuel's role was at the court of Frederick II with respect to the Berlin *Hofoper*. He certainly was not engaged to compose Italian opera seria, which was largely the responsibility of Carl Heinrich Graun. Nor did he evidently have an explicit dispensation excusing him from performing in the orchestra pit, as did Johann Joachim Quantz.[49] One assumes that, as one of the court's two harpsichordists,

46. Manfred Bukofzer developed the concept of "luxuriant" (or "harmonically saturated") counterpoint in chapter 7 of his classic monograph, *Music in the Baroque Era from Monteverdi to Bach* (New York: W. W. Norton, 1947), esp. 221.

47. "Mezendore" was published as no. 12 in Friedrich Wilhelm Marpurg's anthology *Neue Lieder zum Singen beym Clavier* (Berlin, 1756). Regarding Christian's use of the theme from BWV 1029, Ernest Warburton writes: "The parody of the opening of JSB's Sonata in G minor for viola da gamba and obbligato keyboard BWV 1029 (with the mode changed from minor to major) suggests the irreverence more often found in the youngest members of a large family rather than in their older siblings" (*The Collected Works of Johann Christian Bach, 1735–1782: Volume Forty-Eight, Part One: Thematic Catalogue* [New York: Garland Publishing, 1999], 385). Since it is likely that Christian composed the song (published by 1755) sometime after his father's death in 1750, such "irreverence" toward the departed father—if that was in fact Christian's intention—began early indeed.

48. "als in ihm die Bekanntschaften verschiedener ital. Sängerinnen, die Lust erweckten, Italien zu sehen." Ernst Ludwig Gerber, *Historisch-biographisches Lexicon der Tonkünstler* (Leipzig: Breitkopf, 1790), 1:83.

49. "Herrn Johann Joachim Quantzens Lebenslauf von ihm selbst entworfen," in Friedrich Wilhelm Marpurg, *Historisch-kritische Beiträge zur Aufnahme der Musik* (Berlin: Schützens Witwe, 1754), 1:197–250, English translation in Paul Nettl, *Forgotten Musicians* (New York: Philosophical Library, 1951), 280–319 (quote on 318). Emanuel's roles at court, including a discussion of the opera and other musical venues in which he performed, are further discussed in Mary Oleskiewicz's chapter in the present volume.

Ex. 2a. J. C. Bach, Mezendore ("Herr Nicolaus Klimm erfand"),
Warb H1 (Berlin, 1756).

Ex. 2b. J. S. Bach, Sonata in G Minor for Viola da Gamba and Obbligato Harpsichord,
BWV 1029, movement 1.

Ex. 3a. J. C. Bach, Sonata No. 1 in B-flat Major for Violin and Piano, op. 10, no. 1, Warb
B2, Allegro (London, ca. 1773).

Ex. 3b. J. S. Bach, Partita No. 1 in B-flat Major, BWV 825, Praeludium (Leipzig, 1726).

Emanuel was regularly obliged to play continuo in opera performances at the newly built opera house in Berlin. But neither in his autobiography of 1773 nor in his *Versuch* does Emanuel Bach explicitly refer to his participation in opera seria performances. He calls attention instead to his performing in the king's chamber music soirées at the royal residences. In his extensive discussion of accompaniment in the second part of the *Versuch*, where one would most expect to find at some point advice specifically on playing continuo in the context of opera, the closest Philip Emanuel comes to mentioning the topic appears in paragraph six of the section on recitative, where he has some suggestions about playing "in intermezzos and comic operas with much noisy action and other works for the theater where the action often occurs backstage."[50] That is perhaps indicative, for it is quite certain that Emanuel Bach took part specifically in the performance of such small-scale musical dramas at Sanssouci, Potsdam, and Charlottenburg. Mary Oleskiewicz reports that "a small select group of virtuosos performed in the king's evening concerts. . . . The keyboard players were [Christoph] Schaffrath (until 1745) . . . Emanuel Bach (1741–67), Nichelmann (1745–55), and Carl Friedrich Fasch (1756–86)"; that the concerts took place "from 1746 in the Potsdam *Stadtschloß* and from 1747 in Schloß Sanssouci"; furthermore, that "in 1745, Friedrich had Knobelsdorff build a small theatre for the performance of comic intermezzos as part of the renovations of the Potsdam Stadtschloß. . . . Music was supplied by select members of the Hofkapelle."[51] Such explicit testimony does not seem to be available with regard to Emanuel's role in the great Berlin opera house.

What does seem certain is that Emanuel was not pleased with the music his half-brother ultimately created nor with developments in Italian opera, at least at the time of his brother's successes. He reportedly told Matthias Claudius shortly after Emanuel settled in Hamburg in the late 1760s that "at bottom Christian's most recent music is nothing. It pleases the ear but leaves the heart empty. That is my opinion of the new music and the new comic music, which, Galuppi told me, is now fashionable in Italy, too."[52]

---

50. Carl Philipp Emanuel Bach, *Versuch über die wahre Art das Clavier zu spielen* (Berlin: Winter, 1762), 2:316. English version from the translation by William J. Mitchell under the title *Essay on the True Art of Playing Keyboard Instruments* (New York: W. W. Norton, 1949), 422 (see David Schulenberg's chapter in the present volume).

51. Mary Oleskiewicz, "The Court of Brandenburg-Prussia," in *Music at German Courts, 1715–1760: Changing Artistic Priorities*, ed. Samantha Owens, Barbara M. Reul, and Janice B. Stockigt (Woodbridge: Boydell Press, 2011), 79–130 (esp. 98–100).

52. "Hinter . . . meines Bruders itziger Komposition ist nichts. . . . Sie fällt hinein und füllt es [das Ohr] aus, läßt aber das Herz leer, das ist mein Urteil von der neuen Musik, der neuen komischen Musik, die auch in Italien, wie mir Galuppi gesagt hat, Mode ist." Cited by Geck, *Die Bach-Söhne*, 55.

If the great mystery in Wilhelm Friedemann's life is why he failed so miserably, then the great mystery in Johann Christian's life is how he became so successful; or, more specifically, how he got to Italy (i.e., in the manner described by Gerber or otherwise); how he became an opera composer; and how, while serving as a young, newly minted church organist at no less a venue than the Milan Cathedral, he managed to garner some extremely prestigious opera commissions from both Turin and Naples.

Unlike his brothers and his father, Christian succeeded in going abroad. The other brothers dutifully followed their father's career path in not doing so. Ironically, this is a testimonial to Christian's Sebastianian sense of purpose, mission, and independence; it suggests that he was, after all, most like Johann Sebastian in this one fundamental way. There is also an irony in that Christian had gone to Italy to fulfill an (unspoken) purpose, or *Endzweck* (to use his father's powerful term), which he as a young man had famously used at a similar point in his career to proclaim his ultimate goal of creating a "well-regulated church music" ("regulirte kirchen music")—a Lutheran church music, needless to say—"to the Glory of God."[53] In Christian's case it was the very secular goal of becoming an opera composer. The irony is all the richer when one recalls that Christian had at first become a church organist like his father and his half-brother Wilhelm Friedemann—but in the service of the Roman Catholic Church.

Christian's half-dozen years in Italy from 1755 to 1761 are intriguing in a number of ways, many of which suggest that his repudiation of his father's legacy was profound indeed. To begin with, there were his studies with Padre Martini, who was not only obviously a father surrogate of sorts but also the aesthetic antipode to Sebastian (insofar as Martini's Palestrinian ideal of counterpoint played a respected, but definitely subordinate, role in J. S. Bach's contrapuntal universe). In this connection it is worth observing that, once he left the country of his birth, Christian composed church music in Latin, operas in Italian and French, and songs in English, but, apparently, nothing in German.[54] That is, nothing in the language central to his father's vocal music legacy. Evidently, neither the biblical texts of Martin Luther nor the verses of the great German hymn poets of the sixteenth and seventeenth centuries—often the animating impulse of his father's inspiration—played any role for Christian Bach during the years of his artistic maturity.

At least as stunning as Christian's neglect of his mother tongue, and perhaps even more poignant, was his conversion from his father's, indeed, from his forefathers', deep-rooted Lutheran heritage to Roman Catholicism. As insincere and opportunistic as his conversion might have been, could there have been any more profound expression

---

53. BDOK I:19, no. 1; NBR, 57, no. 32.

54. Two early songs date from Christian's Berlin years: "Der Weise auf dem Lande," Warb H2, dated April 16, 1755, and "Mezendore," Warb H1, published in 1756 by Marpurg in Berlin. See above.

of—if not aesthetic, then, certainly, spiritual—patricide? When annotating his copy of the Bach family genealogy for J. N. Forkel, ca. 1774–75, Emanuel Bach added the following to the entry on Johann Christian: "[He] is now in England in the service of the Queen—between us, he has managed differently from honest Veit." As Hans T. David and Arthur Mendel observed in the original edition of *The Bach Reader* (an observation retained by Christoph Wolff in *The New Bach Reader*), "Philipp Emanuel's remark: 'inter nos, machte es anders als der ehrliche Veit' has been interpreted as a disapproving allusion to Johann Christian's having embraced Roman Catholicism." The editors proceed, it is true, to express their doubts as to that interpretation, preferring instead to see Emanuel's comment as an expression of pride in Christian's great success in England.[55] The earlier understanding is far more persuasive. Veit Bach, as reported in the very first sentence of the genealogy, was honored by his descendants for having "had to flee Hungary in the sixteenth century on account of his Lutheran religion."[56] Moreover, if Emanuel Bach was "expressing pride in the success and fame" of his half-brother, as David and Mendel suggest, then it is difficult to fathom why he thought it was necessary to whisper his pride—*inter nos*—to Forkel.

To follow up with another paradox, Charles Burney points out yet one more similarity between Johann Sebastian and Johann Christian Bach; namely, both were "deprived" (to use Burney's word) by their father's death when they were still young. Both then went off to live with a much older brother: Sebastian with Johann Christoph Bach, fourteen years his senior, and Johann Christian with Philipp Emanuel, twenty-one years his senior. As with Emanuel, Burney also makes a case for Christian as an original innovator, writing:

> [J. C.] Bach seems to have been the first composer who observed the law of *contrast*, as a *principle* [original italics]. Before his time, contrast there frequently was in the works of others; but it seems to have been accidental. Bach in his symphonies and other instrumental pieces, as well as his songs, seldom failed, after a rapid and noisy passage to introduce one that was slow and soothing. His symphonies seem infinitely more original than either his songs or harpsichord pieces, of which the harmony, mixture of wind-instruments, and general richness and variety of accompaniment, are certainly the most prominent features.[57]

55. Hans T. David and Arthur Mendel, *The Bach Reader*, revised with supplement (New York: W. W. Norton, 1966), 211; also NBR, 293–94, no. 303.

56. David and Mendel, *The Bach Reader*, 203; also NBR, 283, no. 303.

57. Charles Burney, *A General History of Music from the Earliest Ages to the Present Period (1789)*, ed. Frank Mercer (London: G. T. Foulis, 1935; reprint, New York: Dover, 1957), 2:866.

Once again, a son of Johann Sebastian Bach demonstrated, by virtue of his extraordinary craftsmanship and originality, that—despite the outward appearance (or sound) of things—in the final analysis he was his father's authentic artistic heir.

We can conclude with a final irony. Johann Christian Bach went to Bologna, studied with Padre Martini, and soon thereafter shed all traces of his father's musical idiom. A few years later, Wolfgang Amadeus Mozart went to Bologna, studied with Padre Martini, and discovered the music of Johann Sebastian Bach (some of which Martini, a true admirer of J. S. Bach, may have acquired from J. C. Bach). Over the remaining decades of his life, Mozart absorbed its lessons into his own works and triumphantly demonstrated its enduring, "unkillable" relevance to posterity.[58]

58. On the impact of J. S. Bach's music on Mozart, which he may have seriously and systematically studied for the first time in 1770 under Martini's tutelage, see Robert L. Marshall, "Bach and Mozart's Artistic Maturity," in *Bach Perspectives 3: Creative Responses to Bach from Mozart to Hindemith*, ed. Michael Marissen (Lincoln: University of Nebraska Press, 1998), 47–80 (esp. 55–57).

Keyboards, Music Rooms, and the Bach Family at the Court of Frederick the Great

Mary Oleskiewicz

FOR WALTER MAYHALL, IN MEMORIAM

Capellmeister Bach had arrived at Potsdam and was waiting in His Majesty's antechamber for His Majesty's most gracious permission to listen to the music. His August Self immediately gave orders that Bach be admitted, and went, at his entrance, to the so-called Forte *and* Piano.
—*Spenersche Zeitung*, Berlin, May 11, 1747 (NBR, 224)

In what palace and in which rooms did Johann Sebastian Bach encounter King Frederick the Great on the evening of Sunday, May 7, 1747? On which of the king's fortepianos did Bach improvise that night, and, for that matter, just how many fortepianos by Gottfried Silbermann did the king really possess? Years earlier, on his first trip to Berlin in 1719, precisely where did Sebastian Bach appear before Margrave Christian Ludwig? And in 1738, when Emanuel Bach accepted his first "call to Ruppin," where and upon what kind of keyboard instrument(s) did he perform for Frederick, then Crown Prince? After Frederick became king in 1740 and moved to Berlin, in what palaces, music rooms, and with which keyboard instruments did Emanuel's sinfonias, flute sonatas, organ sonatas, and other works at court reverberate? On October 28, 1753, where did Emanuel debut Johann Hohlefeld's so-called *Bogenflügel* for the queen? Furthermore, what do we know about court appearances and keyboard instruments played by other Bach family members active in Berlin, such as Johann Christian Bach, Emanuel's half-brother, who studied there with Emanuel from 1750

This essay has been expanded from a paper read at the annual meeting of the American Bach Society in Rochester, NY, September 29, 2012. I am grateful to Pieter Dirksen, Joachim Homann, John Koster, Andrus Madsen, Annette Richards, and David Schulenberg for helpful comments made during the genesis of this version; to Dan Melamed, the general editor; to Klaus Dorst, Afra Schick, Claudia Sommer, and the staff of the Stiftung Preußische Schlösser und Gärten Berlin-Brandenburg; and to Emily Chapman for invaluable assistance. My research for this project was generously supported by a two-year fellowship in Germany from the Alexander von Humboldt Foundation.

to 1755, or Emanuel's older brother Wilhelm Friedemann, a pupil of Johann Gottlieb Graun (1703–71), who may have first visited the court with his father in 1747 and who, in 1774, relocated to Berlin? Like Emanuel, Friedemann was for a while admired by the king's youngest sister, Princess Amalia (1723–87), as well as by Frederick William II (1744–97), the king's nephew and the future king of Prussia.[1] Finally, did particular keyboard instruments at court directly influence works by Bach and his sons?

In order to answer these questions, it is necessary to review the musical roles of the Bach family at court and to identify all of the many music rooms in the Prussian royal palaces, taking into account archival and other information that identifies the precise locations and musical instruments mentioned in the literature about Johann Sebastian, Wilhelm Friedemann, Carl Philipp Emanuel, and Johann Christian Bach. The court's musical venues, many of them situated within the private living quarters of the king and immediate royal family members, merit discussion not only due to their importance for the history of music and musical performance but also because these are venues where members of the Bach family played and for which they composed music. I provide in this essay updated and corrected information and other important details about the court keyboard instruments, and, when possible, I connect specific pieces of music to particular instruments and musical spaces. An appendix at the end of this essay provides a series of tables to help the reader navigate the many palaces, invoices, and musical instruments under discussion. An online web-companion, found at http://www.press.uillinois.edu/books/oleskiewicz/bp11/, provides essential illustrations, including floor plans and photographs of palace rooms and keyboard instruments. These are indicated at the beginning of each relevant subheading by the icon 🗂, followed by an identifying number.

King Frederick II, "the Great," of Prussia (1714–86), though active as a flutist, was a great collector of keyboard instruments. He is known to Bach scholars first and foremost as the dedicatee of *The Musical Offering* (*Das musikalische Opfer*) BWV 1079, composed in 1747 following Sebastian Bach's visit to court, and as the employer of Carl Philipp Emanuel Bach, who frequently served Crown Prince Frederick beginning in 1738 and then full-time as royal court keyboardist from 1741 until 1767.[2] As chamber

---

1. Much later, Sebastian Bach's grandson Wilhelm Friedrich Ernst Bach became *Kapellmeister* to the Prussian king's widow, Queen Christine. This Bach lies outside the scope of the present essay.

2. Emanuel's autobiography, which outlines his employment, is published in Charles Burney, *Tagebuch einer musikalischen Reise: Vollständige Ausgabe*, 3 vols. in 1, ed. Christoph Hust (Kassel: Bärenreiter, 2003), 3:199–209. For a critical reevaluation of the composer's biography and his relationship to the Prussian court, see Mary Oleskiewicz, "Like Father, Like Son? Emanuel Bach and the Writing of Biography," in *Music and Its Questions: Essays in Honor of Peter Williams*, ed. Thomas Donahue (Richmond: Organ Historical Society Press, 2007), 253–79.

musicians of the king, Emanuel and his colleagues accompanied the flute music and opera arias performed in Frederick's private chamber soirées, which normally took place nightly in the royal apartments of the king's various palaces in Potsdam, Charlottenburg, Berlin, and Breslau (Wrocław), the eighteenth-century capital of Silesia and Lower Silesia (Table 1).

King Frederick was highly interested in new developments in technology, and this interest extended to keyboard instruments; he had begun his musical studies on the harpsichord with Gottlieb Hayne before learning the flute.[3] From his letters we also know that Frederick, who wrote a large number of flute works, liked to compose at the keyboard, which he felt improved his results.[4] Once king, he became a significant collector of all types of keyboards and furnished his numerous private and larger salons or semipublic palace music rooms with the newest, technologically most advanced keyboard instruments available. He also financed the purchase of organs and other types of keyboard instruments for the music rooms of his closest family members.

The Royal Prussian Music Rooms 🗇 1

Music rooms were among the accoutrements required by French prescriptions for palace living quarters.[5] Frederick had music rooms in the style of a *petit salon* constructed

---

3. Gottlieb Hayne, cathedral organist in Berlin and musician in the queen's service, also taught keyboard to Princess Amalia. Frederick apparently played harpsichord well enough to accompany Franz Benda's audition at Rheinsberg: as the violinist himself reported in his autobiography, "Ihro Hoheit befahlen mir gegen Abend zu Ihnen zu kommen, wo Sie so gnädig gewesen mir Selbst auff den Clavier zu accompagniren und hiermit trat ich Meinen Nunmehrigen Dienst an" (In the evening, His Highness ordered me to go to him and graciously accompanied me at the keyboard; herewith I entered his service). See the "Autobiographie Franz Bendas" of 1763, reproduced in Franz Lorenz, *Die Musikerfamilie Benda: Franz Benda und seine Nachkommen* (Berlin: De Gruyter, 1967), 138–59, quotation on 148.

4. Letter from Frederick to his sister Wilhelmine, Rheinsberg ("á Remusberg"), 29 October 1736, BPH Rep. 47, no. 305, vol. 3, fol. 14r: in speaking of a flute concerto he has just composed, Frederick writes, "Je creins fort quil ne reussira pas, car j'ai trop negligé le clavesein pour pouvoir produire quelque chose qui y' soit aplicable et brillent" (I am afraid that it will not succeed, for I have neglected the keyboard too much to produce something that is playable there and brilliant).

5. Jacques-François Blondel, *De la distribution des maisons de plaisance, et de la décoration des édifices en general*, 2 vols. (Paris: Jombert, 1737), 1:31, and on p. 156 he writes: "Dans un Edifice un peu considérable, on a coutume d'appeller pieces d'honneur les Salons, les Salles d'assemblée, les Salles de compagnie, Cabinets, Salles de concert, les Galleries, &c. sans parler des Vestibules, des Porches, des Peristilles & autres pieces qui servent à la communication de ces appartemens" (Within a somewhat substantial building, it is customary to call reception rooms the salons, assembly halls, meeting rooms, cabinets, concert halls, and galleries, not to mention vestibules, porches, peristiles, and other rooms that provide connections to the apartments).

within every one of his private apartments, and in every palace the apartments of his various family members also included small music rooms where private music making, sometimes involving court musicians, took place. His large residential palaces, with their many suites of apartments, featured not one but multiple music rooms of varying size. Original floor plans show that there were also larger concert halls in each abode, and it was in these spaces that the entire court orchestra (*königliche Kapelle*) regularly performed sinfonias, opera arias, concertos, and other works. Details of each palace and its music rooms are discussed below.

Many of the royal residences have since been structurally modified or were destroyed in World War II. However, the physical spaces at court where music was made, as well as the lost and surviving keyboard instruments in them, can be largely determined by studying previously overlooked sources, including eighteenth-century architectural floor plans, palace inventories, and historic photographs made before World War II.

The grand court concerts (called *grosse Hofkonzerte*) took place in the larger salons at court. They were hosted by the queen mother, Sophia Dorothea of Hanover (1687–1757), at her palace Schloss Monbijou, at Schloss Charlottenburg, and at the Berlin Stadtschloss (her own suite on the second floor did not, however, feature a music room); more rarely by the king in Charlottenburg or the Berlin Stadtschloss; by Queen Elisabeth Christine in the Berlin Stadtschloss and in her personal summer residence, Schloss Schönhausen; by the king's youngest sister, Princess Amalia, in the Berlin Stadtschloss, occasionally in Monbijou, and from 1767 in her own palaces and in the Neues Palais (New Palace); and less frequently by other members of the royal family.[6] The performers sometimes included royal family members themselves, including Princess Amalia and, before her departure for Bayreuth, Princess Wilhelmine, who in 1728 accompanied a solo performed by the violinist Locatelli.[7] These concerts also were the only ones open to members of the court and to guests, which sometimes included visitors to the city.

Every one of Frederick's palaces, of course, also had a *petit salon* in the king's quarters for his private use. Admission to the king's soirées was rare and granted by special permission only—even for the court *Kapellmeister*. Thus, it can in no way be taken

---

6. Mary Oleskiewicz, "The Court of Brandenburg-Prussia," in *Music at German Courts 1715–1760: Changing Artistic Priorities*, ed. Samantha Owens, Barbara M. Reul, and Janice B. Stockigt (Woodbridge, UK: Boydell Press, 2011), 99. Prince August William (1722–58), brother of King Frederick and father of the future King Frederick William II, also occasionally held *Hofkonzerte* in his palace on Unter den Linden, which would later become the palace of his son. His residences are beyond the scope of this essay. It should be noted that the surviving inventories of the queen mother's palace, Schloss Monbijou, do not include descriptions of a music room or items such as musical instruments.

7. Ibid., 83–84, and note 16.

for granted that J. C. Bach, during his studies in Berlin with Emanuel Bach, "could have frequently heard the king playing his flute, accompanied by Philipp Emanuel" on Gottfried Silbermann fortepianos, although this might have been possible on some occasion.[8]

Dramatic spectacles—comic operettas, oratorios, and opera seria—and other festive music were performed at the king's palace theaters in Potsdam (the Stadtschloss, the Neues Palais), at the Berlin Stadtschloss, and from 1741 at the large opera house in Berlin on Unter den Linden. In summer months, musical productions often took place on makeshift or semipermanent stages in the orangeries at the palaces of Charlottenburg and Sanssouci (neither of which had a permanent theater), when the structures were emptied of fruit trees, and at Monbijou, Schönhausen, and Breslau. At the end of the 1760s, the orangerie next to Schloss Sanssouci was converted into the elegant Neue Kammern (New Chambers), built to entertain guests at Sanssouci; its second largest room, the Ovidgallerie (Ovid Gallery), which measures 19.2 meters long by 9.5 meters wide, was a highly resonant marble hall similar in scale to the one in Rheinsberg, but more resplendent. Although it bore no special designation in any inventory or floor plan as a "music room," its décor, featuring expensive gilt reliefs of scenes from Ovid's *Metamorphosis*, unmistakably defines its function as a musical space, like the music rooms of Rheinsberg, Sanssouci, Charlottenburg, and the New Palace. The small permanent theaters in the Potsdam Stadtschloss and the New Palace each possessed a harpsichord, whereas the large opera house on Unter den Linden was equipped with two.[9]

Details about the keyboard instruments at court and the historical spaces in which they were used must be pieced together from palace inventories, descriptions of palaces in eighteenth-century travel guides, eyewitness accounts, court records of purchases and payments, inventories, and historical photographs. These instruments included clavichords, harpsichords, fortepianos, and organs, as well as less common types such as the *Bogenflügel*. Some keyboards can be traced to purchases recorded in the *Schatullrechnung*, the monthly account of the king's personal expenditures (see Table 2). However, because the ledger begins only in 1742, it by no means presents a complete picture. The Rheinsberg years and Frederick's first two years as king are completely unaccounted for; moreover, records for certain months and years thereafter are missing.

Through contemporary eighteenth-century reports and by way of circumstantial evidence, we know that several members of the Bach family had, or likely had, access to court keyboards in certain residences on certain dates or at various times. Since few court documents record specific performances or explicitly define the complete range of duties assigned to any of the royal musicians, external evidence, period literature,

8. As suggested by Michael Latcham, "Pianos and Harpsichords for Their Majesties," *Early Music* 36.3 (2008): 361.

9. See notes 12 and 167.

autobiographies, and other sources will help to clarify where and when Emanuel Bach, for example, would have been regularly called upon to perform. In this regard it is important to remember that the king never simultaneously employed more than two keyboardists in the *Hofkapelle*.[10] Therefore, Emanuel alternated systematically with another full-time royal keyboardist for the king's soirées; similarly, he would have been called upon to rotate as accompanist in the grand court concerts frequently hosted by various members of the royal family. Emanuel appeared in these at least once as soloist, according to one newspaper and a court memo.[11] In addition, the entire *Hofkapelle* was regularly called upon to play for the serenades and festival music performed for the numerous birthdays, name days, and weddings of members of the royal family.

During performances of the *Hofoper*, Emanuel also must have been obligated to play one of the two harpsichord parts.[12] These performances took place in Berlin twice a week during the six weeks of Carnival (December to January), in October for Princess Amalia's name day, in March when the season's premiere was again performed for the queen mother's birthday, for royal weddings, and occasionally during the summer or for visits by special guests: "In both months [December and January], [opera] is performed every Monday and Friday. The remaining days of the week, during Carnival, alternate Redouten, Concerts, Operettas [*Comoedien*], and other entertainments at court. Otherwise, every evening from 7 to 9 in the chamber of the king a proper concert takes place, in which His Majesty is accustomed to presenting, in his own insightful and tasteful manner, his exceptional accomplishments on the flute."[13]

10. For the names, dates, and status of the keyboardists who served in the *Hofkapelle* beginning in 1740, see Oleskiewicz, "The Court of Brandenburg-Prussia," 98.

11. Manuel Bärwald, "'. . . ein Clavier von besonderer Erfindung': Der Bogenflügel von Johann Hohlefeld und seine Bedeutung für das Schaffen Carl Philipp Emanuel Bachs," BJ 94 (2008): 282. See the discussion of this performance below.

12. Since the court *Kapellmeister*, Heinrich Graun, directed from the first harpsichord, the second continuo part would have been played, alternately, by Emanuel Bach and his current colleague. See Louis Schneider, *Geschichte der Oper und das königlichen Opernhauses in Berlin* (Berlin: Duncker und Humblot, 1852), 71, which reports that, "according to an old manuscript," the orchestra consisted of "2 harpsichords [2 Flügeln], 12 Violins, 4 Violas, 4 Violoncellos, 3 Contrabasses, 4 Flutes, 2 Bassoons, 2 French horns [2 Waldhörner], 4 Oboes, 1 Theorbo, and 1 harp"; on 109, Schneider cites further testimony to the use of two harpsichords: "Zwei Männer in rothen Mänteln unterschieden sich in demselben vor allen übrigen Tonkünstlern. Es waren die beiden Grauns. Der Capellmeister [C. H. Graun] sass *vor dem ersten Flügel* [emphasis added] und der Concertmeister [J. G. Graun] auf dem ersten Platze der Violinisten" (Two men in red coats distinguished themselves from all the other musicians. They were the two Grauns. The Capellmeister [C. H. Graun] sat at the first harpsichord and the concert master [J. G. Graun] at the first place of the violinists).

13. Friedrich Wilhelm Marpurg, "Nachricht von dem gegenwärtigen Zustande der Oper und Musik des Königs," *Historisch-Kritische Beyträge zur Aufnahme der Musik* 1 (1754): 75–84 (esp. 75–76): "[Opera] wird in den beyden Monathen alle Montage und Freytage gespielet. Die übrigen Tage der Woche,

After the king moved his primary residence to Potsdam, Emanuel Bach and select other royal chamber musicians commuted, in rotation, from Berlin to accompany the king's soirées—a fact documented by records of payments made to the "Potsdam Musici" for per diem expenses.[14] There they joined a small number of resident Potsdam court musicians to form the orchestra that performed for the comic operas given at the small palace theaters in the Potsdam Stadtschloss and, from 1767, in the New Palace. Bach and his colleagues were thus kept busy working in numerous locations within the royal palaces and in other venues discussed below.

The only musician exempt from any of the above-described duties was the king's flutist and royal chamber composer, Johann Joachim Quantz (1697–1773), who proudly declared that he had "the freedom not to play in the orchestra, but only in the royal chamber music, and to take orders from no one but the king."[15] By default, this privilege excused him from performing in the *Hofoper*, comic operas, and grand court concerts. Had Emanuel Bach—or, for that matter, any other musician in the *Hofkapelle*—enjoyed such a rare privilege, surely he too would have made a similar boast in his own autobiography. Franz Benda, for example, who was the lifelong concertmaster of the king's chamber music and the Potsdam comic opera orchestra, could state only that he accompanied the king in over ten thousand flute concerts.[16] Similarly, although it was no small honor, Emanuel Bach could at most claim that the king "graciously had

<hr />

während [*sic*] Carnevalszeit, werden mit Redutten, Concerten, Comödien und andern Lustbarkeiten bey Hofe abgewechselt. Sonst aber wird alle Tage des Abends von 7 bis 9 in der Kammer des Königs ein ordentliches Concert aufgeführet, in welchem Sr. Majestät selbst von ihrem Einsichtsvollen schönen Geschmack und ihrer ausnehmenden Fertigkeit auf der Flöte Proben darzulegen gewohnt sind."

14. The king's *Schatullrechnung* records payments of per diems for the Potsdam Musici; a few invoices record that the keyboard players (including Emanuel Bach), a harpist, bassoonist, and several string players rotated in Potsdam on a staggered, roughly four- to six-week basis, during which time they would have been on call for both the royal chamber concerts and the comic opera. The *Schatullrechnung* (GStA PK) has been published in full online at http://quellen.perspectivia.net/bestaende/spsg-schatullrechnungen /jahre (N.B.: my citations follow the original sources, which may contain spellings that occasionally diverge from the online transcriptions). At one point a dispute over per diem payments for travel and lodging arose, as Frederick's primary residence was Potsdam, and many of the instrumentalists, including Bach, chose to reside in Berlin.

15. "Herrn Johann Joachim Quantzens Lebenslauf, von ihm selbst entworfen," in *Selbstbiographien deutscher Musiker des XVIII. Jahrhunderts*, by Willi Kahl (Cologne: Staufen, 1948), 248: "die Freyheit nicht im Orchester, sondern nur in der Königlichen Kammermusik zu spielen, und von Niemands als des Königs Befehl abzuhangen."

16. Lorenz, *Die Musikerfamilie Benda*, 154: "Es ist für mich Keine Geringe Satisfaction dass ich die Gnade gehabt bey diesen in warheit grossen Friedrich in Diensten zu stehen und durch alle die Jahre wenigstens biss 10000 Flöten-Concerte S. Maj. zu accompagniren" (It gives me no small satisfaction that I had the grace to serve this truly great Frederick and to have accompanied him over the years in at least ten thousand flute concerts).

me accompany, quite alone on the harpsichord [*Flügel*], in Charlottenburg, the first flute solo that he played as King."[17] Even J. F. Reichardt, the king's last *Kapellmeister*, boasted that he had earned the special privilege of attending the king's private chamber concerts, which was in fact a great honor but not on a par with that which Quantz enjoyed. Thus, there can be no doubt that Emanuel, like every other member of the *Hofkapelle*, was required to perform for the opera and wherever else the *Hofkapelle* was commanded to appear.

SCHLOSS RHEINSBERG 🗍 2

In 1738, when Emanuel Bach received his "unexpected and gracious call" to Ruppin,[18] precisely where and on what instrument did he play? At this date, Crown Prince Frederick had been living for two years in the palace at Rheinsberg, overlooking Lake Grienerick. Previously, he had resided in a modest abode in the nearby town of (Neu)Ruppin, and both accommodations were located in a rural area of Brandenburg called Ostprignitz-Ruppin. Since at the time Bach could have visited Frederick only at the Rheinsberg palace, it must be to this larger geographical area ("Ruppin") that Bach's autobiography refers. As soon as Frederick's father purchased the castle in 1734, architectural renovations and an expansion began, initially under the direction of Johann Gottfried Kemmeter (d. 1748). Kemmeter was succeeded in 1736 by Georg Wenzeslaus von Knobelsdorff (1699–1753) upon the latter's return from Italy. The plans naturally included spaces for music making.

Frederick and his wife, Elisabeth Christine of Brunswick-Wolfenbüttel-Bevern (1715–97), moved into the palace in 1736 while construction was ongoing. The earliest surviving Rheinsberg palace inventories, of 1742 and 1745, document in "His Royal Majesty's Music Chamber . . . a large, lacquered harpsichord, having a music desk fitted with two candlestick holders [and] 5 lacquered music stands," precisely the number needed to perform a flute concerto in the manner that would remain typical at court throughout Frederick's lifetime.[19] Undoubtedly a double-manual instrument, the harpsichord was situated inside a small music room within Frederick's private apartments, which would have been the precise place where Bach accompanied, or played

---

17. Emanuel Bach's original German is given in Burney, *Tagebuch einer musikalischen Reise*, 3:200: "Die Gnade hatte, das erste Flötensolo, was Sie als König spielten, in Charlottenburg mit dem Flügel ganz allein zu begleiten."

18. Ibid., 199–200.

19. SPSG Plansammlung, Inv. 843 (1742), *Inventarium aller auf hiesigen Königl: Schloß dem Stall und Domestiquen hause befindlichen Meublen . . . 4ten Sept. 1742*, 9–10, room 4, "Derer Königl: Majestet Music Kammer," containing, among other things, "ein grosser lacquirter Flügel nebst dem Pulpet und 2 Geridons[;] 5 lacquirte Pulpets." The information is repeated in Inv. 844, *Revidiertes=Inventarium . . . Decembri 1745*, fol. 97. This room, unique in having three windows, measured 5.72 meters long by 5.26 meters wide.

before, the Crown Prince and also the place where he subsequently played as a visiting artist. In a letter of 1739, Frederick's close friend Baron Jakob Friedrich von Bielfeld (1717–70), who resided at Rheinsberg and sometimes attended Frederick's soirées as an invited guest, described them as taking place in Frederick's private apartments: "The evenings are dedicated to music. The prince has concerts in his salon, where no one is admitted unless called, and it is a mark of high favor to receive an invitation."[20]

The interior structure of the Rheinsberg palace, still in existence, has been substantially remodeled over time, in part because Frederick gave it to his younger brother Prince Heinrich (1726–1802) upon the latter's marriage in 1752 to Princess Wilhelmine of Hesse-Kassel (1726–1808). However, it is possible to identify the earlier distribution of rooms from Knobelsdorff's floor plan of 1737, coupled with information from the 1742 inventory.[21] The intimate music salon where Emanuel Bach first played for Frederick (and where Bielfeld heard these concerts) was located on the first floor of the south wing but no longer exists; about 1763 it was redesigned and enlarged as a bedroom for Prince Heinrich. It is identifiable on the original floorplan as the only room in the suite having three windows.

Modern restoration to the palace has uncovered architectural and decorative traces of a larger space in Frederick's apartments where music was made, the Spiegelsaal (Hall of Mirrors) with music emblems, located in the southwest corner of the first floor.[22] During Prince Heinrich's renovations of 1763, it was divided up and subsumed under three separate rooms, including the present large picture gallery. The music room and the Spiegelsaal are identifiable in the inventories as the two largest rooms in Frederick's apartments by their greater number of windows and by the fact that they possessed chandeliers with sixteen arms (as opposed to six or fewer, as in those of the other rooms).[23] The Rheinsberg palace's Grosser Marmorsaal (Large Marble Hall), completed in 1740, is located in the northwest corner of the first floor's north

20. Letter VIII to Charles-Étienne Jordan, Rheinsberg, 30 October 1739, in *Lettres familiéres et autres, de Monsieur le Baron de Bielfeld, Tome I*, 2nd ed., revised, expanded, and corrected (Leiden: Luchtmans, 1767), 52: "Les soirées sont consacrées à la Musique. Le Prince a concert dans son salon, où persone n'entre qu'il n'y soit apellé, & c'est une faveur bien marquée qu'une pareille invitation."

21. Details from the inventories, such as the descriptions of abutting rooms, and from the floor plans, which provide the number of windows and directional orientation, have made it possible to identify with precision the location of the music rooms.

22. Detlef Fuchs and Claudia Sommer, eds., *Rheinsberg: Wiederherstellung von Schloss und Park* (Potsdam: Stiftung Preußische Schlösser und Gärten Berlin-Brandenburg, 1996), 43. The room measured 9.6 meters long by 5.56 meters wide.

23. Tilo Eggeling, *Studien zum Friderizianischen Rokoko: Georg Wenceslaus von Knobelsdorff als Entwerfer von Innendekorationen* (Berlin: Gebr. Mann Verlag, 1980), 64.

wing. Intended for music making and spectacles on an even larger scale, it still survives today in its original form.[24] Again decorated with gilt reliefs of scenes from Ovid's *Metamorphosis*, the Grosser Marmorsaal was completed just as Frederick became king and moved his court to Berlin. As a result, it is generally believed that Frederick never had occasion to use the space (as a modern guided tour of the palace informs); however, Bielfeld's letters show, to the contrary, that Frederick and a large entourage of friends, family, and courtiers continued to enjoy lavish summer festivities at Rheinsberg during the 1740s. We must assume, given their magnitude, that these excursions sometimes included Bach and other court musicians: "We passed part of the last two summers, sometimes at Sans-Souci, sometimes at Charlottenburg, sometimes at Oranienburg, and sometimes at Rheinsberg. The queens, the princesses, the princes, and most of the ladies and cavaliers, directly attached to the court, were at these festivities. Everywhere we found . . . prepared pleasures, . . . balls, illuminations, fireworks, food fit for kings, and drinks for the gods. The king has always been in the best humor of the world."[25] The 1741 and 1745 inventories make no mention of a keyboard instrument in either the Spiegelsaal or the Grosser Marmorsaal, and it may be supposed that the harpsichord kept in his private space was temporarily moved there for larger concerts or had been relocated permanently to Berlin.

SCHLOSS CHARLOTTENBURG 🗗 3

Schloss Charlottenburg, with its lavish gardens and situated on the River Spree on the outskirts of Berlin, was initially Frederick's preferred summer residence as king.[26] It had been built for his grandmother Sophia Charlotte of Hanover (1668–1705), a patron of music, a harpsichordist, and the dedicatee of Corelli's op. 5 violin sonatas. Soon after becoming king, Frederick had several existing rooms in the old part of the palace redecorated for himself and ordered Knobelsdorff to construct a splendid new wing that extended to the right of the existing palace.

24. The Marmorsaal (room 16 in the inventory of 1742) measures 12.6 meters long by 9.58 meters wide.

25. Letter LXXV to "M. de M," 15 September 1747, in *Lettres familiéres et autres, de Monsieur le Baron de Bielfeld, Tome II*, 2nd rev. ed. (Leiden: Luchtmans, 1767), 168: "Nous avons passé une partie des deux derniers Etés tantôt à Sans-Souci, tantôt à Charlottenbourg, tantôt à Orangebourg & tantôt à Rheinsberg. Les Reines, les Princesses, les Princes & la plupart des Dames & des Cavaliers, immédiatement attachés à la Cour, ont été de ces fêtes. Partout nous avons trouvé des . . . plaisirs préparés, . . . des bals, des illuminations, des feux d'artifices, une chère toute Royale, & du breuvage des Dieux. Le Roi a toujours été de la meilleure humeur du monde."

26. The official palace website, with images, can be found at http://www.spsg.de/schloesser-gaerten /objekt/schloss-charlottenburg/.

The second floor of Charlottenburg's new wing would ultimately contain two new sets of apartments for the king. The music room of its first set of apartments, completed in 1742, continued themes from his previous music rooms in Rheinsberg: marbled walls overlaid with musical emblems and scenes from Ovid's *Metamorphosis* in gold relief. The room, which measures 10.23 meters long by 5.2 meters wide, was subsequently remodeled by Frederick's successor as a living space, but the earliest surviving inventory of the palace, from 1770/1780, describes its original décor and furnishings.[27] Probably because Frederick no longer used these apartments when it was drawn up, this inventory records no keyboard instrument there. However, we can surmise that the music room had been furnished with his grandmother's black double-manual harpsichord by Michael Mietke,[28] which had been "japanned" by the court lacquerer, Gerard Dagly (fl. 1697–1714), and which is today preserved in Charlottenburg (Table 3).[29] If so, this instrument could have been the one played by Emanuel Bach in Charlottenburg when he accompanied the "first flute solo that [Frederick] played as king."[30] At that early date, however, it may have been kept in one of the redecorated rooms (no. 212 or 213), where Frederick initially resided in Charlottenburg.

During 1746–47 a smaller second set of royal apartments, isolated from the rest of the palace by a series of grand festival halls, was constructed at the end of the new wing.[31] By this time, however, Frederick had come to prefer the more rural Potsdam instead of

27. SPSG Plansammlung, Ak 31, *Inventarium von Mobilibres, im königl. Schlosse Charlottenburg* (p. 4), room 9 (now room 351), "Die Marmorierte Cammer" (the Marbled Chamber). Modern restoration work has uncovered additional details of the original space; see Tilo Eggeling, *Die Wohnungen Friedrichs des Großen im Schloß Charlottenburg* (Berlin: Verwaltung der Staatlichen Schlösser und Gärten, 1978), 9, 22; page 22 (illustration 11) shows a reconstruction of the music room, which was later remodeled by his successor.

28. Mietke (d. 1719) was making harpsichords for the court by 1697. He became the official court keyboard maker to Frederick's grandfather Frederick I in 1707, succeeding Christoph Werner, and in 1712 was paid as *Clavier Stimmer* (keyboard tuner) (Schneider, *Geschichte der Oper*, 55). Three known surviving harpsichords attributed to Mietke include "a single-manual harpsichord, which is signed and dated (Berlin, 1710) . . . in Hudiksvall, Sweden, and a single- and a double-manual harpsichord are preserved in Schloss Charlottenburg, Berlin. The latter two are not signed, probably because they were made for the court" (Dieter Krickeberg, "Mietke," in *Grove Music Online*, http://www.oxfordmusic online.com, accessed 20 April 2015).

29. Harpsichord, ca. 1700, SPSG Plansammlung, Hohenzollern Inv. 2728. There are differing accounts as to when the black Mietke came to Charlottenburg. Gerd Bartoschek et al., *Sophie Charlotte und ihr Schloss: Ein Musenhof des Barock in Brandenburg-Preußen* (Munich: Prestel Verlag, 1999), 248, suggests that the black Mietke could have been the instrument on which Emanuel Bach accompanied the king's first flute solo.

30. Burney, *Tagebuch einer musikalischen Reise*, 3:200. See also note 17.

31. Eggeling, *Die Wohnungen Friedrichs des Großen*, 44–46 (room 364).

Charlottenburg as his primary residence and seldom stayed at Charlottenburg. Thus, the new, second suite consisted of only four rooms with exceptionally plain walls, all designed to function as picture galleries. The inventory of 1770/1780 describes the music room, which measures 6.75 meters long by 9.70 meters wide, as "His Royal Majesty's Concert Chamber" and notes the presence of "1 harpsichord [*Flügel*] and five music stands," just as in Rheinsberg.[32] These items and the rest of the furniture the inventory describes are lost.[33] The absence of an instrument from the first suite's music room at this date suggests that its keyboard (the black Mietke?) might have been relocated to the new apartments.[34] However, as will be discussed below, it is possible that a Silbermann fortepiano stood in the new apartments until about 1765.

Probably during the 1740s, the black Mietke harpsichord was expanded from its original compass of FF–GG–AA–c3 (without FF♯ and GG♯) to its current FF–GG–e3 (without FF♯).[35] The instrument, probably in Charlottenburg by 1700, must have been used for opera performances at Queen Sophia Charlotte's court: a portrait made in 1702 by Anthoni Schoonjans (1655–1726) of the Italian composer Attilio Ariosti, who from 1697 to 1703 was the queen's court composer, shows Ariosti composing while seated at what is almost certainly an artistic rendering of this black japanned instrument.[36] It has been suggested that the black Mietke at one point belonged to Margrave Christian Ludwig of Brandenburg-Schwedt (who during the reign of Frederick William I resided in the Berlin Stadtschloss), Frederick's great-uncle, but there is no compelling evidence for this.[37] However, a perusal of Christian Ludwig's *Nachlass* reveals only one

32. SPSG Plansammlung, Ak 31, *Inventarium von Mobilibres, im königl. Schlosse Charlottenburg*, [p. 2], room 4 (now room 364): "Sr. Königl. Majestät Concert Cammer . . . 1. Flügel, 5. Pulpèts."

33. Afra Schick, "Die Möblierung des Konzertzimmers Friedrichs II. von Preußen im Schloss Charlottenburg—zur Neukonzeption nach 1918," *Jahrbuch Stiftung Preußische Schlösser und Gärten Berlin-Brandenburg* 7 (2005): 126.

34. The suite was destroyed in World War II and reconstructed in 1973. The museum currently does not display any instrument in the room, and the location of the five music stands is unknown.

35. Pitches are indicated using a variation of the Helmholtz system (which derives from German organ tablature), in which CC, C, and c are three, two, and one octaves (respectively) below middle c (c1), and c2 and c3 are one and two octaves (respectively) above. The instrument's compass is given in Sheridan Germann, "The Mietkes, the Margrave, and Bach," in *Bach, Handel, Scarlatti: Tercentenary Essays*, ed. Peter Williams (Cambridge: Cambridge University Press, 1985), 136 and app. C (pp. 144–47), by William Dowd, which gives a full description of both the black and the white Mietke harpsichords in Charlottenburg.

36. See Bartoschek et al., *Sophie Charlotte und ihr Schloss*, 248–49 (illustration of the harpsichord: catalog no. II.40; illustration of the Ariosti portrait on p. 86, catalog no. II.39).

37. Germann goes even further to speculate "that the possibility that the black harpsichord was also owned by Sophie Charlotte is interesting, for if it was hers it has as much chance as the white of having been at the Berliner Schloss in 1719, and therefore of being the harpsichord J. S. Bach played for the

keyboard instrument in his estate at his death in 1734: a blue and silver double-manual harpsichord, which was bequeathed to an obscure descendant of the family.[38]

The only other room that possessed a harpsichord, according to the 1770/1780 Charlottenburg inventory, was located in Princess Amalia's suite on the second floor of the original, central section of the palace. The inventory describes the first of her three rooms, overlooking the garden (formerly those of her grandmother Sophia Charlotte), simply as a "chamber" (*Cammer*) in which stood a "Japanese lacquered harpsichord."[39] The room, Sophia Charlotte's former *Audienzzimmer*, measures 7.3 meters long by 6.75 meters wide; the instrument it contained was the white lacquered single-manual harpsichord built ca. 1702–4 by Mietke and also "japanned" by Dagly.[40] It had been owned and played by Queen Sophia Charlotte before being passed down to her daughter-in-law (Frederick II's mother) Sophia Dorothea of Hanover (d. 1757) and then to her granddaughter Princess Amalia. The instrument's case, in imitation of the white porcelain so prized at the time, depicts Chinese garden scenes with dancing and music-making figures and coordinates with the décor of the room, where it continues to be displayed. Lessons and intimate chamber music in Amalia's Charlottenburg suite would have taken place on this instrument, which therefore Emanuel Bach certainly would have known and played.

A third instrument probably known to Emanuel and previously owned by Queen Sophia Charlotte was a single-manual folding harpsichord that accompanied Frederick on his travels and military campaigns, during which he famously continued to compose and play. This instrument, called *clavecin brisé* and made in Paris by Jean Marius (Table 3), was constructed in three sections and possessed fifty-one keys. Its

---

Margrave" ("The Mietkes, the Margrave, and Bach," 132n46). Germann cites a private communication (dated 1980) that enigmatically claims that the black Mietke "has no historical connection to" Charlottenburg, but more recent literature published by the spsg suggests otherwise (see note 29).

38. Oleskiewicz, "The Court of Brandenburg-Prussia," 109. It has not been possible to determine the precise location of Christian Ludwig's apartments, but due to the limited number of music rooms, they were probably located on the second floor in the suite later occupied by Frederick William II.

39. spsg Plansammlung, Ak 31, *Inventarium von Mobilibres, im königl. Schlosse Charlottenburg*, [p. 36], "Printzes Amalie Königl. Hoheit Cammern," room 111 (now room 206), "ein Flügel Japanisch gemahlet."

40. Harpsichord, ca. 1700, spsg Plansammlung, Inv. V, 104. Images and information about this instrument and about Dagly, court lacquerer and director of the Berlin lacquered furniture workshop, have been published at http://www.spsg.de/nc/presse-foto-film/2015-09-28-gerard-dagly-und-die -berliner-hofwerkstatt/. The instrument is illustrated in Edward L. Kottick, *A History of the Harpsichord* (Bloomington: Indiana University Press, 2003), 208. See Bartoschek et al., *Sophie Charlotte und ihr Schloss*, 250–51, and catalog no. II.48 (illustration). Dating of the white Mietke is from Germann, "The Mietkes, the Margrave, and Bach," 131.

compass, comprising a short G-octave with a split BB/D♯, extended from GG/BB to c3. (There is no GG♯, AA, or BB♭, and in order to play BB one must use the split key between D and E, which plays either BB or D♯, depending on whether one strikes the little key in front or the one in back.) After 1740, the instrument, which had been gifted to Sophia Charlotte in 1704 by her cousin the duchess of Orléans, received Frederick's coat of arms on the underside of its central section. After it was no longer used, the instrument was kept in the *Kunstkammer* of the Berlin Stadtschloss and until it became part of the collection of the Berlin Musikinstrumenten-Museum.[41]

Charlottenburg's *Schlosskapelle*, planned by Johann Friedrich Eosander (1669–1728) before the death of Sophia Charlotte in 1705, was not consecrated until 1706. Its organ, built by the most famous organ builder of the time, Arp Schnitger (1648–1719), was installed in the same year (Table 4).[42] The chapel, following Sophia Charlotte's wishes, was the most elaborately decorated room of the palace and was the location for royal family weddings. These events were followed by lavish festivities, including serenatas, held in the orangerie at Charlottenburg, where Frederick II had a small but exquisite theater installed. We have no documentation of a harpsichord in the orangerie.

Prior to Frederick II's reign, the court organist had been Gottlieb Hayne. From 1740 to 1742 he served as a keyboard tutor to Princess Amalia, and he continued to serve the queen mother in 1752–53.[43] After 1740 either of the court's keyboard musicians, including Emanuel Bach, as well as Princess Amalia's court musician the Bach pupil Johann Philipp Kirnberger (1721–83), also could have been among those who performed for weddings and other occasions on the Schnitger organ.

41. See Bartoschek et al., *Sophie Charlotte und ihr Schloss*, 254, and catalog no. II.59 (illustration). In 1875 it was moved from the *Kunstkammer* to the Berlin Kunstgewerbemuseum and in 1888 entered the collection of the Berlin Musikinstrumenten-Museum.

42. In 1944 the original Schnitger organ at the Charlottenburg *Schlosskapelle* was destroyed by fire and reconstructed by Karl Schuke. For an illustrated history of the chapel and its organ, see Stefan Behrens and Uwe Pape, "Charlottenburg, Schloß Charlottenburg, Eosander-Kapelle, Orgel von Arp Schnitger, 1706, Rekonstruction von Karl Schuke, 1969–70," in *500 Jahre Orgeln in Berliner Evangelischen Kirchen*, ed. Berthold Schwarz, 2 vols. (Berlin: Pape, 1991), 1:70–79. A discography of the Schnitger organ is published at http://www.arpschnitger.nl/sberlineo.html. The original organ's tonal design has been reconstructed in a new instrument at Cornell University; the new instrument's layout and visual design, however, are based on Schnitger's organ case at Clausthal-Zellerfeld in central Germany. See http://music.cornell.edu/about-us/facilities-and-instruments/organs-and-keyboards /organs/anabel-taylor/.

43. Oleskiewicz, "The Court of Brandenburg-Prussia," 81.

Frederick, accustomed to the seclusion of idyllic Rheinsberg, soon tired of city living. Between 1744 and 1746 Knobelsdorff was charged with extensively remodeling and enlarging the Stadtschloss in the more remote Potsdam; the second story included new living quarters for the king.[44] Mainly the artistic work of Johann August Nahl (1710–81), the king's suite was split between the east and west wings on either side of the Grosser Marmorsaal. The east apartment included an exquisite music room, measuring 8.57 meters long by 7.48 meters wide (these dimensions are based on a floor plan of 1809), in Frederician rococo that faced the Lustgarten (Pleasure Garden).[45] The second story also received a new, larger concert hall in the west wing facing Breite Strasse. On the ground floor, Knobelsdorff installed a small theater whose interior was completed in 1748. All three spaces can be identified in the original palace floor plans.

In 1779 and again in 1786 the Berlin chronicler Friedrich Nicolai described the king's music room as having green wooden paneling and gold-leafed Chinese motifs, a fortepiano, and an ornate music stand: "The music stand of the king, by Melchior Kambly, is made of tortoiseshell with gold-leafed iron pictures. A fortepiano by Silbermann also stands here, the best he ever made."[46] Identical stands by Kambly stood in every one of the king's private music rooms; two are still known to exist.[47] The earliest surviving Stadtschloss inventory, from 1780, also confirms the presence of a

44. The palace was partially destroyed in 1945 by Allied bombs and torn down by the Communist government; in 2013 a reconstruction of the entire historic façade was completed, with a modern interior; it now houses the Brandenburg parliament.

45. Hans-Joachim Giersberg et al., *Potsdamer Schlößer und Gärten: Bau- und Gartenkunst vom 17. bis 20. Jahrhundert* (Potsdam: Stiftung Schlösser und Gärten Potsdam-Sanssouci, 1981), 74, 80–81.

46. Friedrich Nicolai, *Beschreibung der königlichen Residenzstädte Berlin und Potsdam und aller daselbst befindlicher Merkwürdigkeiten: Nebst Anzeige der jetztlebenden Gelehrten, Künstler und Musiker, und einer historischen Nachricht von allen Künstlern, welche vom dreyzehnten Jahrhunderte an, bis jetzt, in Berlin gelebt haben, oder deren Kunstwerke daselbst befindlich sind*, 2nd ed., 2 vols. (Berlin, 1779), 2:855: "Das Notenpult des Königes ist von Schildkröte mit vergoldeten erzenen Bildern, von Melchior Kambly. Auch steht hier ein Pianoforte von Silbermann, das beste, so er verfertigt hat." The text is similar in the edition of 1786, 3:1141. The extant music stands by Kambly have gilded rococo bronzework and inlaid pictures of wood and mother-of-pearl. Nicolai's publication of 1779 (in two volumes) was an expanded edition of a publication of the same title (in one volume) in 1769; in 1786 it was expanded to three volumes.

47. Johann Melchior Kambly (or Cambly) (1718–83), not "Rambly," as his name is sometimes mistakenly transcribed, was a Swiss sculptor (particularly of ornamental architectural elements, including wood, bronze, and plaster). From 1745 he contributed to the development of the style of Frederician rococo in Potsdam and Berlin.

"pianoforte of oak" in "His Majesty's Chambers . . . Concert Cammer."[48] The piano was reported here again in 1798, and a palace inventory of 1822 still notes there "a Silbermann pianoforte of Oak, together with a music stand having 2 candle holders."[49]

Insofar as the surviving but incomplete account books show, Frederick customarily purchased a new keyboard instrument for each new music room of every palace. The accounts show that a fortepiano costing 420 Taler, including transport, was recorded in 1746: "to Silbermann for [a] pianoforte" (see Table 2); on June 21 the king ordered payment, and on June 24 Silbermann signed the paid receipt.[50] Undoubtedly purchased for the completion of renovations to the Stadtschloss, this instrument may have been the first Silbermann fortepiano at court, and it is possibly one of the two surviving instruments currently on display in Potsdam (the one dated 1746; another arrived the following year for Sanssouci). Though the Stadtschloss was bombed during World War II and later demolished, a surviving photograph depicts the oak Silbermann fortepiano

48. SPSG Plansammlung, Ak 9, *Inventarium des königl. Schloßes zu Potsdam d. 20 Decbr. 1780 . . . von den im Königl. Schloß zu Potsdam befindlichen Meublen, Betten, sowohl Fürstlichen als für Domestiquen and andere den Castellan Knopf zu Inspektion allergnägdigst anvertrauten Effecten* . . . (unpaginated), designated as room 175 (later room 10): "Concert Cammer, boisiert und laquirt . . . 1 piano forte von eichen Holtz" (Concert chamber, paneled and lacquered . . . 1 piano forte of oak). The inventory indicates that the room was located on the "erstes Obergeschoss / II. Étage / Mittlere Étage" (first upper floor / second story / middle floor).

49. Carl Christian Horvath, *Potsdams Merkwürdigkeiten, beschrieben, und durch Plans und Prospekte erläutert* (Potsdam: Horvath, 1798), 53: "ein vortrefliches Fortepiano von Silbermann"; SPSG Plansammlung, *Inventarium des Königl. Stadt Schlosses zu Potsdam, Vol. 2, welches aus 2te Stockwerk* . . . , Inv. 487 (1822), 42: "Corps de logis Sr. Majestät Friedrich des IIten. / [room no.] 168. Concert. Kammer." In Inv. 479, which is virtually identical, 175, the room number from the old inventory, has been added here in pencil: "ein Silbermannsches Pianoforte von Eichenholz, nebst Pult, u. 2 Leuchterstellen."

50. *Die Schatullrechnung Friedrichs des Grossen*, GStA PK, BPH, Rep. 47, no. 899, fol. 17r, "Extra-Geldausgaben," 1746, item no. 13: "an den Silbermann vor Piano et Forte, 420 Taler"; GStA PK, BPH, Rep. 47, no. 940, n.p.: "Auf Sr: König: Maj. in Preußen allergnädigsten Hohen Ordre, Habe ein Piano et forte, zu Freyburg [*sic*] in Saxen aller untertenigst verferttiget und in Potsdam geliefert, welches nebst den Transport sich ohn maßgeblich beträgt auf 420 RTl. Potsdam, d: 21 Juny 1746. Gottfried Silbermann [Unterschrift]" (According to His Royal Prussian Majesty's most gracious high order, I have, at Freiberg in Saxony, most humbly finished and delivered a Piano and Forte, which, together with transport, comes to 420 Reichstaler. Potsdam, 21 June, 1746. Gottfried Silbermann [signature]). GStA PK, BPH, Rep. 47, no. 940, n.p.: "Diese Rechnung ist richtig bezahlet worden, worüber ich hiermit gebührent quittiere. Potsdam d: 24 Juny, 1746, Gottfried Silbermann [Unterschrift]" (I hereby attest that this bill has been duly paid. Potsdam, 24 June, 1746, Gottfried Silbermann [signature]). John Koster errs in reporting 13 December 1746 as the date of payment to Silbermann ("The Quest for Bach's Clavier: A Historiographical Interpretation," *Early Keyboard Journal* 14 [1996]: 77).

as it was situated in the king's music room.[51] The keyboard's plain oak cabinet stands in stark contrast to the room's elaborate décor.

General Graf Chasôt, a close friend of the king who in the 1740s attended Frederick's concerts in Potsdam, described this elegant private music room with its rounded corners, and he explicitly mentions its Silbermann fortepiano:

> At Potsdam the daily concert would take place in a chamber 24 feet in diameter, with slightly rounded corners, 16 feet up to the cornice; all done up in woodwork with beautiful compartments and magnificently gold-leafed; a very pretty fireplace of red Egyptian marble; and in the middle a superb and a very large rock crystal chandelier culminating below with a crystal ball as large as a head; and, best of all, this chamber was so favorably built, and the furniture so well integrated for music, that we never lost the least bit of sound. The concert consisted in a single first and second violin (rarely doubled), a viola, a violoncello, and for a keyboard a fortepiano of Silbermann, [also] one or two flutes, when the king would play trios with Quantz; one or two castrati and once in a while one of the best singers from the opera would receive orders and a carriage for the journey from Potsdam. In these concerts one heard only voices or flutes; all the other instruments were there only for the accompaniment.[52]

The "slightly rounded corners," visible in the original floor plans and in historical photos (see 4), are not a characteristic of any other Frederician music room and unquestionably confirm the precise location in Chasot's description.

The second floor of the palace was also the location of the second, large music room. The 1780 palace inventory documents this room (designated "Concert Cammer, japanisch gemahlet") as having Japanese motifs on a gold background and furnished with "1 harpsichord."[53] Nicolai, who in 1779 and again in 1786 also described the large music room, identifies this instrument more precisely as "a beautiful harpsichord by Silbermann."[54] The king's *Schatullrechnung* records a good number of harpsichords (see Table 2), many of which are lost and cannot be identified as to maker, but at least

51. Latcham, "Pianos and Harpsichords for Their Majesties," 383 (illustration 16), shows a photograph of this instrument in the king's music room of the Potsdam Schloss but incorrectly identifies the room and instrument as those of Sanssouci Palace.

52. Kurd von Schlözer, *Zur Geschichte Friedrichs des Grossen und seiner Zeit* (Berlin: Wilhelm Hertz, 1856), 212–13.

53. SPSG Plansammlung, Ak 9, *Inventarium des königl. Schloßes zu Potsdam* (n.p.), room 196, "Erstes Obergeschoss / II. Étage / Mittlere Étage / sogenannte Sommer Flügel . . . IX. die Concert Cammer, japanisch gemahlet . . . 1 flügel Clavier" (first upper floor / second story / middle floor). This larger room measured 9 meters long by 7.5 meters wide.

54. Nicolai, *Beschreibung der königlichen Residenzstädte* (1779), 2:859 and (1786), 3:1145, room 18, "Das große Koncertzimmer. . . . Ein schöner Flügel, von Silbermann."

several, including this one and perhaps most, were by Silbermann. This instrument (the second one listed in Table 3B) is undoubtedly one of the instruments documented by the *Schatullrechnung* (Table 2) and probably corresponds to the payment of 200 Taler in June 1746, "dem Silbermann vor ein Clavir" (to Silbermann for a harpsichord), since it was paid for just at the time renovations to the Stadtschloss were complete. The very next instrument paid for was the Silbermann fortepiano for Frederick's private music room in the Stadtschloss, mentioned above.

This larger concert room was remodeled by Frederick's successor as a bedroom;[55] thus no historical photograph helps to identify the instrument further. Unfortunately, neither Nicolai nor the inventories mention the presence of a keyboard instrument in the *Schlosstheater*. By the time of Nicolai's writing, the comic opera had long been disbanded. The inventory of 1780 lists only a stand for a harpsichord ("1 Flügel Clavier Gestelle").

When in 1746 Frederick relocated to Potsdam, many of the musicians who accompanied the king's chamber concerts, including Franz Benda, concertmaster of the chamber music, followed suit. Others, including Emanuel Bach, remained in Berlin and thus commuted to Potsdam in rotation, alternating stays there of roughly four to six weeks. Duties in Potsdam included serving in the twelve-member orchestra that accompanied the Italian comic operettas (*intermezzi*) regularly produced in the new *Schlosstheater*.[56] The Potsdam Stadtschloss remained the king's main residence until the completion of his summer palace, Schloss Sanssouci, in 1747. From then on, Frederick spent the winter months from November to April at the Potsdam Stadtschloss and May through October at Sanssouci.

SCHLOSS SANSSOUCI 5

A second Silbermann piano, delivered to the king no later than April 1747, was purchased through Quantz for 373 Taler, 12 Groschen (see Table 2).[57] The new instrument could only have been acquired for and placed in Sanssouci Palace.[58] The timing could not have been better: the palace's extravagant new music room, an exquisite rococo

---

55. Hans-Joachim Giersberg, *Das Potsdamer Stadtschloss* (Potsdam: Potsdamer Verlag, 1998), 95.

56. The *Schlosstheater*, payments, and the specific duties of the *Hofkapelle* are outlined in greater detail in Oleskiewicz, "The Court of Brandenburg-Prussia," esp. 100.

57. *Schatullrechnung*, GStA PK, BPH, Rep. 47, no. 900, fol. 5r, May 1747, item no. 7: "dem Virtuosen Quantz vor ein Piano et Forte L.Q. 373 Taler, 12 Gr" (47 Taler less than the payment for the piano of 1746, discussed above, which was made directly to Silbermann; it is unclear whether the payment to Quantz included transport). Payments were sometimes recorded well after the invoice was due.

58. The official palace website, with images, is http://www.spsg.de/schloesser-gaerten/objekt/schloss-sanssouci/.

jewel whose decorative interior was completed and invoiced in April,[59] was furnished with a brand new fortepiano just in time for Frederick's summer residency (May to October). This palace, perched atop a terraced vineyard, is where Frederick would spend the majority of every summer season for the rest of his life.

It has usually been supposed that because the interior of the entire palace was not yet finished, the king would not have resided there in May and that his encounter with Bach, whose famous visit occurred that month, must have taken place in the Potsdam Stadtschloss. However, there is no reason to think Frederick waited to occupy Sanssouci: as he did with Rheinsberg and every other one of his subsequent residences, Frederick moved into a new palace as soon as his apartments were ready but before the remainder of the palace was complete. The final payment for the Sanssouci music room's décor, made in April 1747 to the artist Johann Michael Hoppenhaupt (1709–69), provides unequivocal evidence that this new space was ready for use before Sebastian Bach's visit to Potsdam. Perhaps it was no coincidence that the elder Bach elected (or, more likely, was invited) to make his journey at this very juncture.

If indeed Sanssouci was to be inhabited by the king beginning in May, intense pressure would have been on the artisans to have it ready in time for the change of season. Its music room, the most richly decorated of all of Frederick's music rooms and, moreover, the largest space in his elaborate apartments at Sanssouci (the room measures 10.1 meters long by 8.2 meters wide by 6.2 meters high), featured five integral wall paintings by Antoine Pesne, each depicting a scene from Ovid's *Metamorphosis* (continuing the theme from the Rheinsberg and Charlottenburg music rooms). It also featured large mirrors opposite the windows (which overlooked the vineyard and park) and two console tables of Silesian chrysoprase, Frederick's favorite stone. The Ovid theme also inspired a hunt motif here that would be recalled later in the New Palace: a large portrait of the hunting goddess Diana bathing overlooks the room (a clear reference to the Acteon story in book 3 of the *Metamorphosis*); Frederick's favorite Italian greyhound, named Biche, springs into her lap, while additional dogs (in plaster relief) chase rabbits along the room's gilt cornice. Just as in the Potsdam and Berlin palaces, the room's centerpiece is a large Silesian rock crystal chandelier. Sanssouci was the prized and much-anticipated new summer residence of the king; it is thus hard to believe that he would not have wanted to occupy it immediately. There can be little doubt that this palace—and not the old Potsdam Stadtschloss, as has traditionally been believed—was the location of the famous encounter that interrupted the royal chamber concert on the evening of May 7, 1747.[60]

59. Friendly communication by Klaus Dorst, art historian and caretaker of monuments, SPSG.

60. Latcham, "Pianos and Harpsichords for Their Majesties," 382, supposes that "the Silbermann *Hammerflügel* had not yet been installed in Sans Souci"; he thus concludes that "Bach and his son

The king's suite in Sanssouci was located not, as usual, on the second floor but rather on the ground floor of the palace. The music room's décor and its prominent position as the largest room within the entire royal suite (though still relatively intimate) are, however, features typical of his other palaces. The antechamber, a picture gallery that formed the first room of the suite, preceded the music room: this antechamber is where Emanuel Bach and his colleagues waited each evening to be summoned for the royal chamber concerts. This is also where the visitor Charles Burney stood as he listened to the king's concert.[61] And it is surely the very "antechamber" where Johann Sebastian Bach also waited "for His Majesty's most gracious permission to listen to the music."[62] No other keyboard instrument besides this Silbermann fortepiano ever resided in Sanssouci during Frederick's life.

Nicolai's descriptions of Sanssouci palace unfortunately are far more cursory than those of the other palaces; he instead focuses on the neighboring picture gallery, listing in utmost detail the paintings it contained. His earliest description, published in 1769, contains a mere paragraph describing the king's suite, and it can be surmised from the minimal information provided that Nicolai himself probably never personally gained access to the interior. Nevertheless, according to the earliest surviving palace inventory for Sanssouci, in 1782 the "pianoforte" still stood in "das Concert=Zimmer."[63]

BERLIN STADTSCHLOSS 6

The Berlin Stadtschloss, a veritable fortress constructed on a massive scale on Unter den Linden, had long been the official city residence of the Prussian capital. In addition to many rooms and festival halls used for conducting official state business, the palace contained apartments, each complete with a music room, for several members of the immediate royal family: the king; Queen Christine (whose suite had two music rooms); Princess Amalia; and the Crown Prince and Princess of Prussia.

The Berlin Stadtschloss had also been the residence of the king's great-uncle Margrave Christian Ludwig of Brandenburg-Schwedt, the dedicatee of the so-called *Brandenburg Concertos*, until his death in 1734. As Sebastian Bach's 1721 dedication makes

---

[Friedemann] were received by King Frederick in the Stadtschloss" where "the king played his famous theme." I have not been able to locate any contemporary eighteenth-century report that documents the Stadtschloss as the location of the encounter. On the contrary, the preponderance of evidence, both archival and circumstantial, points instead to Sanssouci.

61. A point he neglected to disclose, although it is mentioned by Frederick's last *Kapellmeister*, J. F. Reichardt; see Oleskiewicz, "Like Father, Like Son?," 255 and n. 9.

62. NBR, 224.

63. SPSG, Acta V, *Inventarium. Von dem Königl: Schloss zu Sanssouci, und den neuen Cammern . . . Aufgenommen den 20. Marz. 1782* (n.p. [pp. 3–4]), esp. p. 4, no. 7: "ein Piano forte."

clear, Bach performed before the Margrave while in Berlin during a visit in 1719: "As I had a couple of years ago the pleasure of appearing before Your Royal Highness, by virtue of Your Highness's commands, and as I noticed then that Your Highness took some pleasure in the small talents that Heaven has given me for Music . . . Your Highness deigned to honor me with the command to send Your Highness some pieces of my composition."[64] It has not been possible to identify which of the apartments belonged to him; but since Christian Ludwig necessarily must have occupied one of the suites with a music room, his may have been the one on the second floor that was later inhabited by Crown Prince Frederick William II. Christian Ludwig's music room would have been the location in which Sebastian Bach appeared before him in 1719.

Emanuel Bach and the court's other musicians would have had occasion to play in other multipurpose spaces within the Berlin Stadtschloss as well. The large Rittersaal (Knight's Hall), on the third floor of the palace, was the location on July 17, 1744, of a large royal wedding party—with a "magnificent" *Tafelmusik* by the *Hofkapelle*—to celebrate the marriage of Princess Luise Ulrike (1720–82) to the crown prince of Sweden.[65] The room was situated over the fifth Portale (Portal) and faced the Lust-garten (Pleasure Garden) to the north (i.e., directly above the Balkonzimmer [Balcony Room]). The immense chapel, also located on the third floor over the third Portale (Portal) and facing the Schloßfreiheit (the area flanking the south side of the palace), would have provided yet another venue for occasional music.

It was not until 1745 that King Frederick bothered to have his suite of apartments in the Berlin Schloss decorated. The first four rooms to be furnished, including the concert room, were assigned to the decorator Johann August Nahl. The remaining rooms were taken up in 1747–48 by Johann Christian Hoppenhaupt (fl. 1742, d. 1778–86). As was customary, the music room was the most lavish. Like the much later music room of the New Palace, it featured green-paneled walls ornamented with gold leaf, and—similar to the music room of the king's second set of apartments in the new wing of Charlottenburg that soon would be created—it simultaneously served as a picture gallery, with numerous precious paintings on display. The king's suite, located in the southeastern corner of the second floor, overlooked the Schlossplatz, on one

64. Bach's dedication to Christian Ludwig of the *Six concerts avec plusieurs instruments*, BWV 1046–51, is given in NBR, 92–93, text quote on 92.

65. Christoph Henzel cites the newspaper report in "Das Konzertleben der Preußischen Haupt-stadt 1740–1786 im Spiegel der Berliner Presse," *Jahrbuch des Staatlichen Instituts für Musikforschung Preußischer Kulturbesitz* (2004): 231. The Rittersaal (room 792) measured about 16 meters long by 13 meters wide by 9.75 meters high. See Goerd Peschken and Hans-Werner Klünner, *Das Berliner Schloß: Das klassische Berlin* (Frankfurt am Main: Propyläen, 1982), 476.

side, and the Spree River, on the other.[66] Frederick resided here only for state visits and during brief stays to attend festivities, including his birthday (January 14).

Although Nicolai described the Stadtschloss in Berlin as having five music rooms (including those of King Frederick, Queen Christine, and the future king, Frederick William II, then called the "Prince of Prussia") in his guides of 1769, 1779, and 1786, he took notice of not a single musical instrument in the palace. During the nineteenth century, many of the palace rooms were remodeled, and no photographs survive that depict the music rooms in their original state. The palace was thoroughly destroyed during World War II.

The King's Music Room

Fortunately, Frederick's successor left the king's apartments untouched: the earliest available palace inventory, dated 1793, records that the king's music room still housed "a fortepiano by Silbermann." The fortepiano's whereabouts today are unknown; most likely, it was destroyed in 1945 with the palace, when the building was struck by incendiaries. The inventory also specifies that this room contained "various pieces of music and drawings," a music stand, and, as in all of Frederick's music rooms, a large rock crystal chandelier.[67] Berlin newspapers confirm that the king held his chamber music soirées here on occasion.

Crown Prince Frederick William's Music Room

Crown Prince Frederick William, an important patron of music and a cellist, and his wife, a keyboard player, also enjoyed a small private music room on the second floor of the Berlin Stadtschloss, overlooking the Schlossplatz; Nicolai mentions that it was decorated with red silk damask walls.[68] Unfortunately, no inventory of Frederick Wil-

---

66. Tilo Eggeling, "Die Wohnung Friedrichs des Großen," in Peschken and Klünner, *Das Berliner Schloß*, 69. The author argues that Frederick had little connection to the "lively life" of the city, which is also why he eventually gave up his costly apartments in Charlottenburg, about an hour's carriage ride from Berlin.

67. SPSG Plansammlung, Inv. 44, *Inventarius des Königl. Schlosses zu Berlin aufgenommen im Jahr 1793*, 72–73, room VI (room 216 in the floor plan of 1794): "Im Zimmer überhaupt . . . Ein Piano Forte von Silbermann"; "Verschiedene Noten und Zeichnungen"; "ein Notenpult." In another version of the inventory bearing the same date (Inv. 45), a few items were struck through (at a later date) and noted as no longer at hand, but the fortepiano is not one of them. An earlier inventory of 1777 (Inv. 39) concerns only mundane household items, not furniture or musical instruments. The dimensions of the king's music room (room 659) were approximately 11.4 meters long by 10.5 meters wide by 6.25 meters high.

68. Room 683. According to Peschken and Klünner, the room measured approximately 8.6 meters long by 6.9 meters wide by 6.3 meters high (*Das Berliner Schloss*, 518).

liam's or the other family members' suites is available. However, the king's accounts (Table 2) show that in summer 1765 Frederick purchased a "fortepiano" by an unspecified maker for 300 Taler as a gift to Crown Prince Frederick William's new bride, Elisabeth Christine Ulrike of Brunswick-Wolfenbüttel (1746–1840).[69] This instrument, probably made by the court keyboard maker Christian Friedrich Hildebrandt (ca. 1711–72), was likely destined for their music room in the Berlin Stadtschloss, since their new suite in the New Palace in Potsdam (which also had a red silk damask music room) was fitted with a harpsichord by Burkat Shudi (Tables 2 and 8; and see below).[70]

Queen Elisabeth Christine's Music Rooms

In the summer months from May through October, Frederick's unloved wife, Queen Christine, resided in Niederschönhausen at Schloss Schönhausen in northern Berlin.[71] During the winter months she had a suite of apartments in the Berlin Stadtschloss (her official state rooms) where she received dignitaries and attended to other court business. Located on the third floor of the Berlin Stadtschloss, directly above the king's apartments, her apartments contained both a small private music room and a large concert hall.

In 1779 Nicolai first described the queen's music rooms in detail. Her small music room (*das kleine Konzertzimmer*), located directly above the king's, was decorated with French tapestries sent as a gift from Louis XIV. The large concert hall (*der grosse Cour: und Konzertsaal*), located over the first Portale (Portal) facing the Schlossplatz (Palace Square), featured French tapestries that had been presented by Louis XV. Nicolai does not mention what keyboard instrument either room contained (undoubtedly Silbermann harpsichords), nor do we have an inventory of the queen's suites in the Berlin Stadtschloss or in Schönhausen; thus, there is no documentation about keyboard instruments in any of her music rooms.[72]

---

69. *Schatullrechnung*, GStA PK, BPH, Rep. 47, no. 914, fol. 41r, August 1765, item no. 8: "Für das forte piano der Prinzessin von Preussen, 300 Taler" (For the Princess of Prussia's fortepiano, 300 Taler). The piano was purchased too late (and cost too little) to be an instrument by Gottfried Silbermann.

70. Nicolai, *Beschreibung der Königlichen Residenzstädte* (1769), 1:437, lists "Hildebrand" as a maker of fortepianos.

71. Queen Christine resided at Schloss Schönhausen from 1740 until 1797. The official website of the palace, with illustrations, is http://www.spsg.de/schloesser-gaerten/objekt/schloss-schoenhausen/.

72. Nicolai, *Beschreibung der Königlichen Residenzstädte* (1779), 2:651–53 (the edition of 1769 only states the location of her rooms on the third floor of the palace; see Nicolai, *Beschreibung der königlichen Residenzstädte* [1769], 72). The festival hall in Schönhausen still exists; it features three large windows and measures 13.5 meters long by 7 meters wide. The measurements of her Stadtschloss music rooms were (approximately) 10.5 meters long by 6.6 meters wide by 6.25 meters high (an

The Berlin newspapers reported on the *grosse Hofkonzerte*. Those hosted during the summer by Queen Christine (from about mid-May to the end of October) normally took place in Schloss Schönhausen's large festival hall. During the colder months (and on some rarer occasions in the summer) her concerts took place in the larger concert hall in her suite in the Berlin Stadtschloss, where she resided from October to May.[73] At no time did she have a suite of apartments in Potsdam, nor was she ever permitted to enter Sanssouci. Thus, her large concert hall must be the location where, on October 28, 1753, C. P. E. Bach performed on the novel *Bogenflügel*. A Leipzig newspaper reported:

> On the 28th in the evening the Royal Kapelle performed a concert at Her Majesty the queen's in the presence of Her Majesty the queen mother and the princes and princesses of the royal house. On this occasion the famous artist Herr Hohlefeld introduced a keyboard of special design before Her Majesty. It possessed gut strings stroked by a violin bow, whereby the various tones of violin instruments are imitated. The royal chamber musician Herr Bach played a concerto on this instrument, which received general approval from all the high company present.[74]

A similar report on November 2 in the *Hamburgischer Correspondent* verifies the location of this concert more precisely:

> On this very day Herr Hohlefeld, who, by way of sheer genius, often succeeds in creating new mechanical inventions, had the honor of presenting, in the rooms of Her Majesty the queen [i.e., Queen Elisabeth Christine] and before all the high nobility present, a special type of keyboard on which he made it possible to execute everything

---

estimate of the smaller room, based on the floor plan); the larger room (room 844, also called the Elisabeth-Saal) measured 11 meters long by 16 meters wide by 9.75 meters high (Peschken and Klünner, *Das Berliner Schloss*, 498).

73. With some exceptions, probably when there was a particularly cold May, Queen Christine's and the queen mother's concerts continued to be held in the Stadtschloss to June. Whenever the reports do not specify location, Henzel suggests that Christine's summer concerts were held in the "Stadtschloss?," whereas Schönhausen is the more likely location. He also by default suggests "Stadtschloss?" whenever a host is unstated, but again, this is unjustified (see "Das Konzertleben der Preußischen Hauptstadt," esp. the tables on 229–91).

74. Bärwald, "'. . . ein Clavier von besonderer Erfindung,'" 282: "am 28. Abends die Königl. Capelle bey Ihro Majest. der Königin, in Gegenwart Ihro Majest. der Königl. Frau Mutter und der Prinzen und Prinzeßinnen des Königl. Hauses, ein Concert aufgeführet, der berühmte Künstler, Hr. Hohlefeld, bey solcher Gelegenheit Ihro Majest. der Königin ein Clavier von besonderer Erfindung vorgestellet. Selbiges hat Darm-Seiten, auf welche ein Violin-Bogen streicht, wodurch auf diesem Clavier die verschiedenen Töne der Violin-Instrumente nachgeahmet werden. Der Königl. Cammer-Musicus, Hr. Bach, hat auf solchem Instrumente ein Concert gespielet, das den allgemeinen Beyfall der höchsten und hohen Anwesenden erhalten hat." Hohlefeld's name is sometimes spelled Hohlfeld.

found by virtuosos to be lacking in ordinary harpsichords, namely, the sustaining of tones and the various modification of the same, according to the desired degrees of strength and weakness.[75]

Carl von Ledebur must have erred in stating that this concert took place "at the court of the queen mother," which at this time would have meant not Queen Christine but Sophia Dorothea.[76] One can only guess what works Bach might have performed on this program. His only known composition for an instrument of this type, the Sonata Wq 65/48, was written much later, in Hamburg.[77] Although Friedrich Wilhelm Marpurg reported in 1754 that the king had praised Hohlefeld's instrument, the court did not purchase one until 1770 (see below).

The Comoediensaal

The Berlin Stadtschloss was the location of the Comoediensaal, or first opera theater that Frederick had erected, and that space served for the premiere of C. H. Graun's *Rodelinda*, which took place while the opera house on Unter den Linden was still under construction; it also would have been where Emanuel Bach first accompanied a large-scale opera. Located on the second floor of the palace, the Comoediensaal was situated at the northern end of the central wing, which separated two interior courtyards. In December 1741 and thus at the outset of Carnival season, it was also used as the location of a performance by the *Hofkapelle*.[78] After the permanent opera house was completed, rehearsals still took place in the Comoediensaal in winter to save on heating expenses. The 1793 inventory of the Berlin Stadtschloss also notes the presence in the "Commoedien Saal" of twenty-four music stands and adds that

---

75. Ibid., 283: "An eben dem Tage hatte der Herr Hohlfeld, ein Mann, welchem es durch sein bloßes glückliches Genie schon oft gelungen ist, neue brauchbare Erfindungen in der Mechanik zu machen, die Ehre, *in den Zimmer Ihro Majestät* [emphasis added], der Königinn, und allen daselbst versammleten hohen Herrschaften eine Art eines Clavecins zu zeigen, in welchem er alles, was Kenner bisher an den gemeinen Clavecins vermißt haben, das Aushalten der Töne und die verschiedene Modification derselben, nach beliebigen Graden der Stärke und Schwäche, auf eine besondere Art angebracht hat."

76. "Er [Hohlfeld] hatte 1753 die Ehre, [den Bogenflügel] bei Hofe der Königin Mutter zu zeigen" (He [Hohlfeld] had the honor in 1753 of showing the Bogenflügel at the queen mother's court). Carl von Ledebur, *Tonkünstler-Lexicon Berlin's von den ältesten Zeiten bis auf die Gegenwart* (Berlin, 1861), 253.

77. Concerning the *Bogenflügel* and other works by Emanuel for so-called expressive keyboards, see David Schulenberg's chapter in the present volume.

78. The newspaper report calls it the "Theatersaal im Stadtschloss"; the concert report is cited in Henzel, "Das Konzertleben der Preußischen Hauptstadt," 230.

"the harpsichord and remaining music stands, as well as other things belonging to the theater, are found in the inventory of Baron von Beck, Maître de Spectacle."[79]

Surely Emanuel Bach and other court keyboardists performed in the Berlin Stadtschloss in the king's music room, the Comoediensaal, and the large Konzertsaal. How often they privately served Queen Christine, the Crown Prince and Princess, or Princess Amalia, who had apartments in the palace until at least 1767 (see below), cannot be determined.

THE KEYBOARDS OF PRINCESS AMALIA'S RESIDENCES

Before she became abbess of Quedlinburg in 1755—a title with income that would allow her (in lieu of marriage) to obtain her own residence—Princess Amalia primarily resided in apartments in the Berlin Stadtschloss. As discussed above, from at least 1740 she enjoyed a small suite in Schloss Charlottenburg with a music room and a Mietke harpsichord. From about 1766 she also had summer apartments with a large music room in the New Palace in Potsdam.

Amalia, like the king's other immediate family members, hosted both grand court concerts and chamber soirées in her various living quarters. By the mid-1760s, her music soirées at the Palais Unter den Linden 7, attended by international guests and featuring music of the Bach family and of Berlin composers and no doubt fueled by her extensive music collection of the same, had become a central address for Berlin's musical life. Emanuel Bach, who, in 1768 at his departure for Hamburg, received from her the title of *Kapellmeister von Haus aus* (honorary director of music), no doubt participated in them.[80] Wilhelm Friedemann Bach also enjoyed Amalia's patronage from 1774 until 1778, the year in which he dedicated to the princess his eight fugues without pedal, Fk 31.[81]

---

79. The inventory of Baron von Beck is referred to in SPSG Plansammlung, Inv. 44, *Inventarius des königl. Schlosses zu Berlin aufgenommen im Jahr 1793* (p. 208). A nearly identical copy of the inventory with this title is found under Inv. 45, with the same date.

80. David Schulenberg, *The Music of Carl Philipp Emanuel Bach* (Rochester, NY: University of Rochester Press, 2014), 180. Contrary to what one sometimes reads, Kirnberger never possessed the title of *Kapellmeister* to the princess.

81. David Schulenberg, *The Music of Wilhelm Friedemann Bach* (Rochester, NY: University of Rochester Press, 2010), 121–22. A letter of Princess Amalia to King Frederick dated 24 March 1774 extols Friedemann's genius: "This man unites all the knowledge of his father with the taste of the late Graun; he is the only composer living who will serve as a model through the centuries, he composes in all genres.... Let me express to you, my dear brother, my enthusiasm, but I am not exaggerating, for he is excellent and raises up again this great art that has fallen into decadence." Cited in Peter Wollny, "'... welche dem größten Concerte gleichen': The Polonaises of Wilhelm Friedemann Bach," in *The Keyboard in Baroque Europe*, ed. Christopher Hogwood (Cambridge: Cambridge University

Amalia's first organ, which was contracted with Peter Migendt (1703–67) but completed by his student Ernst Marx as his *Meisterstück* at age twenty-seven, cost 2,000 Taler.[82] It was much larger than a typical chamber organ and was installed in the large Balkonzimmer (Balcony Room) over the fifth Portale (Portal) of the Berlin palace's Lustgarten Flügel (Pleasure Garden Wing).

As the original floor plans show, the Balkonzimmer directly abutted Amalia's apartments on the second floor of the palace.[83] Its location is further confirmed by a letter of December 8, 1755, written by Amalia to her sister-in-law Princess Wilhelmine of Hesse-Kassel, wife of Prince Heinrich: "In 8 days my organ will be completed. It is being tuned right now. [Several days later:] Today I have played my organ for the first time. The Countess Schwerin said it's a little loud, naturally, but the tone is charming. . . . The boys in the street did not stop to listen, even though the *balcony doors* were open [emphasis added]. This proves that the instrument is less powerful than one for a church. I am going to practice so that I can accompany my brother in a solo."[84] Her letter refers to the room's balcony doors. Moreover, a period illustration by Johann David Schleuen (1711–71) corresponds to the architectural features and disposition of her apartments in the Berlin Stadtschloss and depicts the organ in the spacious balcony room with its large doors to the right. The organ's date of construction precludes any possibility that it could have been created for Amalia's first palace at Unter den Linden 7, which she first acquired in 1764, nine years after the organ was finished. Renovations to the palace that would accommodate the organ were not completed until 1767, at which time the organ was relocated.[85] The palace became the location of the Russian embassy.

Press, 2003), 178. Martin Falck outlines the details concerning Bach's intrigue against Kirnberger and his consequent fall from royal favor (*Wilhelm Friedemann Bach: Sein Leben und seine Werke, mit thematischem Verzeichnis seiner Kompositionen* [Leipzig, 1913], 52–53).

82. The organ survives in the Kirche zur frohen Botschaft in Berlin. For further details of the organ's disposition and history, see Stefan Behrens and Uwe Pape, "Karlshorst, Kirche zur frohen Botschaft, Orgel von Ernst Marx und Peter Migendt, 1755," in Schwarz, *500 Jahre Orgeln*, 1:123–35. The organ, as built (p. 126), possessed "22 klingenden Stimmen" (22 sounding voices) (as shown in Table 5), though it had been first conceived with twenty-five. The introduction to CPEB:CW, 1/9, *Organ Works*, xii, incorrectly reports the organ's constructed disposition as being that of the initial, conceptual draft.

83. The location of her former apartments is described in Nicolai, *Beschreibung der königlichen Residenzstädte* (1786), 2:875–76. The "so-genannte Balkonzimmer" (so-called balcony room) was located "über dem Flügeleingang in unmittelbarer Nähe zur Zimmerflucht der Prinzessin" (over the entrance to the wing, right next to the rooms of the princess) (Behrens and Pape, "Karlshorst, Kirche zur frohen Botschaft," 127).

84. Cited by Behrens and Pape, "Karlshorst, Kirche zur frohen Botschaft," 127, my translation.

85. Behrens and Pape report that when Amalia moved to her new palace in the Wilhelmstrasse in 1776, the organ remained at Unter den Linden 7, where it fell into a state of decay ("Karlshorst, Kirche zur frohen Botschaft," 127, 129).

Kirnberger seems to have influenced unusual features of the organ, whose original disposition is given in Table 5. In order to accommodate chamber music, it was tuned to chamber pitch (*Kammerton*).[86] The organ's manual also possessed a wider range than was typical: four and a half octaves from C to f3, including C♯ (organs of the time did not normally exceed c3). Its higher range no doubt reflected the instrument's use as a concert instrument and Amalia's training as a keyboardist. Emanuel Bach must have taught Amalia organ lessons in the Balkonzimmer, and he also would have known the instrument from Amalia's chamber soirées. Passages in his organ sonatas, Wq 70/2–7, not only require this atypical high range, but four of them, Wq 70/3–6, composed in 1755, originated in the same year as the organ. Johann Nikolaus Forkel, biographer of J. S. Bach, moreover, affirms that these four sonatas were produced expressly for Amalia. All but one of the sonatas (Wq 70/7) avoid the pedals altogether.[87] Several English harpsichords purchased by the king for the New Palace during the 1760s and having connections to Amalia also possessed an extended range; these are discussed below (see Table 7).

In 1776 Ernst Marx built a larger house organ for Amalia that was designed for the organ hall on the third floor of her subsequent palace in the Wilhelmstrasse.[88] The new organ, also paid for by the king, must have reflected, like the first one, Amalia's

86. Behrens and Pape confirm that her organ, like the one then in the Berlin Dom, "stood in *Kammerton* for ease of ensemble playing" (ibid., 126). The organ's chamber pitch may have been a' = 415 Hz; see Mary Oleskiewicz, "The Trio in Bach's Musical Offering: A Salute to Frederick's Tastes and Quantz's Flutes?," in *Bach Perspectives 4: The Music of J. S. Bach, Analysis and Interpretation*, ed. David Schulenberg (Lincoln: University of Nebraska Press, 1998), 100 and n. 52.

87. The organ sonatas have been published in cpeb:cw, I/9, where further musical and tonal connections between Bach's sonatas and the organ are drawn. See also Darrell Berg, "C. P. E. Bach's Organ Sonatas: A Musical Offering for Princess Amalia?," *Journal of the American Musicological Society* 51.3 (1998): 477–519.

88. Stefan Behrens and Uwe Pape, *Die Orgel der Prinzessin Anna Amalie in der Kirche zur frohen Botschaft in Berlin-Karlshorst* (Berlin: Pape-Verlag, 1991), 15: an "28stimmigen Orgel von Ernst Marx" (an organ possessing 28 sounding voices by Ernst Marx). The maker must have been Ernst Marx, as there was no other maker in Berlin during the 1770s. The specifications given by them differ somewhat from those given in Martin Rost, "Die Orgeln der Anna Amalia von Preußen von Migendt und Marx," in *Carl Philipp Emanuel Bach: Musik für Europa. Bericht über das Internationale Symposium vom 8. bis 12. März 1994 in Frankfurt (Oder)*, ed. Hans-Günter Ottenberg (Frankfurt an der Oder: Konzerthalle Carl Philipp Emanuel Bach, 1998), 411. The palace, constructed under Frederick William I, had originally served as the residence of the Baron Vernezobre de Laurieux (1690–1748); it was located in the historic Friedrichstadt (present-day Kreuzberg, near Potsdamer Platz). The palace was destroyed by bombs in 1944. However, "after [Amalia's] death the organ was gifted to the Reformierte Kirche at Frankfurt/Oder" and "in the 1880s was replaced with a modern instrument by the Sauer firm" (see Behrens and Pape, "Karlshorst, Kirche zur frohen Botschaft," 127).

continuing preference for chamber music of an earlier period, which comprises so much of her music library (Table 6).[89] Like the earlier organ, the new one also stood in chamber pitch. It featured a compass from C to f3 and a pedal range of C to d1. Although Emanuel Bach was no longer at court, Friedemann Bach, who resided in Berlin during the last ten years of his life (1774–84), must have known both this and the earlier organ through his connections to Amalia.

At her death in 1786, Amalia's instruments still included the two organs described above. Her palace in the Wilhelmstrasse also contained two harpsichords (*Flügel*), one in her Orgelsaal (Organ Hall) and another in the Marmor-Kammer; one fortepiano in the first green chamber; a "Clavier" (clavichord?) in the second green chamber; and a gamba in the third chamber on the second floor; as well as three lutes and twelve music stands (*Pulpets*).[90]

Frederick's Keyboards by Shudi, Silbermann, and Hohlefeld

Beginning in 1765, King Frederick began collecting innovative harpsichords by the Swiss-born London harpsichord maker Burkat Shudi (1702–73). These harpsichords were equipped with special features and, as this essay shows for the first time, were placed in locations that connect them directly with Princess Amalia. Although Emanuel Bach would spend only a few more years in Berlin, these instruments may explain

---

89. Tobias Debuch writes: "Paßt schon im Jahr 1755 eine Hausorgel nicht mehr in die musikalische Landschaft, so muß der Bau einer Hausorgel im Jahr 1776 geradezu anachronistisch gewirkt haben" (If her first house organ of 1755 already did not fit into the musical landscape, the second one must have seemed downright anachronistic) (*Anna Amalia von Preussen: Prinzessin und Musikerin* [Berlin: Logos, 2001], 82). This, however, overlooks the fact that house concerts were still performed midcentury in Berlin with house organs, Janitsch's music academy serving as an example. See *Johann Wilhelm Hertel: Autobiographie*, ed. Erich Schenk (Graz: H. Böhlaus Nachf., 1957), 33: "So freudig war sein Betrieb in der Musik; daher er auf seiner neuen Orgel, die er sich auf eigne Kosten zur musikalischen Akademie in seinem Hause hatte setzen laßen, die erste Zeit fast Tag und Nacht spielte u. dieß so lange trieb, daß die Nachbarschaft drohte, die Abstellung seiner nächtlichen, Schlaf stöhrenden Uebungen auf derselben beym König nachzusuchen" (So enthusiastic was his musical activity that at first he played almost day and night on his new organ, which he had set up at his own expense for the musical academy in his house; and this went on for so long that the neighbors threatened to complain to the king to stop his nocturnal sleep-disturbing practice).

90. Eva Renate Blechschmidt, *Die Amalien-Bibliothek: Musikbibliothek der Prinzessin Amalia von Preußen (1723–1787)* (Berlin: Merseburger, 1965), 26, quotes from Amalia's *Nachlassverzeichnis*: "Zwei Orgeln, je ein Flügel im Orgelsaal und der Marmor-Kammer, ein Fortepiano in der ersten grünen und ein Clavier in der zweiten grünen Kammer, eine Gambe in der dritten Kammer der zweiten Étage, drei Lauten, ferner zwölf Pulpete." Michael O'Loghlin misinterprets Amalia's *Nachlass* as including "two organs, three fortepianos, a harpsichord, a viola da gamba and three lutes" (*Frederick the Great and His Musicians: The Viola da Gamba Music of the Berlin School* [Burlington, VT: Ashgate, 2008], 53).

peculiar features of works both by him and by Wilhelm Friedemann Bach. In addition, the recent rediscovery of a lost Shudi instrument of the king kept in the former royal palace at Breslau may help to explain one of Charles Burney's puzzling observations about these instruments.

THE BRESLAU SCHLOSS AND SHUDI'S HARPSICHORDS 7

In 1750, following his victory in the Silesian wars, Frederick purchased in Breslau a nobleman's palace with a garden, to which was added in 1751 a long, two-story rear wing that contained his apartments: these included a rococo music room (*Concert-Zimmer*, room 53), designed by J. M. Hoppenhaupt,[91] and an only slightly larger adjacent concert hall (*Concert-Saal*, room 52), identified in the 1835 inventory as a throne room. In September 1752 the king resided in his newly finished suite for the first time. It is not known what kind of keyboard instrument initially furnished the music room. However, during 1765 and 1766 Frederick purchased several harpsichords by Shudi, one of which was destined for Breslau (see Table 7).

An eighteenth-century affidavit signed in 1767 indicates that four instruments built for Frederick were completed by Andrew Clark and John Broadwood working under the direction of Shudi himself.[92] Three of the instruments have been identified with serial numbers 496, 511, and 512. The first of these, number 496, was purchased during the 1760s for Frederick's palace in Breslau. At this time Frederick also purchased several more Shudi harpsichords for the New Palace, his final architectural project. All were exceptional in their construction and possessed the latest features available from Shudi's shop.

An early nineteenth-century inventory of the Breslau palace records in the king's private second-floor music room "a harpsichord by Burkat Tschudi, double manual, in a mahogany case with gold leaf, four feet and pedal, and a mahogany music rack."[93] A later entry in the same inventory notes that the stand was *erneuert* (renovated) in

---

91. According to a floor plan of 1900 (SPSG, no. 11604), the king's music room (room 53) measured approximately 8.52 meters wide by 8.95 meters long. The floor plan of 1834/35 gives the dimensions in Ohlau feet as 27 feet 6 inches wide by 33 feet 6 inches long.

92. David Wainwright and Kenneth Mobbs, "Shudi's Harpsichords for Frederick the Great," *Galpin Society Journal* 49 (1996): 85–86.

93. SPSG Plansammlung, Inv. 199, 1835, 109: "Grosser Seitenflügel, Zweites Stockwerk [Raum] Nr. 53. Concert=Kammer. . . . Ein Flügel von Burkat-Tschudi, mit 2 Klaviaturen, in Mahagony Kasten, mit Vergoldung verziert, mit 4 Füßen und Pedal, dazu: ein Pult von Mahagonyholz." A twentieth-century addition in the margin states that the instrument was gone. The inventory also notes a cedar music stand with two bronze candlestick holders: "Ein Notenpult von Zedernholz, mit 2 messingen Leuchter=Armen à zwey Tillen."

1850. This instrument (no. 496) had arrived in Potsdam in 1765 before being shipped almost immediately to Breslau. An entry for July 1765 in the king's *Schatullrechnung* records 15 Taler for the freight from London to Potsdam. In August an additional 9 Taler are recorded for instrument's transport from Potsdam to Breslau.[94] Purchase of the harpsichord was transacted on behalf of the court by the *Kaufmann* (merchant) Bachmann in Magdeburg, who received reimbursement for his services that October.[95] The price for this mahogany instrument (presumably including Kaufmann's fee) was 800 Taler, about three times that of a good German instrument.

In 1765 the *Allgemeine Augsburger Zeitung* reported on the purchase of this instrument and described its novel machine-stop mechanism: "The celebrated Klaviermacher, Burkhardt Tschudi, a born Swiss of Schwanden in the canton Glarus, had the honour to make a harpsichord with two keyboards for His Majesty the King of Prussia, which was very much admired by all who saw it. It was remarked as an extraordinary thing that Tschudi has placed all the registers in one pedal, so that they can be taken off one after the other, and the decreasing and increasing of the tone can be produced at will, which crescendo and decrescendo harpsichord-players have long wished for."[96] This harpsichord was pictured and again described in a 1932 museum catalog of the royal palace in Breslau, which notes that it was signed and dated "Burkat Tschudi Nr. 496 Fecit Londini 1765."[97] A two-manual instrument, it featured a compass with an unusually extended low register: CC–f3. This extended compass and the machine stop are special features of all three of Frederick's surviving Shudi instruments (see Table 7).[98]

94. *Schatullrechnung*, GStA PK, BPH, Rep. 47, no. 914, fol. 36r, July 1765, item no. 20: "Für Fracht des Flügels aus Engeland [*sic*], 15 Taler" (For freight for the harpsichords from England, 15 Taler); and BPH, Rep. 47, no. 914, fol. 41r, August 1765, item no. 20: "die Fracht für den Flügel von Potsdam nach Breslau, 9 Taler" (the freight for the harpsichord from Potsdam to Breslau, 9 Taler).

95. *Schatullrechnung*, GStA PK, BPH, Rep. 47, no. 914, fol. 51r, October 1765, item no. 5: "An den Kaufmann Bachmann für den Flügel aus Engelleand [*sic*], 800 Taler."

96. Wainwright and Mobbs, "Shudi's Harpsichords," 80.

97. Erwin Hintze, *Führer durch das Schlossmuseum in Breslau* (Breslau: Schlossmuseum, 1930), 16–18; the harpsichord is illustrated in plate 3. A 1932 publication entitled *Führer und Katalog zur Sammlung alter Musikinstrumente: Schlesisches Museum für Kunstgewerbe und Altertümer* by Peter Epstein and Ernst Scheyer also contains a description of the harpsichord and its location at the time: "Im Musikzimmer des Breslauer Schlosses, aus dem Besitz Friedrichs des Großen, bezeichnet: Burkat Tschudi Nr. 496 Fecit Londini 1765, Höhe 96, Breite 103, Länge 270. London 1765. Staatseigentum. Schloß Inv. Nr. 73."

98. Not all of Shudi's instruments at the time were so equipped. Another surviving Shudi harpsichord of 1767, not from Frederick's collection, features only a single manual, three hand stops and no machine stop, and the more conventional five-octave compass, FF, GG–f3 (no FF♯). See Albert

Shudi number 496 disappeared in the years following World War II. Until recently, only a photo of the instrument and an early twentieth-century palace museum catalog description survived. The instrument resurfaced recently and is now on display at the Museum of Musical Instruments in Poznań.[99] An inspection of the instrument shows that its soundboard was replaced with one numbered 497 and signed by the maker; the less than ideal quality of this later workmanship strongly suggests that it was not undertaken in the Shudi workshop. Could the soundboard have been replaced during the renovation of 1850 mentioned in the inventory? Was number 497 the "missing" fourth instrument purchased by Frederick and perhaps delivered in 1765 together with or shortly after number 496?[100] If so, why have we no evidence for its purchase or transport? Was it sent as a gift from Shudi to the king? Could the instrument have been damaged beyond repair during shipping, then later used for spare parts?

A partial solution to the puzzle may lie in Charles Burney's account. During his tour of the New Palace, he was told that one of the king's Shudi harpsichords had been badly damaged during transport and since then had been rendered unusable. At the time, Burney assumed that this anecdote referred to Shudi harpsichord number 511, which he had personally viewed in the New Palace.[101] But that instrument shows no evidence of damage. Perhaps Burney misunderstood, and the story he was told instead applies to the mysterious missing instrument, number 497. If Emanuel Bach ever played number 496, it would have been during its brief time in Potsdam before it was shipped to Breslau or on a subsequent journey to the Silesian residence. The remaining Shudi harpsichords were all designated for the New Palace, where he would have had better access to them.

Rice, *Four Centuries of Musical Instruments: The Marlowe A. Sigal Collection* (Atglen, PA: Schiffer Publishing, 2015), 11. I am grateful to Marlowe Sigal for kindly granting access to his private collection to see and hear this and several other instruments.

99. An initial report of the discovery by Patryk Frankowski and Alina Mądry, "A 1765 Harpsichord by Burkat Shudi (No. 496) Rediscovered in Poland," was published in the *Galpin Society Newsletter* 34 (October 2012): 5–6, together with color photographs of the keyboard manuals and faceplate.

100. Wainwright and Mobbs, "Shudi's Harpsichords," 85. I am grateful to Patryk Frankowski and Alina Mądry, curators at the Museum of Instruments in Poznań, for generously providing me with their unpublished manuscript detailing the presence of the soundboard no. 497 in Shudi no. 496.

101. Charles Burney writes: "This instrument which cost 200 guineas, was sent to Hamburg by sea, and from thence to Potsdam, up the Elb and the Havel, which, I was told, had injured it so much, that it has been useless ever since; however, it is natural to suppose, that some jealousy may have been excited by it, and that it has not had quite fair play from those employed to repair it; for I never heard of any one of the great number of harpsichords, which are annually sent from England to the East and West Indies by sea, receiving so much damage as this is said to have done, in a much shorter passage" (*The Present State of Music in Germany* [London: Becket, 1773], 2:145–46).

At least one work by Emanuel Bach, the Concerto in C Major, Wq 112/1, one of the few pieces Emanuel Bach composed specifically for "cembalo solo" and printed in 1765, may have been composed in July of that year in response to the arrival of this newfangled instrument.[102] The work's three levels of rapid dynamic changes (*piano*, *forte*, and *fortissimo*) are absolutely impractical on an ordinary two-manual instrument; this strongly suggests that they were inspired by the presence of a machine stop.

THE NEW PALACE AT SANSSOUCI 🗐 8

The remaining Shudi harpsichords all were purchased for Frederick's last residence, called during the eighteenth century the Neues Schloss bei Sanssouci (New Palace at Sanssouci).[103] This palace was first conceived in 1755 to serve as a spacious summer palace that, in contrast to the intimate Sanssouci, would offer all the comforts needed for family, princely guests, and a splendid court culture. Delayed by the Seven Years' War, construction was begun in 1763 and not completed until 1769.[104] It has usually been assumed that Frederick did not reside in the New Palace until 1767. However, the king's suite of apartments was sufficiently complete by 1765 that in that year Frederick could drink his first cup of coffee in them. Moreover, in 1767 and 1768 hefty payments were already recorded in the *Schatullrechnung* for the tuning of keyboard instruments in the New Palace; given Frederick's habit of paying his invoices months later, these payments also may have included tunings from the previous year.[105]

Like the Berlin Stadtschloss, the New Palace at Sanssouci was a representational palace suitable for grand affairs of state, and Frederick resided there for about four weeks each summer. The palace contained five music rooms plus a theater (on the same intimate scale as the one in the Potsdam Stadtschloss). Only the first three rooms were called "Concert Cammer" in the original floor plans, but all five rooms were already furnished with keyboard instruments during the early period of construction (Table 8). Although these circumstances may seem peripheral to musical activities by members of the Bach family, during the summer months of 1765–67 Emanuel Bach would have accompanied some of the king's concerts here. Members of the *Hofkapelle*

---

102. As suggested in Christine Blanken and Wolfram Enßlin, eds., *Unterwegs mit Carl Philipp Emanuel Bach: Musikalisch-biografischer Reiseführer zu seinen Lebensstationen* (Berlin: Lehmann's Media, 2014), 136.

103. The official palace website, with images, is http://www.spsg.de/schloesser-gaerten/objekt/neues -palais/.

104. C. F. Foerster, *Das Neue Palais bei Potsdam* (Berlin: Deutscher Kunstverlag, 1923), 10.

105. *Schatullrechnung*, GStA PK, BPH, Rep. 47, no. 916, fol. 15v, September 1767, item no. 38: "Das Clavier zu stimmen im neuen Palais, 7 Taler, 8 Gr." (For tuning the keyboard in the New Palace, 7 Taler, 8 Gr.); and September 1768, item no. 58: "das Clavier zu stimmen im neuen Palais, 14 Taler, 4 Gr." (for tuning the keyboard in the New Palace, 14 Taler, 4 Gr.).

would also have participated in performances of opera and oratorio in its theater, whose ceremonial dedication took place on July 19, 1768. Included was a private performance of Hasse's oratorio *La conversione di Sant' Augustino*, attended by Frederick and his siblings Princess Amalia and Prince Heinrich.

The New Palace was also open to the public for tours on application for admission to the palace castellan: even without his connections to Princess Amalia and the Crown Prince, Wilhelm Friedemann Bach could have viewed the many keyboards of the palace just like any other member of the public. More likely, both Friedemann and Emanuel would have had the opportunity to play the Shudi instruments—if not with the permission of Frederick, then via the king's sister Princess Amalia and probably also by way of the Crown Princess, both of whom (as Burney pointed out) also enjoyed one of the (five) suites with a music room in the palace. At least one composition by Friedemann may be closely associated with these Shudi harpsichords.

Although it has been claimed that "nothing is known of the locations of the four [*sic*] Shudi harpsichords in the Neues Palais,"[106] a detailed description of each of the music rooms makes it possible to untangle the number and locations of the keyboards and the occupants of each suite (confusingly hinted at by Burney). Palace inventories and other evidence show conclusively that the Shudi harpsichords had been acquired for three of these music rooms already at the time of the palace's construction, excluding King Frederick's music room, which received a Silbermann fortepiano (Table 8). The following discussion clarifies, insofar as possible, which rooms received which instruments.

The Music Rooms of the Oberes *and* Unteres Fürstenquartiere

Two "English harpsichords" were purchased for each of the New Palace's lavish apartments called the upper and lower *Fürstenquartiere* (princely quarters). These instruments (nos. 511 and 512), which arrived in Potsdam in 1766, were (like the instrument for Breslau) acquired via the *Kaufmann* Bachmann.[107] The *Schatullrechnung* records a payment of 36 Taler for freight for the two instruments in June, an amount slightly more than twice the cost of the freight for a single Shudi instrument (no. 496) in the previous year.[108] Shudi harpsichord number 511, moreover, was decorated specifically

---

106. The text quote is from Latcham, "Pianos and Harpsichords for Their Majesties," 384.

107. *Schatullrechnung*, GStA PK, ʙᴘʜ, Rep. 47, no. 915, fol. 24r, December 1766, item no. 6: "An den Kaufmann Bachmann in Magdeburg für zwey englische Clavire, 1600 Taler" (To Merchant Bachmann in Magdeburg for two English keyboards).

108. *Schatullrechnung*, GStA PK, ʙᴘʜ, Rep. 47, no. 915, fol. 11r, June 1766, item no. 21: "die Fracht für die aus Engelland [*sic*] gekommene[n] Flügel, 36 Taler" (transport for the harpsichord that arrived from England, 36 Taler).

to coordinate with the decorative theme of the *Oberes Konzertzimmer* (upper music room, in the *Oberes Fürstenquartier*).

The music room of the lower *Fürstenquartier* (or Apollo-Saal) was conceived as a temple to the Greek god of music. Situated on the ground floor of the palace, it was completed ca. 1767–68 by Johann Christian Hoppenhaupt after an older design by his brother, J. M. Hoppenhaupt.[109] In addition to its five stunning integral wall paintings by Jacques van Schuppen (1670–1751) on themes of Ovid's *Metamorphosis*, the room featured an overall Apollo / sun god motif, gold draperies, and gold-gilt reliefs. The "English Fortepiano" with a "wood and bronze decorated stand," mentioned in the palace inventory of 1784, no doubt refers to the mahogany Shudi harpsichord (no. 512), which itself featured matching gold-gilt bronze embellishments and hardware.[110]

In poetic contrast to the golden theme of the lower *Fürstenquartier*'s temple to Apollo, the sun god of music, the silver-gilt music room in the upper *Fürstenquartier*—located on the second floor of the New Palace—was envisioned as a temple to the moon goddess and hunter, Diana; it featured pale yellow lacquered walls covered with silver reliefs so extravagant they border on the grotesque. A uniquely spectacular Shudi harpsichord (no. 511) was destined for this room (Tables 7, 8). Unlike Shudi number 512, the exterior of number 511's case features silver bands. The bronze hardware of its mahogany stand and its ball-and-claw feet, frame, and hinges were completely painted with oxidized silver (possibly upon its arrival in Berlin) to match the ostentatious silvering of the room's walls.[111] As in Sanssouci's music room, the Ovidian mythologi-

109. Both the upper and lower *Fürstenquartiere* measure 11.2 meters long by 10.38 meters wide. According to Nicolai's *Beschreibung* (1786), 3:1242 and 1239, the rooms were numbered 46 and 17 (now 260 and 161).

110. SPSG Inv. 398, *Inventarium von sämtlichen . . . Pretiosen*, Tableaux, Mobiliar-Sachen, als Gardinen Sopha's, Canapées, Fauteuils, Stühlen, . . . *im königlich. Neuen=Palais . . . 18 October 1784*, 8: "1 Fortepiano" [inserted by another hand: "englisch"] mit holzernenen mit Bronze decorirte Gestell." In 1786 Nicolai, like the inventory, described this room as paneled (*boisiert*), with gold decorations and possessing a chandelier of Berlin porcelain. By the time of writing, however, Nicolai noted that this music room currently housed a Silbermann fortepiano, evidently the one that had been previously in the king's suite (see below), which in the same inventory currently lacked its piano. See Nicolai, *Beschreibung der Königlichen Residenzstädte* (1786), 3:1239. (Why it was moved to this room is unclear, except that the king in his last year of life resided solely at Sanssouci and no longer played music; perhaps a family member had requested to use it.) An 1896 palace inventory, however, indicates that the Silbermann piano had by then been returned to its original position in the king's music room; SPSG: "Ein Flügel-Fortepiano von Silbermann, auf einem ganz geschnitzten und vergoldeten Rococogestell mit 7 verbundenem Füßen, mit einem Kasten von polirtem Eichenholz" (A keyboard-fortepiano by Silbermann, on a carved and gilded rococo stand with seven bound feet, with a case of polished oak). Friendly communication of Klaus Dorst.

111. Today, no. 511's original silvered stand and pedal are missing. They can be observed in historic photographs and are pictured by William Dale, *Tschudi the Harpsichord Maker* (London: Constable

cal hunting theme is highlighted by a parquet floor with an elaborately inlaid central motif of dogs pursuing a rabbit.

The extravagance of this room and its matching Shudi harpsichord was noted by Charles Burney, who toured the palace in 1772: "In another apartment, there is a most magnificent harpsichord, made by Shudi, in England; the hinges, pedals, and frame are of silver, the case is inlaid, and the front is of tortoise-shell."[112] The 1784 palace inventory likewise describes this room's instrument as a "harpsichord with a gilt silver stand."[113] In his guide to the New Palace, Nicolai (1786) further confirms the identification of the instrument in the upper *Fürstenquartier* as "the harpsichord made in England by Shudi that Burney describes."[114] The tortoiseshell front mentioned by Burney is a misunderstanding; the front of the instrument is veneered in "strongly-figured wood" that Burney mistook "at a quick glance . . . for tortoise-shell."[115]

Museum records indicate that the Shudi harpsichords of 1766, numbers 511 and 512, were placed on display in the Berlin Hohenzollern Museum in Monbijou Palace beginning in 1884. In 1923 they were returned to the New Palace; in 1945, after World War II, number 512 was removed from the lower *Fürstenquartier* by the Red Army and was deposited in the Mikhail Glinka Museum for Culture in Moscow, where today it remains on display.[116] Observers of that instrument have noted that it

---

and Co. Ltd., 1913), albeit incorrectly labeled as no. 512. Latcham reproduces the same photograph as Dale on page 385, now correctly labeled, and offers a plausible explanation for the historical mix-up of stands ("Pianos and Harpsichords for Their Majesties," 385–86).

112. Burney, *The Present State of Music in Germany* (1773), 2:145.

113. SPSG Plansammlung, Inv. 398 (1784), 28a: "1 Flügel mit versilberten decorierter Fuß."

114. Nicolai, *Beschreibung der Königlichen Residenzstädte* (1786), 3:1242: "Hier steht der in England verfertigte Flügel, von Schudi, den Burney beschreibt."

115. Wainwright and Mobbs, "Shudi's Harpsichords," 84.

116. No. 512 is currently displayed with an inelegant replacement stand (depicted most recently in *CIMCIM Bulletin* 1 [June 2016] on p. 3). However, its original stand, with ball-and-claw feet, is the one currently displayed with no. 511 in the New Palace; at some point the stand's pedal (shown in older photographs) went missing. Curiously, a Shudi harpsichord pictured in Paul Seidel, "Die von Burkart Tschudi in London erbauten Klaviere Friedrichs des Großen," *Hohenzollern Jahrbuch* 17 (1913): 249–50, does not appear to be either no. 511 or no. 512: its case features gold or silver bands, like no. 496 and no. 511, but unlike no. 511, it lacks engraved plates over the stops; like no. 496, it also lacks no. 511's elegant carved floral garland under the cheek. The stand is similar or identical to the one original to no. 496 and no. 512, with pedal and partially gilt ball-and-claw feet. Whether it is in fact a photograph of the Breslau Shudi no. 496 or perhaps the lost no. 497 is at this time impossible to say.

possesses a machine stop with "lute, octave, buff [*recte* harp], first unison, and second unison" but no Venetian swell.[117]

Neither Burney's account nor palace inventories clearly indicate which suite was occupied by Princess Amalia or the Prince of Prussia; however, according to Burney, each inhabited a suite of apartments that included one of the original five rooms with a keyboard instrument: "There is a *suite* of rooms appropriated to almost every branch of the royal family. Those of the king, of his sister princess Amelia, and the prince of Prussia, *are the most splendid* [emphasis added]. In each of these apartments, there is a room dedicated to music, furnished with books, desks, a harpsichord, and with other instruments."[118] The Prince of Prussia was a title reserved for the Crown Prince, namely, the future Frederick William II.[119] His suite consisted of three rooms on the second floor (directly over the king's apartment); however, since these did not contain a music room, Burney must therefore have been describing the music room of the Crown Princess, Frederick William's spouse, which directly abutted his apartments (hers were the Obere rote Kammern; see below). For Amalia, this leaves only two remaining possibilities: one of the two lavish *Fürstenquartiere*. It has routinely been supposed (without clear evidence) that Amalia's apartments must have been located on the second floor directly above those of her brother Prince Heinrich and his wife (whose suite contained one of the five music rooms). However, two pieces of information preclude that location: (1) those apartments did not feature a music room, and (2) like Heinrich's suite, they comprised the smallest rooms in the palace. In no way could they have been considered to be "among the most splendid," as Burney described. While it may be questioned that a sister of the king would have enjoyed so lavish an apartment as one of the *Fürstenquartiere*, it should be noted that Amalia, Frederick's closest and dearest relative, served him in lieu of the queen (who was unwelcome at the palace) as the hostess for grand court visits, arriving early to receive

---

117. Wainwright and Mobbs rely on observations and photographs made by members of the Galpin Society who studied the instrument during a visit to the Glinka Museum in 1987 ("Shudi's Harpsichords," 81–82). Shudi's Venetian swell was invented too late (1769) to have been included on Frederick's instruments. A surviving instrument, no. 899, made by Shudi and John Broadwood and dated London, 1781, possesses both the machine stop and the Venetian swell. See Rice, *Four Centuries of Musical Instruments*, 13; see also Eric Halfpenny, "Shudi and the Venetian Swell," *Music and Letters* 27 (1946): 180–84.

118. Burney, *The Present State of Music in Germany* (1773), 2:144.

119. Latcham misidentified the Prince of Prussia (whom Burney points out as having a Shudi harpsichord in the New Palace) as the king's brother Prince Heinrich ("Pianos and Harpsichords for Their Majesties," 383). Furthermore, Burney is mistaken, for it was not Prince Heinrich but rather his wife who had a music room in the New Palace; moreover, her room was furnished not with a Shudi harpsichord but with a different keyboard instrument (see below).

and greet guests and make everything ready. Moreover, she is known to have hosted grand court concerts at the New Palace and must have commanded a large space for these events, such as that afforded by the music rooms of the *Fürstenquartiere*.[120]

The Obere rote Kammern and the Princess of Prussia (Crown Princess)

A third, spacious, and elegant (if less ornate) suite with a keyboard instrument, the Obere rote Kammern (Upper Red Chambers), belonged to the Crown Princess of Prussia.[121] At the time of Burney's visit this person was no longer its first occupant (Frederick William's first wife, Elisabeth Christine Ulrike, a favorite of the king and for whom a fortepiano had been purchased in 1765) but rather his second wife, Frederika Louisa of Hesse-Darmstadt (1751–1805), whom the Crown Prince had married on July 14, 1769.[122] This suite is located on the upper floor of the south wing, courtyard side, abutting Frederick William's apartments.[123] The 1784 palace inventory describes its music room as having walls covered in red silk damask, similar to those of the Crown Princess's music room in the Berlin Stadtschloss. In 1786 Nicolai noted that it contained "a harpsichord by Shudi."[124] It cannot be definitively determined whether her instrument was at that time number 512 or, as is more likely, the fourth (lost) instrument, number 497 (see Table 8). Either way, Friedemann Bach seems to have been in good standing with the Crown Prince during the 1770s and therefore also may have interacted with the Crown Princess and her Shudi harpsichord; he may also have known her Hildebrandt piano.[125]

---

120. Carl Eduard Vehse, *Die Höfe zu Preussen, Friedrich II., der Grosse 1740–1786*, ed. Wolfgang Schneider (Leipzig: Kiepenheuer 1993), 2:265: "Nach dem Frieden pflegte sie [i.e., Princess Amalia], wenn der König Fremde in Potsdam bei sich hatte, die Zeremonienmeisterin zu machen" (After the peace she acted as master of ceremonies when the king had foreign guests in Potsdam). See GStA PK, Berlin, I. HA, Rep. 36, no. 851, fol. 30 ("grosses Konzert bei Amalia" on 15 July 1775).

121. According to Nicolai's *Beschreibung der Königlichen Residenzstädte* (1786), 3:1245. Her music room was room 59 (now room 246); it measured 9.3 meters long by 8.82 meters wide.

122. For information on this fortepiano, see note 69.

123. Foerster, *Das Neue Palais*, 56. Her rooms were still more elaborate than those of the Lower Red Chambers (which had no music room).

124. Nicolai, *Beschreibung der Königlichen Residenzstädte* (1786), 3:1244–45, "Nun die Zimmer von der Prinzessin von Preussen K. H."; "[room] 59): Konzertkammer. Rother Damast und Gold . . . ein Flügel von Shudi."

125. On 2 January 1779 Crown Prince Frederick William submitted a recommendation on behalf of Friedemann Bach for the newly vacated organist position at the Marien-Kirche in Berlin. Whether this was at Bach's request or at Princess Amalia's is not known. The magistrate, however, declined, citing Bach's "weird behavior [*sonderbares Betragen*], inappropriate vicissitude [*unanständlicher Wandel*],"

Music Room in the Suite of "Princess Heinrich" (Wilhelmine of
Hesse-Kassel) and Hohlefeld's Bogenflügel

If the rooms of the king's favorite sister (Amalia) were among the most spacious and elaborate, then it should not be at all surprising that those of his despised brother Prince Heinrich (1726–1802) and his wife since 1752, Princess Wilhelmine, located on the ground floor of the north wing, were unusually small. Completed in about 1769, the music room of "Princess Heinrich" (as Wilhelmine was called in the inventory and in other contemporary documents) was a narrow, rectangular music room with unusual silver rococo gilding (like that used in the music room of the upper *Fürstenquartier*); the floor plans designate the room simply as a "chamber."[126] In it, the palace inventory identifies "1 musical instrument that resembles a harpsichord, with very few slightly torn gut strings and possessing a silver stand" that matched the room's gilding.[127] The inventory's odd, cursory description suggests that the instrument might have been a *Lautenwerk*, a type of instrument that J. S. Bach owned at his death and for which there are few if any surviving examples. More likely, however, it was the *Bogenflügel* by Hohlefeld, which debuted at court in 1753 but which Frederick purchased for the New Palace only in 1770, just after the completion of this music room. The king's *Schatullrechnung* records the price of the *Bogenflügel* as 200 Taler,[128] with additional transport charges of only 1 Taler, 12 Groschen.[129] This verifies J. G. Sulzer's report that in 1770 the king had Hohlefeld bring the instrument to the "New Palace at Sanssouci."[130]

---

and "demonstrated obstinacy [*bewiesener Eigensinn*]," which prevented him from keeping his organ positions in Dresden and Halle. A discussion and transcription of the magistrate's letter are given in Christoph Henzel, "Zu Wilhelm Friedemann Bachs Berliner Jahren," BJ 78 (1992): 108–9.

126. The music room of "Princess Heinrich" is labeled room 24 in the inventory and measures 9.29 meters long by 6.56 meters wide. See Foerster, *Das Neue Palais*, 50. Throughout his memoirs, Count Lehndorff (*Kammerherr* to Queen Christine) also refers to her as Princess Heinrich. See *Die Tagebücher des Grafen Lehndorff: Die geheimen Aufzeichnungen des Kammerherrn der Königin Elisabeth Christine*, ed. Wieland Giebel (Berlin: Berlin Story, 2007), e.g., 271. The room had fallen into a state of decay and was closed to the public for renovation at the time of my visit in 2009. My thanks to Klaus Dorst of the Stiftung Preußische Schlösser und Gärten for permitting access.

127. SPSG Plansammlung, Inv. 398, 10–10a: "1 Musicalisches Instrument—einen Flügel gleichend mit sehr wenigen und sanft zerrissenen Darmsaiten bezogen, und mit ungestrichenen und versilberten Gestell."

128. *Schatullrechnung*, GSta PK, BPH, Rep. 47, no. 919, fol. 2r, February 1770, item no. 14: "für den Bagen [*sic*] Flügel, 200 Taler" (for the Bogenflügel, 200 Taler).

129. *Schatullrechnung*, GStA PK, BPH, Rep. 47, no. 919, fol. 4r, March 1770, item no. 71: "Fracht für den Bogenflügel, 1 Taler, 12 Gr." (freight for the Bogenflügel, 1 Taler, 12 Gr.).

130. Bärwald, "'. . . ein Clavier von besonderer Erfindung,'" 290. This article cites the source for the above quote as J. G. Sulzer, *Allgemeine Theorie der Schönen Künste*, 2nd ed. (Leipzig, 1792), 2:206 [*sic*];

In volume 2 of his *Versuch* (1762), Emanuel Bach acknowledged the merit of the *Bogenflügel* and expressed what a shame it was that the instrument was not more generally in use. King Frederick's purchase of Hohlefeld's instrument, two years after Bach's departure for Hamburg, could not have been the inspiration for Bach's sonata for *Bogenklavier*, Wq 65/48, since Bach didn't compose the work until 1783.

His Majesty's Music Room

The king's apartments in the New Palace were, as at Schloss Sanssouci, located on the ground floor facing Sanssouci garden. Despite his enthusiasm for the new Shudi harpsichords, the king did not purchase one for his own music room. This space was instead equipped in the usual manner with a Silbermann piano that, as will be shown, likely came from Schloss Charlottenburg. The 1784 palace inventory describes the royal "Concert Cammer" as "lacquered Green with gold-gilded decorations and without window dressings." Having furnishings similar to the music room of Sanssouci, it contained, among other items, "1 fortepiano with gold-gilt stand" and "1 music stand on a pedestal with tortoiseshell and mother-of-pearl, gold-gilt bronze, decorated with two candlesticks."[131] The court sculptor, Schwitzer, who was responsible for the musical emblems on the walls, created an elaborately carved and gilded rococo keyboard stand to replace the original one, to match the room's décor.[132] According to an inventory of 1780, the original stand for this fortepiano was kept in an unused room in the Potsdam Stadtschloss.[133]

---

it is in fact found under the article "Fantasiren; Fantasie," 2:205–6, esp. 206n4. It is possible that Kirnberger, who drafted many of the entries on music with his pupil J. A. P. Schulz, was responsible for this information. See Schulenberg, *The Music of Carl Philipp Emanuel Bach*, 343n22.

131. SPSG Plansammlung, Inv. 398 (1784), 4–4a: "Concert Cammer grün lackirt mit vergoldten Decorationen und ohne Fenster Gardinen . . . , 1 Fortepiano mit vergoldten Gestelle . . , 1 Notenpult en gueridon und von Schildkröte mit Perlmutter und vergoldter Bronze decorirt nebst 2 Tillen." In the margin are notations that certain items were moved to Sanssouci, including the king's music stand, at the request of Frederick William II following Frederick's death, but the fortepiano was not one of them: "Den 25ten July 1787 ist der Notenpult auf Sr. Majst: Befehl nach Sans Souci geholet." The king's music room measures 10.59 meters long by 7.25 meters wide.

132. *Schatullrechnung*, GStA PK, BPH, Rep. 47, no. 918, fol. 2v, February 1769, item no. 28: "An den Maler [Friedrich] Bock ein Piano forte-fuß, 30 Taler." For the attributions of the keyboard stand and wall and ceiling sculpture, see Foerster, *Das Neue Palais*, 39: "Die Bildhauerarbeiten von Schwizer, die vergoldeten Zieraten und Musikembleme der weiß und grün getönten Decke von Sartori" (The sculptures by Schwizer, the gilded ornamentation and the musical ensemble of the white and green tinted ceiling by Sartori).

133. SPSG Plansammlung, Ak 9, *Inventarium des königl. Schloßes zu Potsdam d. 20 Decbr. 1780* . . . , "XV. Erstes Obergeschoss / II. Étage / Mittlere Étage . . . die sogenannte Fredersdorffsche Cammer . . . 1 Flügel Fuß, wovon das Clavier im neuen Palais befindlich" (XV. First upper floor / second story / middle floor . . . The so-called Fredersdorf room . . . 1 keyboard stand belonging to the clavier found in the New Palace).

In 1772, when Charles Burney visited Potsdam, he toured the New Palace, viewed the king's private music chamber, and noted its Silbermann fortepiano: "His majesty's concert room is ornamented with glasses of an immense size, and with sculpture, partly gilt, and partly of the most beautiful green varnish, by Martin of Paris; the whole furniture and ornaments of this room are in a most refined and exquisite taste. There is a *piano forte* made by Silbermann of Neuberg, beautifully varnished and embellished; and a tortoise-shell desk for his majesty's use, most richly and elegantly inlaid with silver."[134] Nicolai in 1786 also described the king's music room but mentioned no keyboard instrument there. By this date the king no longer played the flute and so had ceased to use the room. But the fortepiano had not vanished; according to Nicolai, it was now temporarily displayed in the music room of the *Unteres Fürstenquartier* (or Apollo-Saal).[135] A later inventory indicates that the piano was returned to its original location. The fortepiano was still reported in this music room as late as 1798.[136]

WILHELM FRIEDEMANN BACH AND SHUDI'S HARPSICHORDS

As demonstrated above, Friedemann Bach would have known one or more of Shudi's harpsichords, including those played by Princess Amalia and the Crown Princess of Prussia. The Shudi harpsichords acquired by Frederick, including one delivered in 1765 for the Breslau palace, featured two manuals and an extended keyboard of five and a half octaves (see Table 7). As noted above, each possessed a machine stop, described in the *Allgemeine Augsburger Zeitung* of 1765: "Tschudi has placed all the registers in one pedal, so that they can be taken off one after the other, and the decreasing and increasing of the tone can be produced at will, which crescendo and decrescendo harpsichord-players have long wished for."[137] David Schulenberg notes (in chapter 3 of this volume) that J. C. Bach would have become familiar with Shudi's instruments in London after 1762 and points to the effectiveness of J. C.'s and Emanuel Bach's symphonic keyboard sonatas on such an instrument, due to the special machine stop. The very low compass of the king's Shudi harpsichords was also quite extraordinary: few eighteenth-century harpsichords and pianos exceeded the usual five octaves from FF to f3 or e3. It is, moreover, rare to find music that calls for the highest and lowest notes of this more common compass. Up to the 1740s, even very large German key-

134. Burney, *The Present State of Music in Germany* (1773), 2:144.

135. Room 17, ground floor, north wing, garden side. Nicolai, *Beschreibung der Königlichen Residenzstädte* (1786), 3:1239: "17) Konzertzimmer. Boisirt mit Gold. . . . Hier steht ein Silbermannsches Pianoforte."

136. Horvath, *Potsdams Merkwürdigkeiten*, 183–84: room 6: "Das Konzertzimmer . . . ein Flügel von Silbermann."

137. Wainwright and Mobbs, "Shudi's Harpsichords," 80.

board instruments had a typical range of FF to d3,[138] which was still used by Gottfried Silbermann for a piano in 1746. Despite Emanuel Bach having certainly known the court's Shudi's harpsichords, all of which were purchased before his departure for Hamburg in 1768, none of his keyboard compositions descend below FF. On the other hand, it can hardly be a coincidence that a version of Friedemann Bach's Concerto in G Major for unaccompanied keyboard, Fk 40, was later revised in Berlin to include several extremely low notes in the left hand.

Fk 40 exists in two versions: an early one written in Dresden (Fk 40a / BR A 13a) of ca. 1740, and a much later revision (Fk 40b / BR A 13b) of ca. 1775, made soon after the composer's arrival in Berlin, that contains the peculiar low notes.[139] Its first movement has been rewritten to include more elaborate passagework in the right hand; passages in the original left-hand part have been embellished and transposed down an octave, with new downward octave leaps that include the notes GG (mm. 6 and 63), AA (m. 42), and DD (m. 26) (see Example 1). David Schulenberg has puzzled over the low DD as "a note found on few if any keyboard instruments of the period."[140] While on rare occasions very large keyboards, including some by the Dresden maker Johann Heinrich Gräbner, were made with additional low notes,[141] every one of Shudi's harpsichords at court was built with an extended range.

Friedemann Bach's revision fits well chronologically with both his move to Berlin in 1774 and his associations at the Prussian court. Given Amalia's interest in extended compasses, as already seen on her organs, perhaps the revision of Fk 40a was made at her request to take advantage of the Shudi's extended low range. Observers who have played the instruments in the New Palace have noted the "rich and magnificently loud [volume] . . . no doubt due in part to a larger area of soundboard vibrating because of the extra compass in the bass."[142]

---

138. John Phillips, "The 1739 Johann Heinrich Gräbner Harpsichord: An Oddity or a *Bach-Flügel?*," in *Das deutsche Cembalo: Symposium im Rahmen der 24. Tage Alter Musik in Herne 1999*, ed. Christian Ahrens and Gregor Klinke (Munich: Katzbichler, 2000), 130.

139. Both versions are published in Wilhelm Friedemann Bach, *Klaviermusik I*, ed. Peter Wollny, *Gesammelte Werke*, 1 (Stuttgart: Carus, 2009). D-B, Mus. ms. Bach P 365 Fascicle XIII, which contains Fk 40b, is in the hand of the Berlin scribe J. F. Hering.

140. Schulenberg, *The Music of Wilhelm Friedemann Bach*, 93.

141. See, for example, Phillips, "The 1739 Johann Heinrich Gräbner Harpsichord." Another exceptionally large instrument with a six-octave compass from CC to c4, belonging to the Weimar organist Johann Caspar Vogler, a pupil of J. S. Bach, was advertised for sale in a Leipzig newspaper of 1766. See Carl G. Anthon, "An Unusual Harpsichord," *Galpin Society Journal* 37 (1984): 115–16.

142. Wainwright and Mobbs, "Shudi's Harpsichords," 85.

Ex. 1. Wilhelm Friedemann Bach, first movement of Concerto in G Major for Solo
Keyboard, Fk 40, versions A (mm. 49–56) and B (mm. 25–28).

EMANUEL BACH AND THE SILBERMANN HARPSICHORDS AT COURT

An equally unusual work by Emanuel Bach, the "Sonata per il Cembalo à 2 Tastature,"
Wq 69, composed in 1747 in Berlin, was written for a special two-manual harpsichord
with highly variegated and colorful registrations. The detailed instructions indicate the
use of different stops in each hand during the first two movements and for the theme
and each variation in the finale. The work calls for stops such as Cornet and Spinet,
whose nasal sound was produced by jacks placed close to the nut, as well as Flute and
"buff" (Example 2).[143] John Koster, who has deduced that the special instrument required for Wq 69 would have had a minimum of four registers acting on three 8-foot

143. Sebastian Bach's lute-harpsichord was also equipped with a cornet stop, which, when drawn
together with the lute stop, could "almost . . . deceive even professional lute players" (NBR, 366).

Ex. 2. Carl Philipp Emanuel Bach, Sonata per il Cembalo à 2 Tastature, Wq 69,
Allegretto, measures 1–5.

or standard-pitch and one 4-foot or octave sets of strings, has linked such instruments
to Sebastian Bach's *Goldberg Variations*, another work that appeared in the 1740s.[144]

In June 1746 the court paid Silbermann 200 Taler "for a Clavier" whose high price
suggests it might have possessed the stops needed to execute Wq 69. Additional keyboard instruments purchased from Silbermann include a "Clavecien" for 322 Taler,
obtained in 1748 through Quantz (discussed further below).[145] Other payments for
instruments, possibly harpsichords, were made to Johann Friedrich Rost (1706–59),
who received 600 Taler in January 1744; the payment must have been for at least two
instruments.[146] Rost had been appointed court keyboard maker by 1740 alongside
Hildebrandt, who later was entrusted with upkeep of the Silbermann fortepianos. The
account books also record payment for the repair of a "Cedar harpsichord."[147]

SILBERMANN PIANOS AT FREDERICK'S COURT

Late eighteenth-century reports provide exaggerated and conflicting information
as to how many Silbermann pianos were at court, and discussion about the actual
number is sprinkled throughout the Bach literature. The highest number suggested

144. John Koster, "The Harpsichord Culture in Bach's Environs," in Schulenberg, *Bach Perspectives*
4, 69.

145. *Schatullrechnung*, GStA PK, BPH, Rep. 47, no. 901, fol. 4r, March 1748, item no. 4: "an den
Virtuosen Quantz für ein Clavecien, 322 Taler, 20 Gr." (to the virtuoso Quantz for a keyboard, 322
Taler, 20 Gr.).

146. *Schatullrechnung*, GStA PK, BPH, Rep. 47, no. 897, fol. 1r, January 1744, item no. 34: "an den
Instrumentenmacher Rost L[aut].Q[uittung]., 600 Taler" (to the instrument builder Rost, per Receipt, 600 Taler).

147. *Schatullrechnung*, GStA PK, BPH, Rep. 47, no. 899, fol. 5r, May 1746, item no. 7: "an den Tischler
Böhmer in Berlin vor dass Cedern Clavicein in Potsdam und andere Kleinigkeiten. L.Q., 118 Taler"
(to the cabinetmaker Böhmer in Berlin for the cedar keyboard in Potsdam and other miscellanea,
per Receipt, 118 Taler).

was by Forkel: "The pianofortes manufactured by Silbermann, of Freyberg, pleased the King so much that he resolved to buy them all up. He collected 15. I hear that they all now stand, unfit for use, in various corners of the Royal Palace."[148] As there is usually a kernel of truth to every story, perhaps there were indeed fifteen *keyboard* instruments at court by Silbermann, but if so, they included harpsichords and probably other types of claviers.

Johann Friedrich Agricola (1720–74), member of the royal *Hofkapelle* and Sebastian Bach's pupil, reported that after Silbermann improved his pianos, one was sold to the court at Rudolstadt, and "shortly thereafter His Majesty the King of Prussia commissioned one and, as the instrument found royal favor, [the king] commissioned *several more* [emphasis added]," implying at least three.[149] This is corroborated by court records, which indicate that Frederick owned at least three—but more likely four—fortepianos by Gottfried Silbermann (see Table 9). Palace inventories show that near the end of his life, a fortepiano still stood in each of the royal private music rooms in Potsdam: in the Stadtschloss, Sanssouci, and the New Palace. There is also compelling evidence that a fourth stood during his lifetime in the Berlin Stadtschloss.

The well-known newspaper report of Sebastian Bach's visit to the Prussian court on Sunday, May 7, 1747, and published shortly thereafter in the *Spenersche Zeitung*, provides the most objective account of the events:

> His Majesty was informed that Capellmeister Bach had arrived at Potsdam and was waiting in His Majesty's antechamber for His Majesty's most gracious permission to listen to the music. His August Self immediately gave orders that Bach be admitted, and went, at his entrance, to the so-called F*orte* and P*iano*, condescending also to play, in His Most August Person and without any preparation, a theme—for the Capellmeister Bach, which he should execute in a fugue. . . . On Monday, the famous man let himself be heard on the organ in the Church of the Holy Spirit at Potsdam. . . . In the evening, His Majesty charged him again with the execution of a fugue, in six parts.[150]

148. NBR, 429n.

149. Published in Jakob Adlung, *Musica mechanica organoedi*, 2 vols. (Berlin, 1768), 2:116. The passage reads: "Da Hr. Silbermann wirklich viele Verbesserungen, sonderlich in Ansehung des Tractaments gefunden hatte, verkaufte er wieder eins an den Fürstlichen Hof zu Rudolstadt. . . . Kurz darauf liessen des Königs von Preussen Maj. eines dieser Instrumente, und als dies Dero allerhöchsten Beyfall fand, noch verschiedene mehr, vom Hrn Silbermann verschreiben" (Since Herr Silbermann had really discovered many improvements, especially with regard to the action, he sold one again to the Princely Court at Rudolstadt. . . . Shortly thereafter, His Majesty the King of Prussia had one of these instruments ordered from Silbermann, then several more after it received his highest approval). The Rudolstadt instrument was purchased in January 1745 for 352 Taler, 22 Groschen (see Koster, "The Quest for Bach's Clavier," 77).

150. NBR, 224.

Bach's obituary of 1754 compresses the two-day chronology of the 1747 newspaper account into one, stating that Bach developed the king's fugue subject "on the pianoforte" and "hereupon" was commanded to execute "a fugue with six obbligato voices . . . using a theme of his own."[151]

Forkel's particularly fantastic account, published in 1802, was presumably related to him by Wilhelm Friedemann, who was no doubt responsible for certain elements of exaggeration.[152] Written over fifty years after the fact, it is, moreover, the earliest account to mention Wilhelm Friedemann's presence. Whether or not Friedemann actually witnessed the scenarios described, Forkel's account dramatizes the events in other unlikely ways, stating that, rather than waiting in the antechamber of the palace to be announced (as reported by the newspapers), "old Bach, who had alighted at his son's lodgings, was immediately summoned to the Palace" with not even enough "time to change his traveling dress for a black cantor's gown."[153] Further, Forkel claims that Bach was invited "to try [the king's fortepianos, made by Silbermann, which stood in *several rooms of the Palace* [emphasis added]" and was then led "from room to room . . . to try them and to play unpremeditated compositions" upon them.[154]

As palace inventories unambiguously show, none of the royal palaces ever housed more than a single Silbermann piano, and at this time Frederick had no more than two pianos in the city of Potsdam, one in each palace (the New Palace had not yet been built). Moreover, of the two Potsdam palaces, the Stadtschloss had only two music rooms (excluding the theater), and Sanssouci had only one. For Bach to have been led "from room to room" to play so much as a second Silbermann fortepiano, he would have had to visit both Sanssouci and the Potsdam Stadtschloss. Like the obituary, Forkel likely produced a conflation with the next day's events, when Bach performed an organ recital, improvised a work in six parts, and might have been taken to additional instruments, including the Silbermann fortepiano in the Potsdam Stadtschloss. The remaining fortepiano(s) were twenty-eight to thirty-four kilometers away, in Berlin. Forkel also claims that at the king's request, "Bach was taken to all the organs in Potsdam as he had before been to Silbermann's fortepianos."[155] Yet Forkel makes no mention of Bach's organ recital the next day.

---

151. Ibid., 302–3.

152. On the unreliability of testimonies by Wilhelm Friedemann, see Robert L. Marshall's chapter in this volume.

153. NBR, 429.

154. Ibid.

155. Ibid., 430.

In an earlier attempt to settle the question about the number of Silbermann pianos, Conny Restle argued that (1) there were never more than two fortepianos by Silbermann at court (namely, those that remain today in Potsdam), and (2) no Silbermann piano ever stood in Sanssouci until after World War II. However, these hypotheses can no longer be maintained.[156] As shown above, both points are contradicted by contemporary palace inventories, which Restle did not take into account.

Although it is true that payments for only two Silbermann fortepianos are documented unambiguously in the *Schatullrechnung*, the king's private account books cannot be considered complete with regard to instrument purchases. Accounts are missing for 1740, 1741, and the period of the Seven Years' War, as well as for certain months of other years. Payments could also have come from accounts other than the king's purse. There is, in addition, one further payment listed in the *Schatullrechnung*, made to Quantz, which has not yet been considered in this context: in March 1748 Quantz was reimbursed 322 Taler, 20 Groschen for a "Clavecien." This instrument cost only 51 Taler less than the 1747 Silbermann fortepiano he had obtained on behalf of the court, but it was a whopping 122 Taler more than was paid for the previous Silbermann harpsichord recorded.[157] If this "Clavecien" was not a harpsichord but in fact a fortepiano, the fifty-Taler difference in price from the previous fortepianos by Silbermann might be explained by details of construction. The two extant Silbermann pianos in Potsdam both possess mutation stops, which are not only difficult but expensive to build.[158] Given variations in terminology used by the king's various bookkeepers, it is conceivable that the instrument paid for in 1748 was not an extravagant Silbermann harpsichord (as suggested above) but a fortepiano, possibly one with neither a mutation stop nor a transposer.[159] Of the two Silbermann pianos extant in Potsdam today, the one dated 1746 possesses a keyboard compass of FF to d3, whereas the other (paid for in 1747?) spans FF to e3; both feature a special ivory mutation stop that Stewart Pollens describes as producing a hammered-dulcimer sound (resembling a pantalon) when

156. Conny Restle, "Gottfried Silbermann und die Hammerflügel für den Preussischen Hof in Potsdam," *Jahrbuch des Staatlichen Instituts für Musikforschung Preussischer Kulturbesitz* (2001): 189–203.

157. See note 145.

158. Friendly communication of Barbara and Thomas Wolf of The Plains, Virginia, who have studied and copied the Silbermann pianos.

159. Furthermore, eighteenth-century documents as late as Emanuel Bach's Nachlassverzeichnis (estate catalog) of 1788 still refer to hammered instruments as a type of "clavecin," such as the "Fortepiano oder Clavecin Roial [*sic*]" owned by Emanuel at his death in 1788. A facsimile of the Nachlassverzeichnis is published online at https://loc.gov/item/ihas.200212334. The quoted text is from a list of his instruments on page 92.

used with the dampers raised (Table 9).[160] The more expensive piano displayed today in Sanssouci but purchased for the Potsdam Stadtschloss possesses a transposer and a slightly narrower compass.[161] As shown in the palace inventories, these pianos were placed exclusively in Frederick's private suites and did not replace the harpsichords used elsewhere in court performances.

But in addition to the inventories, there is another basis for arguing for the existence of more than two or three fortepianos at court: the king's lifelong practice of creating a copy of his personal surroundings and possessions in each of his residences, not only duplicating the colors, materials, decorative motifs, chandeliers, tables, and other furniture in his private rooms, particularly in his music rooms, but also placing identical copies of books in each palace library and duplicating his collection of flute music, his flutes, and his music stands. Available evidence suggests this duplication also extended to the keyboards in his private suites. The one exception to this was the palace at Breslau, which received a Shudi harpsichord because no Gottfried Silbermann pianos were available.

The New Palace, which was not completed until after Silbermann's death, did not receive a brand new fortepiano; instead, one of the king's existing fortepianos had to be relocated there between 1765 and 1769, when the instrument was fitted with a new, elaborately carved, gold-gilt rococo stand created by one of the court's craftsmen (mentioned above). Where did the instrument come from? Nicolai firmly establishes in 1786 that Silbermann instruments still stood in both the New Palace and in the Potsdam Stadtschloss, and Carl Christian Horvath, whose stated purpose was to update Nicolai's work, continued to report them as being in these locations in 1798. The earliest surviving inventory of the Berlin Stadtschloss, made in 1793 during the reign of Frederick William II, indicates that at this date the music room of the late King Frederick still contained a fortepiano by Silbermann.[162] An inventory

160. Stewart Pollens, *The Early Pianoforte* (Cambridge: Cambridge University Press, 1995), 179, 183. In the nineteenth and early twentieth centuries it was sometimes called a "cembalo stop" (friendly communication from John Koster).

161. The instrument, dated 1746 (see Table 9), is presently the one displayed in Schloss Sanssouci. Following World War II, many museum artifacts in Berlin and Potsdam were returned to different locations, a situation that continues to the present day. On the latter topic, see Mary Oleskiewicz, "A Museum, a World War, and a Rediscovery: Flutes by Quantz and Others from the Hohenzollern Museum," *Journal of the American Musical Instrument Society* 24 (1998): 107–45. For further discussion of Silbermann's pianos and the use of low chamber pitch at court, see Oleskiewicz, "The Trio Sonata in Bach's Offering," 98–99.

162. spsg Plansammlung, Inv. 44, *Inventarius des Königl. Schlosses zu Berlin aufgenommen im Jahr 1793*, 72: "Im Zimmer überhaupt / . . . Ein Piano Forte von Silbermann" (In the room / . . . a pianoforte

for Schloss Sanssouci indicates that in 1782 a fortepiano was still in its music room as well.[163] If we assume for the moment that during the 1740s or 1750s a fortepiano also had been housed in one of the king's two music rooms at Schloss Charlottenburg, and if we take into account that the Charlottenburg palace inventory of 1770 mentions the presence of a harpsichord (*Flügel*) in "His Royal Majesty's Concert Room" (in his second suite only),[164] we can surmise that as the palace was rarely used at that time by the king, the Charlottenburg fortepiano was moved to the New Palace and replaced by the harpsichord. This is precisely what happened with the king's manuscript copies of flute music labeled "pour Charlottenbourg." Instead of creating new copies of flute music for the New Palace in 1765, the works by Quantz and himself composed up to this date (and until then kept in the music room at Charlottenburg) were relocated to the music room of the New Palace; henceforth, only copies of newly composed works were made with the label "pour le nouveau Palais" (for the New Palace).[165] If the latter hypothesis is correct, then there were precisely four Silbermann fortepianos at court, and all of the king's music rooms are accounted for in terms of what instruments they possessed. But in any case, the preponderance of all evidence strongly supports the presence of four such instruments.

Conclusion

The venues, instruments, and contexts for musical instruction, performance, and concert attendance by the Bachs and their students in the Prussian king's palace residences were numerous and highly varied. The dimensions, acoustics, and purposes that characterized each unique musical space must have been as influential on prevailing style and practice as were the varying types of keyboard instruments available. Frederick

---

by Silbermann). A copy of the inventory is found under Inv. 45 with the same date. However, in this copy a few items have been struck through and noted as no longer on hand. (The fortepiano is not one of them.) An earlier extant inventory of 1777 (Inv. 39) concerns only mundane household items and does not list furniture or musical instruments.

163. See note 63.

164. SPSG Plansammlung, Ak 31, *Inventarium Von Mobilibres, im Königl. Schlosse Charlottenburg*, [p. 2]. The inventory indicates that the harpsichord was located in the king's music room (in his newer, second suite), room 4 (this room is today numbered as 364). See also note 32.

165. The catalogs of "solos" (flute sonatas) "pour Sans Souçi" (D-B KH M 1574) and "pour le nouveau Palais" (D-B KH M 1575) and of concertos "pour Sans Souçi" (D-B KH M 1572) and "pour le nouveau Palais" (D-B KH M 1573) are still extant. All were made ca. 1765, when Frederick took up residence in the New Palace. The copies made for palaces destroyed in the war (Potsdam Stadtschloss, Breslau Schloss, and Berlin Stadtschloss), along with all traces of the copies of flute music labeled for those palaces, are missing.

collected a large number of diverse keyboard instruments, and those that we can document show not only that he was concerned with having instruments equipped with the latest technology but also that his taste in soundscapes was diverse and far-reaching. The *petits salons* in Frederick's apartments, with their ornamental parquet floors and large, acoustically reflective mirrors, were designed for neither a large ensemble nor an audience but rather for the enjoyment of the participants. Chasôt, an eyewitness, noted the fine acoustic properties of the king's music room in the Potsdam Stadtschloss. As he documents, these spaces required an approach to performance—using a small ensemble of soloists—different from that of large concert halls and festival rooms where the entire *Hofkapelle*, an ensemble of thirty-five to forty instrumentalists, performed.[166] Halls of the latter type, designed with highly reflective surfaces, including large mirrors and windows and sometimes marble floors, would have depended on the presence of numerous spectators to absorb some of the resonant sound. Likewise, the intimate palace theaters also required forces quite distinct from those used in the royal opera house, whose orchestra pit was generous enough to contain an orchestra with two harpsichords.[167]

That Frederick chose to equip only his small, personal music rooms—and not the larger ones—with Silbermann fortepianos must reflect the instruments' tonal qualities and suitability for chamber music. His decision to do so is consistent with contemporary descriptions of the instruments. As Jakob Adlung reported, "[The Silbermann piano] is not as strong as other keyboards: it is a chamber instrument and should not be used for loud music." On the other hand, he notes that on at least one occasion, a Silbermann piano was used to good effect in the *Hofoper* in Berlin: "Once [a Silbermann piano] was used with success in Berlin at the opera."[168] Perhaps it was reserved for the recitatives, in place of one of the harpsichords.

The instruments furnished by King Frederick in each of these historical spaces must have helped shape both the approaches to keyboard playing and the writings, compositions, and performance style of Emanuel Bach and his colleagues. We know from various reports that Johann Sebastian Bach tested and ultimately gave his approval of

---

166. On the exact size and constitution of the Hofkapelle during Frederick's lifetime, see Oleskiewicz, "The Court of Brandenburg-Prussia," 111–26.

167. The *Schatullrechnung*, GStA PK, BPH, Rep. 47, no. 908, fol. 4r, March 1755, item no. 36: "An den Baron von Svëerts [Ernst Maximillian von Sweerts (1710–57), *Intendant*] vor reparation derer Clavicembali im Opern-Hause, 49 Taler" (To Baron von Sweerts for repair of the harpsichords in the opera house, 49 Taler) records repairs to these two harpsichords (see Table 2).

168. "So stark wie andere Claveßins geht es nicht, und ist ein Kammerinstrument, und daher zu keiner starken Musik zu gebrauchen"; "Man hat es gleichwohl einsmals in Berlin in der Oper mit gutem Erfolge gebraucht" (Adlung, *Musica mechanica organoedi*, 2:117).

Silbermann's pianos, that he played one or more of them during his visit to the Prussian court in 1747, and that in 1749, at the end of his life, he was involved in the sale of at least one Silbermann piano.[169] But Sebastian Bach's estate did not contain a piano at his death, and there is "no reason to think that Bach owned or played a particular harpsichord by Silbermann."[170] Emanuel Bach, however, would have been required to perform accompaniments nightly on Silbermann fortepianos in multiple locations beginning in 1746, if not before, and on harpsichords by various makers, including Silbermann, on other occasions. From the introduction to volume 2 of his *Versuch*, we know that by 1762 the piano and clavichord had become his preferred instruments for realizing accompaniments that "require the most elegant taste," an assessment that must have come from the experience of accompanying flutes and voices daily on Silbermann's pianos at the king's private chamber concerts.

While it is not possible to connect pieces composed by Emanuel Bach at Berlin to a fortepiano, many of his Berlin pieces from the late 1740s onward were probably written with the clavichord in mind. Schulenberg notes the use of *Bebung* (an indication for clavichord) in the *Probestücke* Wq 63/4 and 63/6 and in the Sonata Wq 55/2,[171] composed at Berlin in 1758 on Bach's famous Silbermann clavichord, which he had acquired in about 1746, just when the court was also procuring instruments from Silbermann. Only one continuo part in a work by Quantz specifically calls for "Cimbalo, Piano e Forte," yet even this part contains no feature, apart from dynamics, that would exclude performance on a harpsichord.[172] The generic idiom described by Schulenberg and found in most Bach family works for keyboard before 1750 is characterized by a style of composing or notating music that was fundamentally independent of the medium,

---

169. For a chronology of Bach and the Silbermann pianos, see Koster, "The Quest for Bach's Clavier," 77–78.

170. Germann, "The Mietkes, the Margrave, and Bach," 120. Germann suggests that the only possible exception would have been the large veneered harpsichord mentioned in the inventory of Bach's estate in 1750, but the Silbermanns were not known for making veneered instruments, and this was more likely an instrument of central or southern German origin. A better candidate for the maker of that instrument, according to Germann (120n4), is Johann Nicolaus Bach, Sebastian's cousin, who was praised by Adlung for his *Lautenklavier* (two of which are mentioned in Bach's estate inventory, together with five harpsichords and a spinet).

171. See David Schulenberg's chapter in the present volume and Schulenberg, *The Music of Carl Philipp Emanuel Bach*, 126 and 227.

172. The work is the Concerto in F Major for Flute and Strings, QV 5:162. The autograph piano part contains the first movement of the concerto and is meant to replace the first movement of the more generically labeled "basso continuo" part. It differs from other Quantz continuo parts in that the keyboard doubles certain passages of the first and second violins. Both keyboard parts contain numerous dynamic markings that would be impossible to realize on a harpsichord.

leaving it to the player to take advantage of the specific capabilities of the instrument used for a given performance.[173] Certain works, such as Wq 69, Wq 70/2–7, Wq 112/1, BWV 1079/1,[174] and Fk 40b, suggest that on specific occasions members of the Bach family took advantage of the remarkable diversity of instruments and performing spaces in the various royal palaces to compose special pieces and execute them in an appropriate manner.

173. Schulenberg points out that Emanuel Bach resembled his contemporaries in being "slow to adapt his keyboard writing for specific types of instrument" and that "even the presence of mulitple levels of dynamics in the Württemburg Sonatas [Wq 49] does not make them uniquely suited for the [clavichord or fortepiano]" (*The Music of Carl Philipp Emanuel Bach*, 84).

174. Peter Williams, in the preface to his edition of *J. S. Bach: Musikalisches Opfer* (London: Eulenberg, 1986), xii–xiii, points out a number of features that would make the three-part ricercar from *The Musical Offering* especially suited to the early piano (discussed in Schulenberg, *The Keyboard Music of J. S. Bach*, 392).

Appendix

Table 1. Frederick II's residences and dates of occupancy

Palace	Date	Occupancy
Schloss Rheinsberg	1736–ca. 1752	Residence as crown prince until 1740; thereafter as king occasionally during the 1740s
Schloss Charlottenburg	1740–86	Primary residence until 1745; contained apartments for Princess Amalia
Stadtschloss Berlin	1745–86	Used mainly by the king for state visits and during Carnival, but rarely after ca. 1763; winter residence of queen and close relatives in Berlin, including Princess Amalia
Stadtschloss Potsdam	1745–86	Primary residence 1745–47; after 1747 the king occupied it only during the winter months (November through April)
Schloss Sanssouci, Potsdam	1747–86	Intimate private Lustschloss used in summer months (May through October) beginning in 1747
Schloss Breslau	1752–86	Inhabited by Frederick on visits to Silesia beginning in 1752
Neues Palais at Sanssouci, Potsdam	1765–86	Large representational palace used occasionally by the king in summer months (May through October); housed dignitaries, close family, extended family members, and other guests

Table 2. Keyboard instrument payments recorded in Frederick II's *Schatullrechnung*

Date	Amount	Remark	Instrument	Maker
January 1744	600 Taler	"An den Instrumenten-macher Rost"	Not specified; for two harpsichords?	Rost
May 1746	118 Taler	"An den Tischler Böhmer in Berlin vor dass Cedern Clavicein in Potsdam"	One cedar harpsichord	—
June 1746	200 Taler	"Dem Silbermann vor ein Clavier"	One harpsichord	Silbermann
"Extra Expenses" June 1746	420 Taler	"An dem Silbermann. vor Piano und Forte"	One fortepiano	Silbermann
May 1747	373 Taler, 12 Groschen	"Dem Virtuosen Quantz vor ein Piano et Forte"	One fortepiano	Silbermann
March 1748	322 Taler, 20 Groschen	"an den Virtuosen Quantz Für ein Clavecien"	One harpsichord	[Silbermann?]
March 1755	49 Taler	"An den Baron von Svëerts vor reparation derer Clavicembali im Opern-Hause"	Repair of (two) harpsichords in the opera house	[Silbermann?]
August 1765	300 Taler	"Für das Forte piano der Printzessin von Preussen"	One fortepiano	[Hildebrandt?]
October 1765	800 Taler	"An den Kaufmann Bachmann für den Flügel aus Engelleand [*sic*]"	One harpsichord from England	Shudi
December 1766	1600 Taler	"An den Kaufmann Bachmann in Magdeburg für zwey englische Claviere"	Two harpsichords from England	Shudi
February 1770	200 Taler	"Für den Bagen Flügel [Bogenflügel]"	One *Bogenflügel*	Hohlefeld

Table 3. Organs and other keyboards in use at court

A. Extant keyboards (excluding those by Shudi and Silbermann)

Date	Instrument	Maker	Description	Location
Ca. 1703	Harpsichord	Mietke	Two manuals, FF–GG–AA–c3; 8', 4', 8' + coupler; black lacquer with chinoiserie by Dagly; 107 cm high, 238 cm long, 89.5 cm wide	Schloss Charlottenburg
Ca. 1702–4	Harpsichord	Mietke	One manual, GG, AA–c3; 2 x 8'; white lacquer with chinoiserie by Dagly; 97 cm high, 225 cm long, 90 cm wide	Schloss Charlottenburg, Princess Amalia's suite
Ca. 1700	*Clavecin brisé*	Jean Marius	One manual: folding harpsichord in three sections, short G-octave, BB/D♯–c3; painted, with gold leaf; 8.5 cm high, 148.5 cm long (with keyboard pulled out), 69.3 cm wide; underside of midsection bears coat of arms of Frederick II	Berlin Stadtschloss, Kunstkammer; 1875–88 in Kunstgewerbemuseum; from 1888 Musikinstru-menten- Museum, Berlin
1706	Organ	Schnitger	Two manuals: originally C, D, E–c3; pedals C, D, E–d1; disposition, see Table 4; original pitch almost one whole step below modern pitch	Schloss Charlottenburg, Eosander Schlosskapelle
1755	House organ	Ernst Marx	Two manuals: C–f3, including C♯; pedal range C–d1; disposition, see Table 5; in chamber pitch	Stadtschloss, Balcony Room, second floor (Amalia's suite); from 1767, Amalia's palace at Unter den Linden 7
1776	House organ	Ernst Marx	Manuals and pedals as in organ of 1755; disposition, see Table 6; in chamber pitch	Amalia's palace at Wilhelmstrasse 102, Orgelsaal

B. Unidentified keyboards

Date	Instrument	Maker	Description	Location
Ca. 1737	Harpsichord	?	"A large, lacquered harpsichord, having a music desk fitted with two candlestick holders"	Schloss Rheinsberg, Frederick II's private music room
After 1740	Harpsichord	Silbermann	"A beautiful harpsichord by Silbermann" (according to Nicolai, 1779–86)	Potsdam Stadtschloss, large music room

Table 4. Disposition of the Arp Schnitger organ at
Schloss Charlottenburg (1706) ⬛ 3

Hauptwerk (manual 2)	Rückpositiv (manual 1)	Pedal
Principal 8'	Principal 8'	Subbaß 16'
Gedact 8'	Gedact lieblich	Octav 8'
Floite dues 8'	8'	
Octav 4'	Octav 4'	Octav 4'
Violdegamb 4'	Floite dues 4'	Nachthorn 2'
Nassat 3'	Octav 2'	Mixtur 6fach
SuperOctav 2'	Waltflöit 2'	Posaunen 16'
Mixtur 4fach	Sesquialt 2fach	Trommet 8'
Hoboy 8'	Scharf 3fach	Cornet 2'
Vox humana 8'		

Note: Disposition as given by Stefan Behrens and Uwe Pape, "Charlottenburg, Schloß Charlottenburg, Eosander-Kapelle, Orgel von Arp Schnitger, 1706, Rekonstruction von Karl Schuke, 1969–70," in *500 Jahre Orgeln in Berliner Evangelischen Kirchen*, 2 vols. (Berlin: Pape, 1991), 1:74.

Table 5. Disposition of Princess Amalia's organ for the
Berlin Stadtschloss (1755) ⬛ 6

Hauptwerk (manual I)	Oberwerk (manual II)	Pedal
Principal 8'	Principal 4'	Subbaß 16'
Viola di Gamba 8'	Quintatön 8'	Octave 8'
Bordun 16'	Gedackt 8'	Octave 4'
Rohrflöte 8'	Gedackt 4'	Posaune 16'
Octave 4'	Nasat 3'	Baßflöte 8'
Quinte 3'	Waldflöte 2'	
Octave 2'	Sifflöte 1'	
Mixtur 4fach 1⅓'	Salicional 8'	
Flaute dolce 8'		

Note: Disposition (as built) given by Stefan Behrens and Uwe Pape, "Karlshorst, Kirche zur frohen Botschaft, Orgel von Ernst Marx und Peter Migendt, 1755," in *500 Jahre Orgeln in Berliner Evangelischen Kirchen*, 2 vols. (Berlin: Pape, 1991), 1:126.

Table 6. Disposition of Princess Amalia's second house organ (1776)

Hauptwerk (manual 1)	Oberwerk (manual 2)	Pedal
Prinzipal 8'	Prinzipal 4'	Violon 16'
Quintadena 16'	Gedackt 8'	Subbaß 16'
Bordun 16'	Quintatön 8'	Posaune 16'
Violon 8'	Rohrflöte 4'	Quinte 6'
Viola da Gamba 8'	Nassat 3'	Oktave 8'
Salizional 8'	Oktave 2'	Baßflöte 8'
Rohrflöte, 8'	Waldflöte 2'	Sperrventile
Gedackt 8'	Sifflöte 1'	Kalkantenglocke
Flöte douce 8'		Manualkoppel II/I
Oktave 4'		
Quinte 3'		
Oktave 2'		
Mixtur 4fach 2'		
Piffora 2fach 8'		

Note: Organ disposition as given by Martin Rost, "Die Orgeln der Anna Amalia von Preußen von Migendt und Marx," in *Carl Philipp Emanuel Bach: Musik für Europa. Bericht über das Internationale Symposium vom 8. bis 12. März 1994 in Frankfurt (Oder)*, ed. Hans-Günter Ottenberg (Frankfurt an der Oder: Konzerthalle Carl Philipp Emanuel Bach, 1998), 411. This organ no longer survives. Rost notes that the manual and pedal compasses were identical to Amalia's first organ (412).

Table 7. Shudi harpsichords acquired by Frederick II ⬜ 7, 8

Serial no.	Date	Location	Description	Price
496	1765	ex Breslau Schloss → Poznań Museum of Musical Instruments	Two manuals, CC–f3, Standard English disposition: three sets of strings 8', 8', 4'; four sets of jacks, controlled by stop knobs on the nameboard: 8' and 4' on the lower manual; dogleg 8' on both manuals; lute (nasal) 8' on the upper manual (playing the same strings as the dogleg 8'); harp (buff) to the lower-manual 8', controlled by a stop now on the left side of the keywell. No Venetian swell. Signed "Burkat Tschudi No. 496 fecit Londini 1765"; mahogany case; 96 cm high, 103 cm wide, 270 cm long. Played by Mozart on May 13, 1765, in London	800 Taler
497	1765?	?	[Soundboard now in no. 496]	?
511	1766	New Palace at Sanssouci	Two manuals, CC–f3. Standard English disposition, as above. No Venetian swell. Signed "Burkat Tschudi No. 511 fecit Londini 1766"; 95 cm high, 105 cm wide, 270 cm long. Inlaid mahogany case with bronze hardware: oxidized silver hinges, pedals, frame, and ornate pedal (for working the machine stop) positioned between two silvered ball-and-claw feet; HM inventory no. 3698. Bears three small labels engraved with instructions for working the machine stop. Described by Charles Burney, *The Present State of Music in Germany* (London: Becket, 1773): 2:145; see text note 112	800 Taler
512	1766	ex New Palace at Sanssouci → Glinka Museum, Moscow	Two manuals, CC–f3. Standard English disposition, as above. No Venetian swell. Signed "Burkat Tschudi No. 512 Fecit Londini 1766"	800 Taler

Table 8. Music rooms furnished with a keyboard in the New Palace at Sanssouci, from the period of construction ⬚ 8

	tSuite	Inventory designation	Location	Dimensions (meters)	Instrument
1	King Frederick	"Concert Cammer"	Ground floor, garden side of main building	10.59 by 7.25	Fortepiano by Silbermann
2	Unteres Fürstenquartier / Apollo Saal (Lower Princely Quarters / Apollo Room)	"Concert Cammer"	Ground floor, garden side of main building	11.20 by 10.38	Harpsichord no. 512 by Burkat Shudi
3	Oberes Fürstenquartier (Upper Princely Quarters)	"Cammer / eigentliche Concert Cammer"	Second floor, garden side of main building	11.20 by 10.38	Harpsichord no. 511 by Burkat Shudi
4	Princess "Heinrich" (Wilhelmine of Hesse-Kassel [1726–1808], wife of Prince Heinrich of Prussia; see text note 126)	"Cammer"	Ground floor, court side	9.29 by 6.56	? (after 1770, *Bogenflügel* by Hohlefeld)
5	Crown Princess of Prussia; Obere Rote Cammern (Upper Red Chambers)	"Cammer"	Second floor, court side of main building	9.30 by 8.82	Harpsichord (no. 497[?] by Burkat Shudi)
6	Schlosstheater	N/A	Second floor, court side	14.20 by 12.25; stage: 9.7 by 9.7; pit: 9.75 by 2.45	Unknown (one harpsichord)

Note: I determined the dimensions given here using a laser and original architectural plans. For the location of each room, see ⬚ 8.

Table 9. Silbermann fortepianos documented in Frederick II's
private music rooms during his lifetime

Date invoiced	Location	Description	Price
—	Berlin Stadtschloss, ca. 1745 to at least 1793	?	?
June 21, 1746*	Potsdam Stadtschloss, 1746 to at least 1822	One manual, FF–d3; double strung; damper-raising mechanism; ivory and brass mutation stop; transposer; dated 1746	420 Taler
April 1747	Schloss Sanssouci, 1747 to at least 1782	One manual, FF–e3; double strung; damper-raising mechanism; ivory mutation stop; undated	373 Taler, 12 Groschen
—	New Palace at Sanssouci, ca. 1765 (1772) to at least 1798**	?	?

* The instrument purchased for the Potsdam Stadtschloss, dated 1746, bears an inscription on its belly rail: "Dieß instrument: Piano et Forte genandt, ist von den Königl. Pohlnischen, und Churfl. Sächs. Hof und Landt Orgel, und Instrument macher, in Freyberg von Herrn, Gottfried / Silbermann, verfertiget worden, Datum, Freyberg in Meißen den 11. Junij / Anno Christi 1746" (Restle, "Gottfried Silbermann," 194).

** This would have been an older instrument probably moved here from the king's second music room in the New Wing of Schloss Charlottenburg. Of course, the actual instrument moved to the New Palace might have been the surviving undated piano (listed above under Sanssouci).

C. P. E. Bach's Keyboard Music
and the Question of Idiom

David Schulenberg

C arl Philipp Emanuel Bach has always been known above all as a keyboard player and composer for keyboard instruments, and his favorite instrument is usually supposed to have been the clavichord. Recent work has raised doubt about the centrality of keyboard music to his output, at least during the later part of his career. Yet there can be little question that his compositions for harpsichord, clavichord, or fortepiano constitute his most important contribution to European music. Nevertheless, the composer rarely specified the precise instrument for which each piece was intended, nor could these hundreds of pieces, written during a career spanning more than six decades, have been meant for a single variety of keyboard. This essay demonstrates that C. P. E. Bach's writing for stringed keyboard instruments is more diverse than it is generally perceived to be and that it reveals substantial changes over time, even while rarely requiring a particular type of instrument.

Stringed keyboard instruments, as a group, are at least as diverse as any other organo-logical category, yet for much of their history Western composers have treated them generically, writing keyboard music without designating any specific sounding medium. This was as true for Carl Philipp Emanuel Bach as it had been for his father: both tended to designate keyboard pieces as being for unspecified "clavier" or "cembalo." Even music that seems ideally suited for one particular variety of keyboard instrument is often playable on another. In part this must reflect the peculiar status of keyboard instruments as virtual ensembles, capable of playing full scores composed originally for groups of instruments or voices. It must also reflect the adoption of the keyboard during the seventeenth and eighteenth centuries as the primary medium for teaching European musicians, on which even singers and players of melody instruments learned harmony and counterpoint. An additional factor surely was the diversity of keyboard instruments. Even those of a single basic type, such as the organ, existed in a wealth of forms such that nearly every individual exemplar revealed a unique combination of compass, registrational possibilities, and other features.

As a child at Weimar and Köthen during the teens and twenties of the eighteenth century, Emanuel Bach presumably knew the organs, harpsichords, and clavichords available in those towns, as well as music of various types that was being composed for them, above all, his father's. By the time of Emanuel Bach's death in 1788, Mozart had composed nearly all his keyboard sonatas and concertos—the later ones surely conceived for the fortepiano—and the young Beethoven was already writing distinctive music for keyboard instruments. How radically Emanuel Bach's approach to the keyboard had changed during a career spanning nearly sixty years is evident if one compares one of his late published pieces to an early work that must predate the more familiar compositions cataloged by Wotquenne and Helm and acknowledged in the composer's own work lists (Examples 1–2).[1] The later of these pieces, the Rondo in A Minor, Wq 56/5, was one of the composer's rare keyboard compositions to be assigned to a specific instrument, the fortepiano.[2] Composed at Hamburg in 1778 and published two years later, it includes detailed performance markings that explicitly demand an instrument capable of dynamics. A dynamic instrument is also implicit in the occasional *piano* octaves and other details, discussed below, that are unidiomatic for the harpsichord. Notable as well is the constantly changing texture, which in Example 1 ranges from simple polyphony in two or three parts to massed chords and a sort of hocket between the two hands (what the French called *batteries*), all within the space of a few measures. On the other hand, the movement from Bach's early *Sonata per il cembalo solo* (without Wq number) uses an idiom associated today with the harpsichord: it completely lacks dynamic markings, and it is largely in two contrapuntal parts, each confined to a limited tessitura and rhythmic texture (Example 2).[3] Despite the absence

1. The earlier work is absent from two lists of keyboard music acknowledged by the composer and offered for sale by him and his heirs during the latter part of the century: the "Autographischer Catalogus von den Claviersonaten des C. Ph. E. Bach bis zum Jahre 1772 komponirt" (D-Bsa, SA 4261), facsimile in Christoph Wolff, "Carl Philipp Emanuel Bachs Verzeichnis seiner Clavierwerke von 1733 bis 1772," in *Über Leben, Kunst und Kunstwerke: Aspekte musikalischer Biographie; Johann Sebastian Bach im Zentrum*, ed. Barbara Steinwachs et al. (Leipzig: Evangelische Verlagsanstalt, 1999), 217–35; and the *Verzeichniß des musikalischen Nachlasses des verstorbenen Capellmeisters Carl Philipp Emanuel Bach* (Hamburg: Schniebes, 1790), transcription online at http://www.cpebach.org/pdfs /resources/NV-1790.pdf. The so-called *Nachlassverzeichnis* also records places and dates of composition for most works and is the source for information about the latter given in this essay. In addition, it provides a list of instruments that the composer owned at his death, including two large clavichords, a harpsichord, and a fortepiano.

2. As indicated by the title of the publication in which the piece was issued: *Clavier-Sonaten / nebst / einigen Rondos / fürs Forte-piano / für / Kenner und Liebhaber* (Leipzig, 1780). Any doubt that the phrase *fürs Forte-piano* modifies only the noun *Rondos* is dispelled by the layout of the page, with the lines *einigen Rondos / fürs Forte-piano* set off by the use of smaller type. Throughout this essay, the term "fortepiano" is used interchangeably with "piano," the former being used when citing specific documents such as the present title page.

3. As noted by Darrell Berg, the word *cembalo* in Emanuel Bach's scores is evidently an Italian equivalent of the German (originally French) *Clavier* and does not designate a specific stringed keyboard

of dynamic markings, the composer probably expected such a piece to be played on the clavichord, an instrument more likely to be within the financial means of the students for whom this relatively simple composition might have been intended.

Clearly these two examples reflect, or parallel, the profound changes in European keyboard instruments that took place during Bach's lifetime. Whether musical style and technique changed in response to new instruments, or whether instruments were modified or invented to serve new types of music, is a chicken-and-egg question. A musical instrument, however, is not a biological organism that hatches at a particular moment; it is the product of a living maker responding to the needs of contemporary musicians and audiences, as is each composition played on it. Thus in any period we can expect to see parallel developments of both instruments and instrumental idioms. Surely these two pieces were written for and typically performed on distinct instruments. Yet it would be speculative to go beyond this general statement and try to determine on exactly what actual instruments each of these pieces was originally played or on which it might best be performed today.[4] More fruitful will be to focus on the evolving keyboard idiom of Bach's music, that is, its textures, figuration, and any performance styles or techniques for which it seems to call.

Given the centrality of keyboard instruments to Bach's output, it seems strange that he seldom specified the precise medium of this music. Today he is associated with the clavichord, which he indeed proclaimed as the instrument on which a player is best judged,[5] and during his lifetime he was famous for his private performances on it. Charles Burney gave a frequently quoted account of Bach's performance on the

---

instrument such as the harpsichord; see, for example, her "Preface: Keyboard Music," in *Carl Philipp Emanuel Bach: The Complete Works*, vol. 1/8.2, ed. Peter Wollny (Los Altos, CA: Packard Humanities Institute, 2005), xii. Example 2 shows the conclusion of what is edited as movement 3 of a "Suite in G Major," no. 68, in the same volume. The movement is a fragment, lacking its opening portion and therefore its tempo or movement designation. Wollny dates the sole source, fascicle 10 of D-Hs, ND VI 3191, to before 1738; comparison with the composer's acknowledged music from the mid-1730s suggests that this movement was composed before then.

4. Efforts to pin down the precise instrument for which Bach wrote particular pieces include John Henry van der Meer, *Die Klangfarbliche Identität der Klavierwerke Carl Philipp Emanuel Bachs* (Amsterdam: North-Holland Publishing, 1978); and Joel Speerstra, "Towards an Identification of the Clavichord Repertoire among C. P. E. Bach's Solo Keyboard Music: Some Preliminary Conclusions," in *De clavicordio II*, ed. Bernard Brauchli et al. (Magnano: International Centre for Clavichord Studies, 1995), 43–81.

5. "Das Clavicord ist also das Instrument, worauf man einen Clavieristen aufs genaueste zu beurtheilen fähig ist," *Versuch über die wahre Art das Clavier zu spielen*, 2 vols. (Berlin, 1753–62; new edition in CPEB:CW, 7/1–3 [ed. Tobias Plebuch, 2011]), vol. 1, introduction, para. 12. Citations of Bach's *Versuch* will take the latter form, rather than specifying page numbers, in order to facilitate reference to various editions and translations.

Ex. 1. Rondo in A Minor, Wq 56/5, movement 2, measures 9–28.

Ex. 2. Sonata in G Major, without Wotquenne or Helm number,
end of third (?) movement.

clavichord, at the composer's home in Hamburg, of works that included the concertos of Wq 43.[6] Another contemporary reported hearing him perform trios on the same instrument, accompanied by muted violin and cello "played with discretion."[7] But in public he performed—perhaps the same pieces—on harpsichord and piano.[8] Even the six famous volumes of pieces for *Kenner und Liebhaber*, which he published toward the end of his life, are mainly for the generic "clavier"; only the thirteen rondos within these collections are for fortepiano.[9]

A few works, including just one of the sonatas for *Kenner und Liebhaber* (Wq 55/2), call for *Bebung*, a sort of vibrato obtainable on the clavichord (Example 3). Clearly, the presence of notation for this device in any composition suggests that the clavichord is the preferred instrument. Yet this notation, like a number of ornament signs, does not seem to occur in Bach's music prior to his describing it in volume 1 of his *Versuch*. Its presence in pieces from 1753 onward is one of many indications that Bach's keyboard idiom was evolving—and that his notation of specific performance practices was becoming increasingly precise.[10] Yet it remains equally clear that practices such as *Bebung* that were specific to particular instruments were optional, not binding, elements of the musical text. More than in music for other media, that text still had to be completed or realized through adaptations carried out by the player in response to the capabilities and limitations of whatever instrument was used for a given performance.

Example 3 is from a sonata that Bach reportedly composed on his famous Silbermann clavichord, the instrument that Burney heard and that Bach acquired in about 1746.[11]

6. Charles Burney, *The Present State of Music in Germany, the Netherlands, and United Provinces*, 2nd ed., 2 vols. (London: Becket/Robson/Robinson, 1775), 2:271–72.

7. "ein mit Discretion gespieltes Violoncell," anonymous review, *Hamburgischer Correspondent*, 10 October 1777, reprinted in Ernst Suchalla, ed., *Carl Philipp Emanuel Bach: Briefe und Dokumente: Kritische Gesamtausgabe*, 2 vols. (Göttingen: Vandenhoeck & Ruprecht, 1994), 1:632–33.

8. Thus on 6 April 1778 Bach played "ein neues Concert und Trio für Clavier" as part of a concert that also included his setting of Ramler's *Himmelfahrt und Auferstehung Christi*, Wq 240 (*Hamburgischer Correspondent*, quoted by Josef Sittard, *Geschichte des Musik- und Concertwesens in Hamburg vom 14. Jahrhundert bis auf die Gegenwart* [Altona: A. C. Reher, 1890], 107). An earlier advertisement for this concert in the same newspaper (4 April 1778) specifies that the "Clavier" was a fortepiano; see CPEB:CW, 3/9.15 (ed. Douglas Lee, 2009), xii.

9. As specified by the titles of the individual volumes. See note 2.

10. The notation for *Bebung*, described in *Versuch*, vol. 1, chap. 3, para. 20, first appears in two of the *Probestücke* published in conjunction with the *Versuch*, presumably in 1753 (Wq 63/4, movement 2, and Wq 63/6, movement 3); see the author's edition in CPEB:CW, 1/3 (2005).

11. Bach sold the instrument in 1781 after owning it for thirty-five years, according to a document quoted in CPEB:CW, 1/8.1, xvi–xvii; further discussion in David Schulenberg, "When Did the Clavichord Become C. P. E. Bach's Favourite Instrument? An Inquiry into Expression, Style, and Medium in

Ex. 3.Sonata in F Major, Wq 55/2, movement 1, measures 67–77.
Bebung is indicated by dots beneath slurs.

We can identify a small number of other compositions that likewise may have been written with specific instruments in mind. Several pieces are designated for organ, but as they show few features idiomatic to the latter instrument (most do not even call for pedals), they need no further consideration here.[12] A sonata composed in 1747 is preserved with autograph registrations that would have required a special type of harpsichord.[13] Another sonata from 1783 is for *Bogenclavier*, evidently a sort of keyed hurdy-gurdy with gut strings and a mechanism that imitated the sound of a violin.[14]

Eighteenth-Century Keyboard Music," in *De clavicordio IV: Proceedings of the IV International Clavichord Symposium, Magnano, 8–11 September 1999*, ed. Bernard Brauchli et al. (Magnano: Musica Antica a Magnano, 2000), 37–53. An anonymous reviewer mentioned Bach's having composed Wq 55/2 for the Silbermann clavichord (*Hamburgischer Correspondent*, 31 July 1779, reprinted in Suchalla, *Briefe und Dokumente*, 1:763).

12. The idiom of these pieces, especially the organ sonatas Wq 70/2–7, is discussed in the introduction to CPEB:CW, I/9 (ed. Annette Richards and David Yearsley, 2008); see also Mary Oleskiewicz's chapter in the present volume. An additional sonata, Wq 65/24 in D minor, can be tentatively assigned to the organ, as suggested in my *Music of C. P. E. Bach*, 84.

13. The copy of the D Minor Sonata Wq 69 in D-B, Mus. ms. P 772, includes Bach's rubrics for registration; facsimile in *The Collected Works for Solo Keyboard by Carl Philipp Emanuel Bach (1714–1788)*, 6 vols., ed. Darrell Berg (New York: Garland, 1985), 3:319–28. See Mary Oleskiewicz's chapter in the present volume for further discussion of this work.

14. Bach performed on a *Bogenclavier* by the Berlin maker Hohlefeld (sometimes spelled Hohlfeld) in 1753, but the sonata composed thirty years later was evidently for another instrument; see online supplement 10.7 to David Schulenberg, *The Music of Carl Philipp Emanuel Bach* (Rochester, NY: University of Rochester Press, 2014; online supplements are accessible from http://faculty.wagner

A recent discovery suggests that the last piece in the *Kenner und Liebhaber* series, the C Major Fantasia, Wq 61/6, of 1786, was originally for an instrument that combined harpsichord and piano actions used in different sections of the piece.[15] Earlier in his career, Bach composed three sonatas at the spa town of Töplitz on a clavichord with a short octave, evidently a small traveling instrument; each sonata is certainly idiomatic to the clavichord, although some of the bass notes would not have been available on an instrument equipped with any of the usual sorts of short octave.[16]

All these compositions remain playable on ordinary instruments, in keeping with the tradition that keyboard music is for a generic "clavier." Bach directed harpsichordists to ignore dynamic markings that cannot be readily realized, but he avoided the suggestion that pieces incorporating such markings should not be played on the harpsichord.[17] Rather, he counseled players to be prepared to perform any piece on both clavichord and harpsichord. This advice appeared in the first volume of the *Versuch*; presumably he would have mentioned the piano as well a decade or two later.[18]

Clearly Bach and his contemporaries were prepared to perform keyboard music on whatever instruments were available. This explains the puzzling fact that, just as Bach rarely specified the instruments for his keyboard pieces, he wrote very little in the *Versuch* about keyboard touch or technique. One must turn to the treatise on flute playing by his older colleague Quantz, published a year before Bach's, for a detailed account of how J. S. Bach approached the keyboard. Quantz describes a technique that involves a stroking motion of the fingers on the keys rather than a percussive or striking

---

.edu/david-schulenberg/the-music-of-c-p-e-bach-supplementary-text-and-tables/). For a score of Wq 65/48, see the facsimile in Berg, *Collected Works for Solo Keyboard*, 4:223–29. Mary Oleskiewicz's chapter in this volume provides further discussion of this topic.

15. See Peter Wollny, "Carl Philipp Emanuel Bachs Rezeption neuer Entwicklungen im Klavierbau: Eine unbekannte Quelle zur Fantasie in C-Dur Wq 61/6," BJ 100 (2014): 175–87, esp. 181–82; further discussion in Mary Oleskiewicz's chapter in this volume.

16. An instrument with a short octave lacks a full chromatic scale in the lowest portion of the keyboard; Bach mentioned composing six sonatas on such an instrument in a letter of 2 February 1775 to Forkel. The *Nachlassverzeichnis* lists three sonatas as having been composed at Töplitz, and although all require a normal keyboard, two of them (Wq 49/3 and 49/5) include *pianissimo* markings; a third (Wq 65/13) includes legato chords whose particular suitability to the clavichord is discussed in my "When Did the Clavichord Become C. P. E. Bach's Favourite Instrument?," 44.

17. *Versuch*, vol. 2, chap. 29, para. 7; the rules given here concern specifically accompaniment, but they represent a more detailed version of advice given in vol. 1, chap. 3, para. 29 on when and when not to attempt to respond to dynamic markings in performances on a two-manual harpsichord.

18. *Versuch*, vol. 1, introduction, para. 15; in volume 2, published in 1762, Bach expresses greater appreciation for the piano.

attack.[19] Presumably Emanuel was taught to play in the same manner, but his precise touch and technique must have varied with time and depending on the instrument.

We thus have a paradox: the eighteenth-century composer and writer most closely associated with stringed keyboard instruments never adequately described how he played them or even which ones were best suited for his music. We might suppose that he had been trained by his father to think of keyboard music independent of any specific realization in sound. Yet during his long career he made significant innovations in writing for keyboard instruments, and these clearly reflect changes in playing and in the instruments themselves.

The most famous of these innovations involve devices now understood as making music more expressive, allowing the keyboard instrument to "speak" in a way it had not done previously.[20] The idea of the keyboard instrument as representing a metaphorical voice—either a singer or a speaker—emerges in certain pieces that constitute virtual monologues or dialogues. Some of these same pieces also introduce new types of improvisatory or fantasia style. In later works, while continuing to develop these inventions, Bach also adopted approaches that were gaining fashion with younger composers and audiences, among them styles of keyboard writing that can be termed "symphonic" and "comic," respectively. Each of these innovations involved specific keyboard idioms and, perhaps, specific types of instruments on which they were particularly effective.

The most concrete way in which Bach and other composers could give voice to the keyboard was through instrumental recitative. His doing so in the first of his "Prussian" Sonatas—published in 1742 with a dedication to his employer, King Frederick II, "the Great," of Prussia—was doubtless an acknowledgment of the latter's love of opera, as represented in the newly opened royal opera house on Unter den Linden. The imitation of recitative in the slow movement of this sonata (Example 4) is more literal than that in Sebastian's Chromatic Fantasia; its notation as a melody line with figured bass resembles that of recitative movements in sonatas for flute and continuo by Quantz and the king himself.[21] Emanuel also hews closer to actual vocal models by embedding

19. Johann Joachim Quantz, *Versuch einer Anweisung die Flöte traversiere zu spielen* (Berlin, 1752; trans. Edward R. Reilly as *On Playing the Flute*, 2nd ed. [New York: Schirmer Books, 1985]), chap. 17, sec. 6, para. 18 (pp. 259–60 in the translation, where the translator comments in a footnote that the player whose technique is described here is identified in Quantz's index as J. S. Bach).

20. The classic statement of this view, drawing on eighteenth-century precedents, is Arnold Schering, "C. Ph. E. Bach und das redende Prinzip in der Musik," *Jahrbuch der Musikbibliothek Peters* 45 (1938): 13–29; English translation by the present author in *Carl Philipp Emanuel Bach*, ed. David Schulenberg (Farnham: Ashgate, 2015), chap. 2.

21. See, for example, movement 3 of Quantz's Flute Sonata in G Minor, QV 1:116, recorded by Mary Oleskiewicz, flute, with the author and Stephanie Vial, cello, on *Johann Joachim Quantz: Flute Sonatas*

Ex. 4. "Prussian" Sonata No. 1 in F Major, Wq 48/1, movement 2, measures 1–10.

the recitative passages within a larger arioso.[22] By leaving it up to the player to realize his generic recitative notation in idiomatic keyboard style, Emanuel avoids having to write an accompaniment that might be distinctive to any particular type of keyboard instrument. Yet the arioso passages are among many in the "Prussian" Sonatas and in their successors, the "Württemberg" Sonatas of two years later, that raise questions about the instruments Bach used or had in mind for these pieces. Uncertainty arises especially when a sustained melody in the upper register is accompanied by repeated chords in the lower parts. Such chords are not easily subordinated to the melody on a harpsichord, yet the F minor tonality would have made execution of certain intervals problematical on a fretted clavichord.[23]

(Naxos 8.555064, 2003); or movement 1 of Frederick's Flute Sonata in A Minor, in *Frederick II: Four Sonatas for Flute and Basso Continuo*, ed. Mary Oleskiewicz (Wiesbaden: Breitkopf & Härtel, 2012).

22. As in the alternating arioso-recitative movement "Impare Filli" from Hasse's cantata *Quel vago seno* for soprano, flute, and continuo. The recitative movement by Frederick mentioned in the previous note includes an arioso ("adagio") section at the center.

23. For example, in measure 2 the half step $a^{b\prime}$–g' would have had to be detached on many fretted clavichords, on which both notes were produced on the same string; the player would have needed to release the first note entirely before striking the second, breaking the slur and eliminating the effect of an expressive appoggiatura.

Many of Bach's subsequent works of the 1740s and 1750s represent efforts to intensify the metaphorical drama above the quite modest level suggested by Example 4. Only one later work takes up instrumental recitative as such: the C Minor Concerto, Wq 31, of 1753. Here the allusion is to accompanied, not simple (*secco*), recitative, with the strings holding out chords in the recitative passages (Example 5).[24] This frees the keyboard from having to furnish its own realization of the harmony, which is no longer represented by a figured bass. Moreover, instead of a melodic line comprising formulas from actual recitative, the keyboard plays a distinctly instrumental type of improvisatory figuration, chiefly melodic but occasionally involving broken chords in both hands.

Example 5 is from a heavily embellished version of the movement that might date from around the end of the composer's Berlin period.[25] In this version, the keyboard solos reveal a sort of fantasia style, replacing conventional melodic formulas used in actual recitative with longer and more voluble passages similar in style to the written-out embellishments and cadenzas found in some of Bach's later Berlin keyboard sonatas (such as those of the *Probestücke*, Wq 63, and the *Reprisen-Sonaten*, Wq 50). Although a capable player could render either version on both harpsichord and piano, the latter instrument would be better suited for a performance of the revised version, in which the expanded solo passages demand even more of the "light and shade" implicit in any recitative.[26] Indeed, Bach's revision of this and a number of other works during the 1760s could reflect his acquisition around that time of a new keyboard instrument, presumably a piano.[27]

The fantasia style of the revised recitative passages also occurs within earlier works for keyboard alone. In the opening movement of the Sixth "Württemberg" Sonata, composed and published in 1744, Bach imitated the sweeping gestures and sudden

24. In measure 25 the autograph (D-B, Mus. ms. Bach P 711) reads as shown, but possibly a *Schleifer von dreyen Nötgen* was intended in place of a turn, which would repeat the preceding c"–b♭'; see *Versuch*, vol. 1, chap. 2, sec. 7, para. 5, where the discussion of this ornament (signified by an inverted turn sign) is illustrated by an example on this very note, b♭'.

25. The handwriting in the autograph score containing the embellishments (D-B, Mus. ms. Bach P 711) resembles that of other autographs assigned to the 1760s, for example, parts for the concerto Wq 39 in D-B, Mus. ms. Bach St 532, but positive dating must await the report in the forthcoming edition in CPEB:CW, 3/9.10.

26. Quantz and Bach both use the words *Licht und Schatten* to refer, apparently, to small dynamic nuances; see, for example, Quantz, *Versuch*, chap. 14, para. 9; Bach, *Versuch*, vol. 1, chap. 3, para. 29 ("Schatten und Licht").

27. The most concrete basis for this conjecture is the upward extension of the keyboard compass from e''' to f''' beginning with works composed in 1762, as noted by Miklós Spányi, "Performer's Remarks," in liner notes to *C. P. E. Bach: The Complete Keyboard Concertos, Volume 9* (BIS CD-868, 2000), 6.

Ex. 5. Concerto in C Minor, Wq 31, movement 2, measures 17–25.

pauses of a dramatic accompanied recitative, but this was integrated into a regular sonata form (Example 6). Like the C minor concerto, this movement later underwent heavy embellishment that deepened the sense of a wild improvisation embedded within a formal sonata movement.[28] Yet even the "varied" version employs only two dynamic levels (*forte* and *piano*), and although alternating rapidly, they can be managed on a two-manual harpsichord. Other sonatas from the "Prussian" and "Württemberg" sets, however, contain three levels of dynamics—including *pianissimo*—and this eliminates the possibility of simply dividing the music between the louder and softer manuals of a harpsichord. One movement from the "Württemberg" Sonatas

28. Bach's embellishments are from his *Veränderungen und Auszierungen über einige meiner Sonaten* (Wq 68), preserved in D-B, Mus. ms. P 1135; facsimile in Berg, *Collected Works for Solo Keyboard*, 6:161, from which Example 6 has been transcribed.

Ex. 6. "Württemberg" Sonata No. 6 in B Minor, Wq 49/6, movement 1,
measures 1–9 (original and embellished versions).

that calls for *pianissimo* also calls for the rapid shifts between *piano* and *forte* that the composer later advised harpsichordists to ignore.[29] Yet that same set of sonatas could close with a movement whose austere two-part imitative counterpoint clearly echoes that of Sebastian Bach's inventions.[30]

Several movements from other sonatas of the period extend the idea of a metaphorical dialogue that Bach had already broached in the First "Prussian" Sonata. The opening movement of a sonata in F-sharp minor (Wq 52/4), composed in 1744 but not published until nineteen years later, alternates between two very different types of music distinguished by rhythmic texture and dynamic level (Example 7). A G minor sonata of 1746 (Wq 65/17) opens with a dialogue whose interlocutors are distinguished not by dynamics but by an alternation between fantasia style and two distinct but more conventional types of writing: one resembles the unison ritornello of a "rage" aria, the other an ordinary sonata movement (Example 8). Such pieces anticipated Bach's so-called Program Trio of 1749, in which the metaphorical dialogue becomes explicit.[31]

Details in these sonatas again indicate an evolving keyboard idiom. Each of the first two movements of Wq 65/17 (which connect directly to the following movement) closes with a *pianissimo* half cadence. Dynamic markings within the body of each movement, although confined to *piano* and *forte*, occur within, not at the beginnings of, phrases; the placement of dynamics at the end of the second movement implies a gradual crescendo followed by a more prolonged decrescendo (Example 9). In Wq 52/4, the principal theme of the last movement includes several staccato strokes or wedges on accented notes (Example 10). Although unremarkable to a modern pianist, this type of marking is rare in earlier keyboard music.[32] Bach himself described such notes as *gestossen*, that is, "pushed" or "forced";[33] the German word is more expressive of the execution of short, accented notes on the clavichord or on a bowed string instrument than on harpsichord or organ.

---

29. See note 17. The movement in question is the Adagio from the E Minor Sonata, Wq 49/3, especially measures 39–47.

30. The closing Allegro of Wq 49/6, which, unlike the first two movements, entirely lacks dynamics.

31. The C Minor Trio, Wq 161/1, published in 1751, explicitly represents a dialogue between two characters, designated Melancholicus and Sanguineus. Originally scored for two violins and continuo, it can be played with obbligato keyboard substituting for one of the violins ("Sanguineus"). Further discussion in my *Music of C. P. E. Bach*, 103–6.

32. A somewhat comparable example by J. S. Bach occurs in no. 14 of the Goldberg Variations, a work that probably predates Wq 52/4 by only a few years; see the discussion of Example 11 in David Schulenberg, "Versions of Bach: Performing Practice in the Keyboard Works," in *Bach Perspectives 4: The Music of J. S. Bach: Analysis and Interpretation* (Lincoln: University of Nebraska Press, 1999), 129.

33. *Versuch*, vol. 1, chap. 3, para. 17.

Ex. 7. Sonata in F-sharp Minor, Wq 52/4, movement 1, measures 1–21.

Ex. 8. Sonata in G Minor, Wq 65/17, movement 1, (*a*) opening fantasia passage;
(*b*) unison passage, measures 1–7; (*c*) "ordinary" passage, measures 22–25.

Ex. 9. Sonata in G Minor, Wq 65/17, movement 2, measures 50–55.

Ex. 10. Sonata in F-sharp Minor, Wq 52/4, movement 3, measures 1–4.

In the slow movement of Wq 52/4, the principal motive consists of five slurred eighths (Example 11). Again unremarkable to a pianist, this is problematical for a harpsichordist, especially when doubled in sixths within the right hand, as in measure 8. Only on a dynamic instrument can one realize the implicit accent on the dissonant second note of the figure or the decrescendo that follows it.[34] The movement as a whole, moreover, is another sort of metaphorical dialogue, for it is essentially an imitative trio movement modeled not on Sebastian's keyboard sinfonias (three-part inventions) but on a type of duet that was common in opera seria (compare Example 12).[35] Similar movements are found in Emanuel's "Prussian" and "Württemberg" Sonatas as well (Wq 48/3, Wq 49/4–5). All are readily playable on an ordinary two-manual harpsichord, apart from two *pianissimo* markings in Wq 48/3—but a harpsichordist can

34. In measure 1, the second note under the slur (g') forms a fourth with the bass, acting as an appoggiatura that resolves with the next note to the third, f#'. Presumably the appoggiatura should be emphasized and the following note (or notes) played more softly, following the common rule given in Bach's *Versuch* (vol. 1, chap. 1, sec. 2, para. 7) and in Quantz's (chap. 8, para. 4).

35. Such duets, one or two per opera, typically occur at particularly affecting moments between the main characters in the later acts. The work from which Example 12 is taken was premiered at Berlin in 1743; Bach, who surely witnessed it (if he did not perform in it), seems to allude to one of its arias in his D major flute concerto (see my *Music of Carl Philipp Emanuel Bach*, 65, and online example 5.2).

Ex. 11. Sonata in F-sharp Minor, Wq 52/4, movement 2, measures 1–13.

Ex. 12. Carl Heinrich Graun, "Tu vuoi ch'io viva, o care," from *Artaserse*,
GraunWV B:I:8:54, measures 5–11 (without strings).

only imagine that the appoggiaturas and other expressive figures in the two melodic parts are receiving the "light and shade" that they demand.

On the other hand, the two manuals of a large harpsichord seem ideal for representing the dialogue between a louder, more voluble character and a quieter, lyrical one within the first movement of Wq 52/4 (see Example 7). Yet within the lyrical passages of Wq 52/4 one again finds legato writing whose implicit dynamics cannot be fully realized on the harpsichord. When this sonata finally appeared in print in 1763, most purchasers were likely to play it on the clavichord. By then the large unfretted instruments necessary for satisfactory performance of Bach's keyboard music appear to have become relatively widespread in Germany.[36] But most players would have found the clavichord impractical for performances of the sonata when it was first written, for again the key (F-sharp minor) made certain intervals and ornaments impossible to play expressively on the smaller fretted instruments that were probably still the norm in the early 1740s.

It is possible that this work, like the "Prussian" and "Württemberg" Sonatas composed just before it, was not entirely realizable on any of the instruments generally available when it was first written. Like Beethoven half a century later at Vienna, Emanuel Bach was pushing the envelope of his instrumentarium.[37] Within a few years, however, Bach certainly had instruments available to him that allowed him to play things unheard of on either harpsichord or organ. This is clear not only from Wq 65/17, which incorporates passages in fantasia style, but from an actual fantasia of perhaps the same year. This work, H 348, incorporates one or two improvisatory formulas also found in the sonata (Example 13; compare Example 8a). One passage that again seems to imitate accompanied recitative employs four levels of dynamic markings in close succession (Example 14).[38]

It is tempting to associate the innovations in these compositions from around 1746 with the Silbermann clavichord that Bach acquired around this time or with the

36. On the development of the clavichord and its popularity in eighteenth-century Germany, see, for example, part 4 of the article "Clavichord," in *Grove Music Online*, by Edward M. Ripin et al., accessed 19 June 2015, www.grovemusic.com, which cites numerous writings of the time.

37. Beethoven eventually declared that the piano "is and always will be an unsatisfactory instrument" (Es ist und bleibt ein ungenügendes Instrument), as reported by the violinist Carl Holz in a "Mittheilung" of 19 June 1826, included in *Beethoven, Liszt, Wagner: Ein Bild der Kunstbewegung unseres Jahrhunderts*, by Ludwig Nohl (Vienna: W. Braumüller, 1874), 112.

38. Unknown to Wotquenne, the Fantasia in E-flat is identified by its number in E. Eugene Helm's *Thematic Catalogue of the Works of Carl Philipp Emanuel Bach* (New Haven, CT: Yale University Press, 1989); it is edited in cpeb:cw, 1/8.1 (ed. Peter Wollny, 2006). The absence of bar lines prevents references to passages by measure numbers; the "system" designations in the captions for Examples 13 and 14 correspond to those in Wollny's edition.

Ex. 13. Fantasia in E-flat Major, H 348, system g (as designated in
CPEB:CW, vol. 1/8.1).

Ex. 14. Fantasia in E-flat Major, H 348, systems n–o (as designated in
CPEB:CW, vol. 1/8.1).

fortepianos that King Frederick began collecting during this period.[39] But, as is clear
from the examples above, the idiom of his keyboard music had been evolving in this
direction for some time, and whether even the new instruments were adequate for
Bach's music is uncertain. The king's pianos were used primarily to accompany his
private concerts of flute sonatas and concertos, not for solo keyboard music.[40] Despite
the fame of Bach's Silbermann clavichord, he eventually sold it, evidently having come

39. Gottfried Silbermann furnished the court with at least three pianos, the earliest of which is
probably the one now in Sanssouci palace in Potsdam, dated 1746; he was also paid by the court in
June 1746 for a "Clavier." See Mary Oleskiewicz, "The Trio in Bach's Musical Offering: A Salute to
Frederick's Tastes and Quantz's Flutes?," in *Bach Perspectives 4*, 98. For the date when Bach acquired
his Silbermann clavichord, see note 11. Mary Oleskiewicz provides more information on the royal
pianos in her chapter in this volume.

40. One of Quantz's concertos from this period, qv 5:162, includes a part for fortepiano; see Oleskiewicz, "The Trio," 101.

to prefer other instruments by 1781.[41] The piano that Bach evidently acquired in the 1760s probably had a wider compass and broader dynamic range than the king's quiet Florentine-style pianos, making it suitable for public concerts. On the other hand, even the clavichord was hardly confined to quiet or expressive music, especially in its new, larger forms. When Bach played for Burney on his Silbermann instrument, the latter was impressed that Bach "possesses every style," even if he "chiefly confines himself to the expressive."[42]

The fantasia style that first appears in Bach's keyboard music of the 1740s would continue to characterize it to the end of his career. It was, however, only one of several distinct new idioms introduced into his keyboard compositions during these years. Another idiom, less serious but indicative of where the composer's interests were heading at midcentury, can be termed a "symphonic" style. If the fantasia style had a specific relationship to the unfretted clavichord, the symphonic style might be related to other new types of keyboard instruments developed during these decades. The symphony itself, although descended from earlier types of opera overture, was then new as a self-contained genre of instrumental music. Bach wrote his first example (Wq 173) as early as 1741 but did not take it up in earnest until the 1750s, probably for use in public concerts.[43] Soon publishers such as Breitkopf in Leipzig were issuing keyboard transcriptions of actual symphonies; during the Seven Years' War, while the city was under Prussian occupation, Breitkopf published a collection of symphonies and overtures for keyboard that opened with an arrangement of King Frederick's famous D major work.[44]

Such pieces might be merely noisy entertainments, but adapting them or their style to the keyboard could have presented an interesting challenge to an imaginative composer. Bach took up the symphonic style in a significant number of sonatas, although initially these were confined to minor works that circulated only in manuscript or in printed anthologies rather than in his own publications. The first of these sonatas, Wq 62/5 in E, again dates from 1744 but was published only in 1758 or 1759. By then Bach had composed further examples, some coming surprisingly close in style to later

---

41. Surprisingly little is known about Bach's Silbermann clavichord, and not all accounts of it are unstintingly positive. It may not have been particularly large, and its upward compass extended only to e''', according to a 1768 letter of the poet Claudius; see my *Music of C. P. E. Bach*, 229.

42. Burney, *Present State of Music in Germany*, 2:270.

43. Further discussion in my *Music of C. P. E. Bach*, 209–18.

44. *Raccolta delle megliore sinfonie di più celebri compositori accomodate all'clavicembalo: Raccolta I* (Leipzig: Breitkopf, 1761), RISM B/II, 298. The king's symphony had been published in its original form in 1743 by Balthasar Schmidt of Nuremberg a year after the latter issued Bach's "Prussian" Sonatas.

sonatas by Johann Christian Bach, Emanuel's younger half brother. Christian studied with Emanuel in Berlin from 1750 to 1755, perhaps playing works such as another E major sonata, Wq 65/29, of 1755 (Example 15). Here the octaves of the opening phrase, followed by a quieter passage over a dominant pedal (articulated as repeated eighths), allude to moments in actual Berlin symphonies of the period such as Bach's Wq 174–76, all from the same year. Although not very profound, such a piece might have made a splendid effect on several English-style harpsichords with special stops that King Frederick would later collect.[45] Whether or not Christian Bach ever encountered such instruments before leaving Germany, he would become familiar with them after moving to England in 1762.

As he did with the symphony itself, Emanuel quickly learned how to make a sonata in "symphonic" style something more expressive and original than convention demanded. The first movement of a 1758 sonata in E minor—the same key as his famous symphony Wq 177 of 1756—demonstrates how a refined version of this style could incorporate wide-ranging enharmonic modulations. Yet Wq 52/6 shares with many simpler examples the drum bass that is ubiquitous in both keyboard and orchestral music of the period, particularly in the symphonic style. Both quick movements are replete with basses consisting largely of repeated eighth notes, which allow the accompaniment to maintain a sense of motion without challenging the preeminence of the leading melodic part (Example 16).

The drum bass was an early instance of the type of motivic or atmospheric, as opposed to contrapuntal, accompaniment that proliferated in later instrumental music. J. S. Bach almost never used drum basses,[46] nor did Haydn, Mozart, or Beethoven in their keyboard music, although it is common in their orchestral works. Emanuel was aware that playing too many *Trommelbässe* could cause a player's left hand to grow stiff, and he eventually described it as "pernicious banging . . . contrary to the nature of both the harpsichord and the piano."[47] Yet repeated-note basses are an essential part of Emanuel Bach's keyboard idiom throughout his career (see, e.g., Examples 7 and

45. Michael Latcham, "Pianos and Harpsichords for Their Majesties," *Early Music* 36.3 (2008): 380–86, discusses Frederick's harpsichords by Burkat Shudi, but see Mary Oleskiewicz's chapter in the present volume.

46. Rare instances in his keyboard music include brief passages in the gavotte of the Third English Suite (mm. 20–23, perhaps an allusion to an actual drum or *tambour*), and in the C Minor Fantasia, BWV 906/1 (m. 8).

47. "Dieses schädliche Tockiren [from French *tocquer*] ist ferner wider die Natur der Flügel so wohl, als der piano forte"; from a long addendum to *Versuch*, vol. 1, introduction, para. 9, added for the revised edition of 1787 (CPEB:CW, 7/1:11). The original edition has only brief remarks about drum basses (paras. 7, 9).

Ex. 15. Sonata in E Major, Wq 65/29, movement 1, measures 1–16.

Ex. 16. Sonata in E Minor, Wq 52/6, movement 1, measures 1–6.

11). His chief objection appears to have been to the use by other composers of long series of repeated eighth or sixteenth notes in the continuo parts of quick movements; he advises players to simplify these. Yet his own frequent use of repeated-note basses even in expressive slow movements suggests that bass lines of this type need not be played mechanically. Bach famously advised musicians not to play like a trained bird,[48] a dictum that might apply to basses as well as melodies. Even in a symphonic sonata, the crescendos and diminuendos implied by closely spaced dynamic markings (as in Example 16) could be applied to the bass's repeated eighth notes—whether played on clavichord, fortepiano, or harpsichord equipped with a Venetian swell or an English machine stop. Although Bach may never have had firsthand experience with instruments of the latter type, he must have known of them, at least during his Hamburg years, when the dissemination of his music in England and elsewhere (as revealed by the subscription lists in his Hamburg publications) suggests that such devices would have been used by some players of these compositions.

Variable dynamics were certainly a routine part of Bach's keyboard vocabulary by the 1750s, complementing the simple alternation of *piano* and *forte* that constitutes so-called terrace dynamics. Indeed, crescendos and decrescendos were becoming essential parameters of composition, part of the invention or the material of a work, as opposed to a sort of ornamentation. The E Minor Sonata, Wq 52/6, departs from conventional symphonic works by opening quietly; after the initial *piano* phrase it even softens to *pianissimo*. In 1758, to begin any movement softly was a special gesture; to open with a decrescendo would have been especially striking, and of course it could have been projected only on a dynamic instrument.

The new flexibility in the use of dynamics becomes even clearer in that work's slow movement, which is a sort of character piece such as Bach had taken to writing several years earlier (Example 17). Bach's character pieces, although having their roots in the French harpsichord tradition, were surely meant for dynamic instruments, as markings in many of them attest. The title of this adagio, "L'Einschnitt," refers to brief passages, usually marked *piano*, that appear at the ends of phrases, as at the opening (see mm. 1–2 and 4–6 in Example 17).[49] These passages cannot be played on the soft upper manual of a harpsichord, as they generally occur within phrases, sometimes without intervening rests. A harpsichordist following Bach's counsel to leave out impractical dynamic markings in this movement would omit an essential element of its design.

---

48. "Aus der Seele muß man spielen, und nicht wie ein abgerichteter Vogel," *Versuch*, vol. 1, chap. 3, para. 7.

49. By the 1770s the word *Einschnitt*, meaning "incise," had become a technical term for the smallest part of a melodic phrase, as discussed in Johann Philipp Kirnberger, *Die Kunst des reinen Satzes in der Musik*, 4 pts. in 2 vols. (Berlin, 1771–79), 2:137–53.

Ex. 17. Sonata in E Minor, Wq 52/6, movement 2, "L'Einschnitt," measures 1–7.

Equally telling is a passage near the end of this movement, which reaches a harmonic climax on an augmented sixth chord at m. 30 (Example 18). The texture expands to four voices, with the bass doubled in octaves, yet Bach marks it *pianissimo*, and the upper part is slurred. Such writing is unimaginable on the harpsichord. Moreover, to play it well on either clavichord or piano, including the slur that Bach marks in the upper voice, requires sophisticated manipulation of hand and arm weight, a technique familiar to modern pianists but largely irrelevant to harpsichord and organ technique. No eighteenth-century writer on keyboard performance explained how to play such a passage (Bach certainly did not), but writing of this sort strongly suggests a new physical approach to the keyboard. The latter in turn implies a new type of connection between the player's fingertips and the sound issuing from the instrument, prefiguring nineteenth-century Romantic pianism. Indeed, the end of this movement has a nineteenth-century ring to it, thanks to Bach's use of dissonant appoggiaturas and changing notes to decorate the broken chords in the written-out cadenza (mm. 35–37).

Such writing becomes increasingly common in Bach's later keyboard works, including the famous pieces for *Kenner und Liebhaber*. That this idiom could appear even in a "symphonic" sonata suggests that, although a sonata of this sort might once have seemed especially suitable to the harpsichord, by the end of Bach's career the latter instrument was no longer adequate for this type of music. The further development of Bach's keyboard idiom is perhaps best illustrated by an extraordinary sonata composed in 1775 (Wq 65/47). Like the rondos and fantasias for *Kenner und Liebhaber*, which Bach began writing three years later, this sonata is relatively light in character, differing in this respect from both the more serious pieces in fantasia style and the heavier symphonic sonatas. It nevertheless represents the culmination of another trend that had been evident in Bach's keyboard writing since the 1740s.

Ex. 18. Sonata in E Minor, Wq 52/6, movement 2, "L'Einschnitt," measures 29–38.

An early example of this idiom occurs in the C Major Sonata, Wq 62/10, of 1749. Both quick movements open with melodic and bass lines that are fragmented through rests and shifts of register (Example 19). A frequently mentioned feature of Bach's style, this fragmentation combines with the prevailingly thin texture to create an allusive musical surface. The later sonata Wq 65/47 goes much further in this direction, its opening theme seemingly reduced to disconnected little motives that sound in almost Webernesque isolation from one another (Example 20). In fact, neither movement is as disjointed as it may appear on paper, especially not when played at the quick tempos indicated.[50] Both works, moreover, incorporate brief flashes of rapid keyboard figuration even while avoiding the extended sequences of broken chords found in the rondos for *Kenner und Liebhaber*, which Bach began to compose in 1780 (Examples 21–22; compare Example 25a).

The two sonata movements open over the same descending bass line (C♮–B–A). The later work extends that line to a full octave descent, although the fact is not immediately apparent due to the irregular rhythm and intervening rests.[51] The dynamic

50. Live performances by the author of both sonatas, as well as Wq 52/4, 52/6, and the Rondo 56/5, can be heard in a recording of a recital presented by the Boston Clavichord Society on 22 March 2015, online at http://faculty.wagner.edu/david-schulenberg/works_perfs-html/.

51. Opening themes constructed over descending scalar bass lines are a hallmark of Bach's writing and that of many contemporaries; further discussion in my *Music of C. P. E. Bach*, 22–23, and numerous

Ex. 19. Ex. 19. Sonata in C Major, Wq 62/10, movement 3, measures 1–6.

(implied voice-leading)

Ex. 20. Sonata in C Major, Wq 65/47, movement 1, measures 1–8 (with analysis).

Ex. 21. Ex. 21. Sonata in C Major, Wq 62/10, movement 3, measures 30–36.

Ex. 22. Sonata in C Major, Wq 65/47, movement 1, measures 19–22.

markings in the later sonata, interpreted literally, would exaggerate the fragmentation. But although some of these markings could well indicate "terrace" alternations between loud and soft, others might imply a gradual shift in dynamic level. Playing Example 20 on clavichord or piano, one could make a crescendo in measures 5–7, where *piano* leads to *forte*, thereby bringing out the bass progression G–G♯ and rendering the entire passage more coherent. More generally, an imaginative performer on clavichord or piano, as opposed to harpsichord, might discover further ways of projecting the analysis of the voice leading shown beneath Bach's text, demonstrating that what has been viewed as a "capricious" sonata in fact uses the constant interruptions of the bass and melodic lines for expressive purposes.[52]

Expressive and, at the same time, comic, for neither of these two C major sonatas could have been intended entirely seriously. Bach himself might have described Wq 65/47 as *komisch*, using a term that he applied in later years to trivial works by younger contemporaries in which the slow movement is truncated or even omitted.[53] The sonata Wq 65/47, although hardly trivial, has only a brief, transitional Adagio. Bach eventually gave in to fashion, publishing many sonatas and other works of this type, yet he withheld Wq 65/47 from publication, perhaps because he did not expect amateur players to understand or appreciate it. He had waited until 1762 to publish the earlier Wq 62/10, which, however, includes a full-fledged slow movement—albeit an Andante whose compact through-composed binary form and song-like periodic phrases point to middle movements of an even more popular style from the 1750s and later.

What most stands out in both sonatas, however, is the flexible treatment of the keyboard to achieve an idiom that can be described as comic in the most positive sense of

additional examples in David Schulenberg, *The Instrumental Music of Carl Philipp Emanuel Bach* (Ann Arbor, MI: UMI Research Press, 1984), chap. 4 (pp. 31–55).

52. Darrell Berg, who in cpeb:cw, 1/5.1 (2007), xiv, notes the anticipation of Bach's late style in Wq 62/10, earlier described Wq 65/47 as one of the composer's most thoroughly "capricious" sonatas. See Darrell Matthews Berg, "The Keyboard Sonatas of C. P. E. Bach: An Expression of the Mannerist Principle" (Ph.D. diss., State University of New York at Buffalo, 1975), 122.

53. Claudius reported the composer's views on "the new comic music" in his letter of 1768; see my *Music of C. P. E. Bach*, 194–95.

the word. Despite its fragmentation, the first movement of Wq 62/10 is rather rigorous in developing its opening motive. Yet even the contrapuntal manipulation of the latter in the final ("recapitulation") section is rendered light and witty, if not laugh-out-loud comical, by the sudden bursts of quick triplets with which it first alternates and then is combined (Example 23). The later Wq 65/47 likewise treats some of its motivic material—in Example 24 a plain staccato octave—in simple counterpoint. Yet the latter goes almost unnoticed in the midst of seemingly arbitrary filigree, which then gives way to an utterly contrasting *crescendo* series of chromatic chords.

The sharp contrasts of texture, figuration, rhythm, and dynamics within Example 24 would have been inconceivable within the idiom of the early work shown in Example 2. Yet the presence of comparable things in Wq 62/10 or the rapidly fluctuating keyboard idiom and dynamics of the Fantasia H 348 suggests that, even if Bach was rarely writing such things down during the late 1740s and 1750s, by then he was already improvising passages of types that he would routinely notate in his publications for *Kenner und Liebhaber*. Although the rondos of those sets, including the one illustrated in Example 1, were explicitly for the piano, at least one was singled out by a contemporary reviewer for being as suitable for the clavichord as is the sonata that preceded it in volume 4 of the series.[54] Both pieces indeed look like stereotypical clavichord music in their restriction to simple textures and avoidance of busy figuration.[55] On the other hand, several of the sonatas for *Kenner und Liebhaber*, including the "symphonic" ones in A (Wq 55/4) and B-flat (Wq 59/3), might have been regarded as more suitable to the piano than the clavichord.

Still, that none of the keyboard idioms used in this music could be uniquely associated with either instrument is clear from one juxtaposition of a rondo "fürs Forte-Piano" and a "Clavier-Sonate." The A Minor Rondo shown in Example 1 was to have been the final piece in the second collection for *Kenner und Liebhaber*. But during the spring of 1780 the publisher Breitkopf informed Bach that the volume was turning out too short, and the composer consequently added a brief sonata in A major (Wq 56/6) to round out the volume.[56] Its tonality and its position at the end of the set make it a natural complement to the rondo; a brilliant if compact work, the sonata incorporates in its final movement the same type of harmonically inspired passagework that characterizes the late rondos, including the one with which it seems to be paired

54. Carl Friedrich Cramer, in *Magazin der Musik* 1 (1783): 1245–46, on the Rondo in E, Wq 58/3, from the fourth volume for *Kenner und Liebhaber* (published 1783), quoted by Christopher Hogwood in CPEB:CW, 4/4.1 (2009), xix.

55. Another rondo suitable for clavichord was the famous one written on the composer's "separation from his Silbermann keyboard" ("Abschied von meinem Silbermannischen Clavier," Wq 66), a slow, melancholy piece in E minor whose main theme includes indications for *Bebung*.

56. Bach explains himself in his letter to Breitkopf of 13 May 1780, cited in CPEB:CW, 1/4.1, xvii.

Ex. 23. Sonata in C Major, Wq 62/10, movement 1, measures 53–60.

Ex. 24. Sonata in C Major, Wq 65/47, movement 3, measures 48–55.

(Example 25). Although only the rondo is explicitly "fürs Forte-Piano," according to the title of the volume, the following piece seems equally suited for fortepiano despite its generic designation as one of the set's three "Clavier-Sonaten."

In its lack of a slow movement, this sonata again represents the "comic" style, contrasting with the unusually serious rondo that precedes it in the volume. The juxtaposition of the serious with the comic would occur again in one of the composer's very last instrumental works, the pair of movements that bears the famous title "C. P. E. Bachs Empfindungen" (C. P. E. Bach's sentiments), Wq 80. The first movement originated in 1787 as the Fantasia in F-sharp Minor, Wq 67; the second, composed more than two decades earlier, was the final Allegro from one of Bach's last Berlin sonatas (Wq

Ex. 25. (*a*) Rondo in A Minor, Wq 56/5, measures 129–33; (*b*) Sonata in A Major, Wq 56/6, movement 2, measures 39–44.

65/45 of 1766). To both movements the composer added a subsidiary violin part.[57] Bach's title has been taken very seriously, doubtless in response to the prevailingly dark tone of the fantasia. Yet the title evidently embraces both movements, and the inclusion of the Allegro suggests a broad understanding of the idea of sentiment—if it was not also an ironic commentary on the fashionable term *Empfindung*.[58] The piece could have been performed on a clavichord accompanied by a violin (perhaps muted), but both players, not to mention any listeners, probably would have had an easier time using a fortepiano.

57. The work is edited in cpeb:cw, 2/2.2 (ed. Christoph Wolff, 2011).

58. For reflections on the meaning of this term, see Richard Kramer, "Diderot's *Paradoxe* and C. P. E. Bach's *Empfindungen*," chap. 6 in *Unfinished Music* (New York: Oxford University Press, 2008; corrected paperback edition, 2012), 129–49.

Already in volume 2 of the *Versuch*, published in 1762, Bach had mentioned the suitability of the piano for fantasias, especially when played with the "undamped register."[59] By this he surely meant disengaging the dampers completely, as is possible on various types of eighteenth-century instruments—not using a damper pedal to clear the sonority with each chord change, as pianists have done routinely since the later nineteenth century. The effect of blurred figuration and harmonies would have been especially striking in Bach's fantasias, marked as they are by sudden and remote modulations, often chromatic. Distant modulations seem to have been regarded at the time as a window into the sublime (*das Erhabene*), the highest artistic category for Bach's proto-Romantic contemporaries. Critics sensed the sublime in such works as his setting of Klopstock's *Morgengesang* (Wq 239), and his fantasias and rondos might have been perceived similarly, at least in their sometimes counterintuitive modulations.[60] Although Bach never called for it explicitly in a score, the Romantic effect of lifting or disengaging the dampers of a fortepiano during these passages might have invoked the sublime in a way that could not be achieved on any other keyboard instrument.

Of course, it is impossible to know whether or how this effect was heard during the composer's lifetime in either the rondos for *Kenner und Liebhaber* or his *Empfindungen*. Nor do these pieces reach solely for the sublime. The *Empfindungen*, like the rondo-sonata pair at the end of the second *Kenner und Liebhaber* collection, juxtaposes radically contrasting expressive characters, even if the keyboard idioms of its two movements are not entirely dissimilar. In each case, the paired movements represent two sides of C. P. E. Bach's sentiments. These were expressible on both the clavichords and the fortepiano that the composer owned at the end of his life—but they were not even imaginable on the instruments he had known in his youth.

59. "Das ungedämpfte Register des Fortepiano," *Versuch*, vol. 2, chap. 41, para. 4.

60. On the relationship between chromatic harmony and the sublime as perceived in Bach's late vocal works, see Annette Richards, "An Enduring Monument: C. P. E. Bach and the Musical Sublime," in *C. P. E. Bach Studies*, ed. Annette Richards (Cambridge: Cambridge University Press, 2006), 162.

Voices and Invoices

The Hamburg Vocal Ensemble of C. P. E. Bach

Evan Cortens

A s cantor at the Johanneum and director of music for the five principal churches in Hamburg from 1768 to 1788,[1] Carl Philipp Emanuel Bach was required to produce roughly 130 performances annually.[2] This led to the creation of vast quantities of performing material, much now accessible for the first time since World War II thanks to the rediscovery of the Berlin Sing-Akademie's library in 1999. The materials for Bach's occasional music saw limited use, often only once.[3] These parts, especially the vocal ones, tell us a great deal about how they were used and frequently

---

1. Though Bach was appointed to the position in November 1767 (see letters 13 and 13a in Carl Philipp Emanuel Bach, *The Letters of C. P. E. Bach*, trans. and ed. Stephen L. Clark [Oxford: Oxford University Press, 1997], 10–11), he did not arrive in Hamburg until March 1768, for reasons that remain unclear (ibid., xxxiii). The first performance under his direction would take place on 2 April, the day before Easter; his installation as cantor took place on 19 April (Hans-Günter Ottenberg, *C. P. E. Bach*, trans. Philip J. Whitmore [Oxford: Oxford University Press, 1987], 109).

2. The basic calendar for church performances was established in 1657 under then-cantor Thomas Selle, with the *Ordnung der Musik*. This would remain substantially intact until "at least 1786, and most likely" the church music reforms in 1789 (Reginald Sanders, "Carl Philipp Emanuel Bach and Liturgical Music at the Hamburg Principal Churches from 1768 to 1788" [Ph.D. diss., Yale University, 2001], 7–8). However, the total yearly number of sacred music performances in which Bach was involved was probably closer to two hundred (Stephen L. Clark, "The Occasional Choral Works of C. P. E. Bach" [Ph.D. diss., Princeton University, 1984], 3). This number includes the additional performances not directly required by his office.

3. E. Eugene Helm distinguishes between two categories: "major choral works" and "choral works for special occasions" / "occasional choral works" (*Thematic Catalogue of the Works of Carl Philipp Emanuel*

This chapter builds on work first undertaken in my 2008 Boston University master's thesis; my thanks to the readers of that document, Joshua Rifkin and Victor Coelho, for their invaluable feedback. Earlier versions were presented at the AMS Greater New York Chapter, the University of Western Ontario Graduate Music Symposium, and the Bach Colloquium. Further thanks to Andrew Shryock, Caroline Waight, and David Yearsley for their helpful comments on earlier versions, as well as to the editor and anonymous reviewers for this volume.

contain the names of the singer who used them as well as Bach's autograph corrections. The correlation of this information with the detailed pay receipts—bound together today as the Hamburg *Rechnungsbuch der Kirchenmusik* (D-Hsa, Hs. 462)—proves most revealing. Recent research into eighteenth-century choral performance practice has shown that the norm in many parts of Germany was one singer per part (*Stimmblatt*).[4] Although occasionally multiple singers read from a single copy of one of Emanuel Bach's vocal parts, this was the exception—one singer per part was the norm for his performances of liturgical music.

* * *

The performances for which Bach was responsible can be divided into two types: those on the regular church calendar (e.g., the annual Passion performances or weekly cantatas given at the principal churches) and additional occasional performances, mainly ceremonies celebrating the installation of a new pastor. Only rarely are invoices found for performances of the former type, and they tend to be cursory.[5] The most detailed invoices are reserved for occasional works for which Bach received remuneration

---

Bach [New Haven, CT: Yale University Press, 1989], 175, 187). For the purposes of the present study, the important distinction between the two is that the latter were intended for a limited number of performances. However, Helm also distinguishes between the two on the basis that the major choral works contain borrowed material and had a "wide distribution and high reputation during the composer's lifetime." In this chapter, I will not weigh in on the debate as to whether this repertoire is best called "choral" music at all; I am using the term in accordance with CPEB:CW, which classifies all of the works under discussion here in Series 5, *Choral Music* (ed. Darrell Berg, Ulrich Leisinger, and Peter Wollny [Los Altos: Packard Humanities Institute, 2005]).

4. Throughout this chapter, I use the term "part" to mean a physical performance part (*Stimmblatt*) as distinguished from "line," meaning a vocal line in the score. The best-known work on this subject is that by Joshua Rifkin on J. S. Bach; his first presentation of this, at the 1981 American Musicological Society annual meeting in Boston, is reprinted in Andrew Parrott, *The Essential Bach Choir* (Woodbridge: Boydell Press, 2000), 189–208. Jeanne Swack, in an unpublished conference presentation to be included in a forthcoming monograph, has shown one singer per part to be the norm for Telemann in Frankfurt. Daniel R. Melamed (*Hearing Bach's Passions* [New York: Oxford University Press, 2005], 27–29) has further demonstrated that it mostly held in Hamburg as well. Jürgen Neubacher's magisterial *Georg Philipp Telemanns Hamburger Kirchenmusik und ihre Aufführungsbedingungen (1721–1767): Organisationsstrukturen, Musiker, Besetzungspraktiken* (Hildesheim: Olms, 2009) has sustained these conclusions while showing that parts were also occasionally shared.

5. For a representative example, see document number 94 in Ernst Suchalla, ed., *Carl Philipp Emanuel Bach: Briefe und Dokumente: Kritische Gesamtausgabe*, 2 vols. (Göttingen: Vandenhoek & Ruprecht, 1994), 1:223 (hereafter CPEB:B), which specifies that 25 Marks were paid "Für Cantorum" at the Katharinenkirche on 27 March 1771. This performance was for that year's Easter celebration, and Bach likely presented one of his so-called *Quartalsmusiken*.

outside of his regular salary. When Bach was executing the functions of his office, it appears that he was required only to keep a record of the performance. However, when engaging in additional duties, he was required to justify every expense.[6]

A short insert in an unknown hand gives a brief history of the *Rechnungsbuch der Kirchenmusik* and its contents. It was compiled into its current form—a bound volume consisting of 186 numbered pages—by Bach's successor Christian Friedrich Gottlieb Schwencke (1767–1822). The invoices, dating from 1740 to 1800, document performances by Telemann, Bach, and Schwencke and were placed onto uniformly sized sheets of paper—often with more than one on a page—and listed in roughly chronological order in a table of contents.[7] The table of contents also lists invoices that were removed, often by autograph hunters, while the book was in the possession of a Viennese collector. The volume returned to Hamburg in the late nineteenth century.[8]

Of the 115 invoices in the *Rechnungsbuch* from Bach's time, most cannot be connected with a piece of music actually performed. Of those that can, only ten relate to identifiable works with extant original performing materials; these are listed in Table 1. Eight are installation cantatas, and the remaining two are the *Musik am Dankfest wegen des fertigen Michaelis-Thurms* (H 823) and the funeral chorus "Meinen Leib wird man begraben" (H 837).[9]

The level of detail varies greatly from invoice to invoice—some refer only to the date, place, and total cost of the performance. Most invoices are itemized in one of two ways: either by function performed or by name of performer. When broken down by function, the invoice usually specifies the number of performers in a specific role (e.g., "Für 10 Sänger: *x* Marks"). Less often, the function and amount are simply stated (e.g.,

---

6. These disparities in detail also seem to be related to the party financially responsible for the performance. *Einführungsmusik* performances rarely, if ever, list any of the performers by name, whereas large-scale choral performances for municipal events, like Passion performances at smaller churches and the *Michaelis-Thurms Musik*, often itemize their performers; further study is required in this area. Emanuel Bach's exact procedure for submitting an invoice for reimbursement remains unclear. It was perhaps less than obvious, for he wrote to Georg Michael Telemann (see letter number 18 in Clark, *The Letters of C. P. E. Bach*, 15) asking for assistance. Regrettably, Telemann's reply does not survive.

7. The earliest and latest invoices in the *Rechnungsbuch* are on numbered pages 37 and 153, respectively. The Bach portion, 115 invoices with at least one from every year he was in Hamburg, has been transcribed and annotated across both volumes of CPEB:B. For a fuller consideration of the *Rechnungsbuch* in its entirety, see Sanders, "C. P. E. Bach and Liturgical Music," 77–110. The Telemann portion has been transcribed in Neubacher, *G. P. Telemanns Hamburger Kirchenmusik*. At present, I am unaware of a transcription or detailed study of the Schwencke portion.

8. Just after the title page and before the table of contents, a sheet of lined paper has been inserted, upon which a nineteenth-century hand gives a rough provenance, including dates and prices of acquisition.

9. See numbers 547 and 587 in CPEB:B, 2:1182–85, 1256–58.

"Für die Sänger: *x* Marks"). Three invoices fall into this category; they are designated by a question mark following the number of singers in the invoice column. Here, the number of singers employed has been calculated based on an average payment of 2 Marks per singer, an amount analogous to other invoices where the number of singers is explicitly specified.[10] Invoices itemized by name are few and seem to refer to particularly large celebrations.[11]

The invoices not only allow us to reconstruct Bach's performing forces but also provide a means of tracking the careers of various church musicians in Hamburg.[12] Several of the invoices indicate the presence of "Chorknaben" and a "Vorsänger" who did not participate in the performance of the figural music but rather only led the congregation in the singing of the chorale.[13] In a letter, Bach's daughter wrote that the only use her father had made of choirboys was having them carry the score between his house and the church.[14]

The vocal parts for the ten works are labeled with a voice-type designation—either "Canto," "Alto," "Tenore," or "Basso"—which may or may not be followed by "ripieno." Most supply a singer's name at the top of the part; in a few cases, the singer's name is instead given within the part. The autograph scores, surviving for eight of the ten

---

10. In the vast majority of cases, the most frequent payment per singer is 2 Marks. In CPEB:B, numbers 67, 104, 109, 120, 206, 226, 230, 305, 336, 387, 415, 441, 503, 507, and 510, the payment to the singers, when divided by the number of singers listed, equals exactly 2 Marks. Only five cases are present where the payment is either above (no. 384 = 4, no. 447 = 3.25, and no. 547 = 3.4) or below (no. 152 = 1.8 and no. 418 = 1.7). (These figures are given with "metric cents," i.e., 100 cents per Mark. Hamburg Marks actually divide into 16 schillings [ß]). It is perhaps reasonable, then, to use the former figure (i.e., 2 Marks) to calculate the number of singers employed when the invoice only gives a total amount. The results are as follows: CPEB:B, no. 74: 15 / 2 = 7.5 (so, 8 singers); no. 214: 32 / 2 = 16 (the invoice in question is for a large work, probably meaning a payment of 4 Marks each, so 8 singers); no. 315: 16 / 2 = 8 singers; no. 444: 15.5 / 2 = 7.75, rounding up to 8 singers.

11. But see note 6.

12. Peter Wollny has used this sort of evidence to suggest that the copyist Anon. 304 is Otto Ernst Gregorius Schieferlein. The appearance of his name in invoices under Telemann and Bach corresponds exactly with manuscripts in the hand of Anon. 304. See Peter Wollny, review of *Staatsbibliothek zu Berlin—Preußischer Kulturbesitz. Kataloge der Musikabteilung, 1. Reihe, Band 7: Georg Philipp Telemann. Autographe und Abschriften*, ed. Joachim Jaenecke, BJ 81 (1995): 218. Sanders has done this sort of work for all of Bach's instrumentalists and singers in Tables 3.2A and 3.5 of Sanders, "C. P. E. Bach and Liturgical Music," 89, 105–7.

13. Document number 65 in CPEB:B, 1:156.

14. See question/response number 8 from Anna Carolina Bach, transcribed in Sanders, "C. P. E. Bach and Liturgical Music," 160–61.

Table 1. Bach's single-performance choral works with extant invoices and vocal parts

H	Work*	CPEB:B	Sources	Invoice singers	Parts
821a	EM Palm (1769)	74	D-Bsa, SA 711 (score and parts with names)	8?	6
821d	EM Häseler (1772)	109	D-B Mus. ms. P 346 (score with names); D-Bsa, SA 706 (parts with names)	8	6
821e	EM Hornbostel (1772)	120	D-Bsa, SA 707 (scores and parts with names)	8	7
821h	EM Gerling (1777)	305	D-Bsa, SA 710 (score no names; parts with names)	9	7
821i	EM Sturm (1778)	315	D-Bsa, SA 715 (parts with names)	8?	8
821k	EM Jänisch (1782)	418	D-Bsa, SA 712 (score and parts with names)	10	8
821l	EM Gasie (1785)	510	D-Bsa, SA 709 (parts with names)	10	7
823	*Michaelis-Thurms Musik* (1786)	547	D-Bsa, SA 243 (score and parts with names)	10	7
821o	EM Willerding (1787)	566	D-Bsa, SA 705 (score and parts with names)	8?	8
837	"Meinen Leib wird man begraben" (1788)	587	D-Bsa, SA 719 (parts without names)	8?	8

* EM = *Einführungsmusik* (installation cantata).

works, typically provide a singer's name for solo movements, often something along the lines of "Aria für Herr Illert," written above the movement in question.[15]

Most of Bach's performing materials represent "insufficient" vocal parts, meaning fewer parts than there were singers. However, it is worth a brief comment on the opposite situation, namely, musical material present in more parts than would seem to be required. Ulrich Leisinger has observed that in "many cases" in Bach's Hamburg vocal works, the two soprano parts are identical, arguing that there is "probably no

15. Incidentally, not only did the names in the score indicate to the copyist in which part he should copy a movement, but this practice also allowed Bach to keep track of how many arias he had written for each singer: in one case he wrote "2ter Aria für . . ." (second aria for . . .). Bach thus seems to have tried to evenly distribute the solo material among his performers. This can be seen most clearly in the Passions, especially the 1769 *St. Matthew Passion*, in which nearly every singer is assigned two solo movements. In his Hamburg works of the 1760s and early 1770s, he meticulously

other interpretation" than that two boys sang the arias rather than just one.[16] This happens exclusively in soprano parts, not in other voice types. In the nine works under consideration that have solos (H 837 is a single-movement chorus), there are a total of eighteen soprano solos. Six (33 percent) are duplicated in four distinct works: H 821h (movts. 8 and 13), H 821i (movt. 2), H 823 (movts. 5 and 6), and H 8210 (movt. 15).

Names appearing in the parts or the score can help. In H 821h, the aria movement 8 is present in both canto parts (copied by Schieferlein), but above the line in both parts, an autograph insertion reads "Mr. Steinike." A similar situation pertains in the recitative movement 13—although it was copied into both canto parts, an autograph inscription reads "Mr. Siemers."[17] This suggests that the two movements were copied into both parts because they were not yet assigned to particular singers. At some point before the performance, Bach assigned the movements and wrote in names to indicate that the named singer should sing but that the person reading from the other part should not.

The situation for H 821i is slightly less clear. Movement 2 is in both soprano parts, but there are no names. In the score, however, the movement is assigned to "Mr. Steinike." Perhaps Bach gave a verbal direction to indicate which performer should sing. For the two other works, H 823 and H 8210, solo movements are copied into multiple soprano parts, but there are no names in the parts or score to indicate a singer assignment. These works are later, dating from 1786 and 1787, respectively; it is likely that by this time movements were copied into multiple parts to give several options but that Bach no longer wrote out instructions. We cannot rule out the possibility that solo movements were sung by multiple sopranos, perhaps for greater volume or projection, as Leisinger suggests.

* * *

Only in two instances in Table 1—H 821i and H 8210—do the number of extant parts and the number of singers paid appear to be equal: there are eight parts and, assuming

---

marks solo movements for all voice types in this manner. As time progressed, though, he became less concerned with the names of the sopranos and altos, often simply writing, for instance, "für den Alt." Perhaps this is because his roster of tenors and basses was fairly stable (Michel and Illert sang for Bach during his entire tenure), but the altos and especially the sopranos often changed. For more information about Bach's singers, see Sanders, "C. P. E. Bach and Liturgical Music," 148–59; for more on Michel in particular, see Paul Corneilson, "C. P. E. Bach's Evangelist: Johann Heinrich Michel," *Bach: Journal of the Riemenschneider Bach Institute* 41, no. 2 (2010): 1–23.

16. Ulrich Leisinger, "Neues über Carl Philipp Emanuel Bachs Passionen nach 'historischer und alter Art,'" *Jahrbuch des Staatlichen Instituts für Musikforschung Preußischer Kulturbesitz* (2002): 116.

17. Interestingly, both inscriptions are in Latin script, not the German script used for the text underlay.

each singer received 2 Marks, also eight singers. The former is perhaps the clearest case of one-singer-to-a-part in the repertoire under consideration. There are two parts per voice type, and the parts for the three lowest voice types are each headed with the name of a singer.[18] This leaves ambiguity only in the soprano parts. Bach's score specifies that the soprano aria was to be sung by a "Mr. Steineke," but both soprano parts contain all movements: the aria is in both parts, with no indication which part was used in performance.[19] Because sopranos were occasionally paid less than their more senior counterparts, and we have only the total expenditure for singers.[20] There may have been three or even four sopranos singing from the two parts.

H 8210, the other apparent correspondence between an invoice and surviving parts, is more challenging. Again, we are on uncertain ground initially, given that the invoice does not specify the number of singers, only a total payment for them.[21] The payment

18. For *Einführungsmusik* (installation cantata) Sturm, D-Bsa, SA 715 contains the following parts: 1. Canto; 2. Canto; 3. Alto (Delver); 4. Alto (Seidel); 5. Tenore (Hartmann); 6. Tenore (Michel); 7. Basso (Hoffmann); 8. Basso (Illert).

19. Not surprisingly, Sanders, "C. P. E. Bach and Liturgical Music," does not list this particular spelling, "Steineke," among his "musicians who performed with Bach" since it never appears in an invoice. He does, however, list a "Steineg(g)er (Steiniger) senior and junior" (158), which despite the orthographic differences is perhaps close enough in pronunciation, name spelling being rather inconsistent, as mentioned in note 8 with the case of Seidel/Seydel. (In this context, it is worth noting that while Suchalla assigns a date of 14 August 1781 for D-Hsa, Hs. 462, fol. 156 [see no. 406 in CPEB:B, 2:889], Sanders notes that the notice in the *Hamburger Unpartheyischen Correspondent* cited by Suchalla does not mention music [Sanders, "C. P. E. Bach and Liturgical Music," 148]. Sanders therefore assigns it to 14 July 1785.) Leopold August Elias Steineger is listed as a tenor in Illert's 1788 report to the Hamburg Senate (Sanders, "C. P. E. Bach and Liturgical Music," 104), though it is theoretically possible that he may have served as a soprano first, as his birth date is unknown. It is perhaps worth noting here also that the way in which Bach has written the name into the score—between "poco largo" and "ohne Hoboen"—indicates that it was added at some point later. That said, the handwriting is (as far as can be determined) contemporaneous with the rest of the text. CPEB:B, number 152 lists a "Steinke," later crossed out, as a Calcant (i.e., bellows operator). Again, it is hard to know whether this is the same person.

20. In the *Rechnungsbuch*, it is unusual for the payments to the singers to be broken down on a per-son-by-person, or voice-by-voice, basis; in fact, it happens just four times. On three of those occasions (CPEB:B, nos. 152, 447, and 547), the sopranos are paid less than the tenors and basses; on one occasion (CPEB:B, no. 336), all eight singers are paid the same amount. In Illert's report to the Hamburg Senate (Sanders, "C. P. E. Bach and Liturgical Music," 103), the quarterly payments to the two least experienced sopranos are nearly half the quarterly payments to the basses.

21. Anja Morgenstern writes that the invoice for H 8210 "indicates the same total amount as for the Einführungsmusik Gasie [H 821l]" and that therefore there were ten singers in H 8210, the same as for H 821l (CPEB:CW, 5/3.5, xxxv). Morgenstern is referring to the invoice totals exclusive of the payment for the composition of the music itself, 68 Marks in both cases. However, I disagree

of 16 Marks "for the singers" suggests that there were eight of them.[22] In addition, although I have indicated that there are eight extant vocal parts, the reality is more complex. This cantata is in two parts, and the vocal parts (and, for that matter, the instrumental parts) reflect this in having been prepared as two separate booklets, a total of thirteen in all: eight containing the first half of the cantata and five containing the second half (see Table 2).[23]

The canto parts can be divided into two groups: (1) part numbers 1 and 2, together comprising the complete cantata (first and second parts of the cantata, respectively); and (2) part numbers 3 and 4, likewise forming another complete set. Movement 15a, a solo recitative, was copied into both soprano parts, presumably to allow Bach to select the soloist later. In the score Bach wrote "Rec. für den Cant" (rec[itative] for the soprano), referring to a single singer. The first half of the cantata presents no such issue: the two soprano solos (movts. 6 and 9) are copied only into vocal part number 2. The alto, tenor, and bass parts are more challenging, for although there are two complete parts for the cantata's first half for each voice type, there is only one for each voice type for the second half. Either two (or more) singers sang from the parts for the second half of the cantata, or fewer singers performed the second half. First, let's consider the tenor parts. The heading for vocal part number 8, containing part 1 of the cantata, names Kirchner as the intended singer; part number 9, also assigned to Kirchner, contains the cantata's second half. Vocal part number 10 contains the first half of the cantata, but there is no corresponding tenor vocal part for the work's second half. The heading of part number 10 does not name a specific singer; however, in it Bach assigns movements 3 and 7 (which are present only in this part) to [Johann Heinrich] Michel. Since this part was copied by Michel himself, we should not be surprised that he didn't bother to write his own name into the part he would later use. The question remains: What did Michel do for the second half of the performance? Although part number 9 is assigned to Kirchner in the heading, right above movement 15b (a tenor *accompagnato*) is written "H. Michel," meaning that Michel, not Kirchner, was to sing this movement (Figure 1). At the very least, this means that after Kirchner

---

that this means that the number of musicians in the ensemble was the same, since even though the overall totals match, the role-by-role breakdown does not. It would seem inconsistent to pay the eight *Rathsmusici* a total of 12 Marks in both cases, as indicated by the invoice, but to pay the same number of singers 20 Marks for H 821l but just 16 Marks for H 821o. I argue instead that the lower payment indicates the use of fewer singers.

22. See note 10 for the methodology behind this calculation. It is possible that there were actually seven or nine paid singers but unlikely that there were significantly more or less than this figure, as that would mean an exceptionally large or small average payment per singer.

23. CPEB:CW, 5/3.5, 201.

Table 2. Original vocal parts for EM Willerding, H 8210

No.	Voice heading	Folio	Singer	Part 1 movements	Part 2 movements
1	Canto	25			12, 15a, 17
2	Canto	26		2, 4, 5, 6, 9, 11	
3	Canto	28			12, 15a, 17
4	Canto Ripieno	29v		2, 4, 5, 11	
5	Alto	30	[Seydel/Delver]	2, 3, 4, 5, 9, 10, 11	
6	Alt	33			12, 17
7	Alto Ripieno	34		2, 4, 5, 11	
8	Tenor	35	H. Kirchner	2, 4, 5, 8, 11	
9	Tenor	37	H. Kirchner		12, 14, 15b, 17
10	Tenor	39	[Michel]	2, 3, 4, 5, 7, 9, 11	
11	Bass	41	H. Hoffmann	2, 4, 5, 6, 11	
12	Basso	43	H. Hoffmann		12, 13, 16, 17
13	Bass	45	H. Illert	1, 2, 4, 5, 9, 11	

Table 3. Movements in EM Willerding, H 8210

No.	Type	Vocal solos	Text incipit
Part 1			
1	Accompagnement	B	Wer sich rühmen will
2	Chor		Dich rühmen wir, großer Schöpfer
3	Recitativ	T, A	Empor zu deiner Höh
4	Chor		Gebote erleuchten die Seele
5	Choral		Dich predigt Sonnenschein und Sturm
6	Recitativ	B, S	Dich sieht der Mensch
7	Arioso	T	Dich erkennen, Gott der Götter
8	Recitativ	T	Dich kennt der Christ
9	Arie a 4*	S+A, T+B	Dein sanftes Wort der Gnade
10	Recitativ	A	Rufst du uns nicht mit Güte
11	Choral		Dann warden wir uns herzlich freun
Part 2			
12	Choral		Mit Ehrfurcht werfen wir uns nieder
13a	Arioso	B	Wer euch höret, der höret mich
13b	Recitativ	B	Wir hören gern, Herr Zebaoth
14	Arie	T	Früh hast du dich aufgeschwungen
15a	Recitativ	S	Schon eilt mit seinen Segenssprüchen
15b	Accompagnement	T	Du Hirte, den uns Gott zu unsrer Freude gab
16	Arie	B	Tritt hin, den heil'gen Eid zu schwören
17	Choral		Gib deinem Diener
18	Chor [= movt. 2]		Dich rühmen wir, großer Schöpfer

* The movement starts out as a duet for soprano and alto and then becomes a duet for tenor and bass.

Fig. 1. EM (*Einführungsmusik*) Willerding, H 8210, excerpt of movement 15b,
"Du Hirte," assigned to Michel, tenor voice part number 9 (D-Bsa, SA 705, fol. 37v).

sang the tenor aria movement 14, the part was passed to Michel, who sang the tenor
accompagnato movement 17. Michel and Kirchner probably both sang the opening and
closing chorales (movts. 12 and 17) together, reading from the same part.

We can observe an analogous situation with the bass parts (nos. 11, 12, and 13),
but here there are no singers' names in the score or parts to help resolve what took
place in the second half of the cantata. The first part of the cantata is clear: vocal part
number 11 was assigned to [Johann Andreas] Hoffmann and number 13 to [Friedrich
Martin] Illert; in addition, Bach's assignment of solos in the score precisely matches
the assignments in the vocal performing parts. Movement 6, assigned to Hoffmann,
has been copied only into part number 11; movements 1 and 9, assigned to Illert, are
copied only into part number 13. Two possibilities exist for vocal part number 12,
which contains the second half of the cantata. One is that both basses sang the choral
movements together from the same part, with Hoffmann taking the solos, as his name
is in the part's header. The other is that Illert did not sing at all in the second half,
which Hoffmann sang alone. Finally, we need to consider the alto parts (nos. 5, 6, and
7). Although part number 5, which contains music for the first half of the cantata, does
not present a singer's name in its heading, we find two names within it. Movement 3, a
recitative, is marked "H. Seydel." Movement 9 in this part, on the other hand, contains
the music to both lines of a soprano/alto duet and is marked "H. Delver." Movement
10, a recitative, is again marked "H. Seydel." For movement 9, the autograph score
rules out the possibility that [Peter Nicolaus Friederich] Delver sang the canto part of
this duet aria, rather than the alto. In the score (D-Bsa, SA 705, fol. 14v), Bach wrote
"H. Delver" above the "A[lto]." staff (see Figure 2), but no name is given above the
"C[anto]" staff. Throughout the entire score, Bach wrote the name of the soloist either
in the heading of the movement (e.g., movt. 7, "Arioso. H. Michel") or directly above
the staff of the vocal line for that singer (e.g., movt. 1, "H. Illert" is written above the
staff of the bass vocal line). It is thus most likely that Bach intended the "H. Delver"

Fig. 2. EM Willerding, H 8210, autograph score (D-Bsa, SA 705, fol. 14v),
movement 9, opening of duet aria.

on folio 14v to refer to the alto line, as it would be a departure from the conventions
set throughout the remainder of the score for it to refer to the canto line (e.g., the line
above the singer's name), rather than to the alto line below. Finally, if this inscription
in the vocal part indicated the duet partner, it would mean that Delver performed the
soprano line. Although he had sung soprano earlier in his career, in 1785 (two years
before H 8210) his name clearly appears in an alto part for an installation cantata (H
8211, movt. 14, "Da geht er schon"). Thus, he almost certainly would not have been
required to switch roles from alto to soprano during the performance.

The most likely conclusion from this evidence is that two altos, Delver and [Johann
Matthias] Seydel, sang from one part, passing it back and forth between them for their
solo movements, as indicated by their names in the part. They would have then sung
together from this same part during the choruses and chorales, movements that do

not indicate singers' names. Because Delver's and Seydel's names appear in the same copyist's hand as the music, and because the assignments agree with Bach's assignments in the score, it appears that from its very inception the part was intended to be used by multiple singers. If this is correct, then Bach used three altos in the original performance of this piece, with two singing from the part just described and another from the complementary alto ripieno part (no. 4).[24]

In summary, based on the vocal materials and score assignments, Bach's chorus for the performance of H 82 10 most likely included two sopranos, two or three altos, two tenors, and two basses (one of whom may not have sung the second half of the cantata). The most important conclusion here, however, is not how many singers participated in ensemble but rather that two parts (nos. 5 and 9) provide conclusive evidence of having been shared between two singers, and one vocal part (no. 12) was shared quite possibly among three.

How can we account for the eight other performances in Table 1, where the number of singers specified by the invoice and the number of parts do not correspond? We must consider two possible scenarios: either significant amounts of vocal material are missing, or more than one singer read from a part. The former is possible but doubtful, given the excellent state of the instrumental parts.[25] (Although the invoices often list a payment for "copialien" [copying], no breakdown is given, and it is not possible to determine how many parts were made from cost alone.) As for the latter alternative, that of multiple singers reading from a part, H 82 1l (1785) proves especially instructive. There are seven extant vocal parts, but the invoice records a payment of 20 Marks for ten singers.[26] Each of the tenor and bass parts, two apiece, has a singer's name at the top left corner in the hand of Michel, their copyist. This clearly suggests that each was intended for use by just one person. The upper voice parts present a different situation. The parts for canto, canto ripieno, and alto do not contain any names in their headings. Furthermore, in the canto ripieno part (no. 2), there is no name to be found within the part itself either, suggesting that it was not intended for a specific person.

24. As noted above, however, part number 4 only contains the first half of the cantata. It is unclear what this putative third alto would have done during the second half. Could three singers have sung from a single part?

25. Some libraries, for instance, the Österreichische Nationalbibliothek in Vienna (A-Wn), have had a practice of disposing of doublettes. However, given that in every case all of the violin doublettes are extant, it would be odd for the library to have disposed of only some of the vocal doublettes. Furthermore, whereas the two first violin parts are virtually identical, two vocal parts may differ significantly in what movements they contain; thus, disposing of one would lead to a loss of music.

26. The invoice is given as number 510, CPEB:B, 2:1096–98. The original vocal parts, in D-Bsa, SA 709, are as follows: 1. Canto; 2. Canto Ripieno; 3. Alto; 4. Tenor (Rosenau); 5. Tenor (Michel); 6. Basso (Hoffmann); 7. Basso (Illert).

In the canto part (no. 1), under the clef for the fifth movement, a soprano aria, there is an insertion in Bach's hand (the remainder of the part is in Michel's hand) for "Mr. Schumacher." This is the only part in which this aria is entered—it is not present in the canto ripieno part. If Bach had intended this part to be sung by Schumacher alone, why not indicate this at the top of the first page, as was done with the tenor and bass parts? Further, the choral movements in the same part have no names. Thus it would appear that the presence of the name was an instruction to other singer(s) not to sing this movement: Schumacher alone was to sing the aria. The alto part is even more interesting. Again, there is no name in the heading, but there are two names within it, and both are in Michel's hand: the fourth movement (recitative) is marked "Hr. Seydel," and the fourteenth movement (arioso) is marked "Herr Delver."[27] Though the indications are in different halves of the cantata, the part is written on one bifolio. Seydel might have passed the part to Delver after the first half concluded, but this might have been more clearly indicated by writing the singers' names at the top of the part and, furthermore, by writing the parts as separate booklets. It is more likely that the two sang from one part. Thus it appears that in H 82 1l two singers sang from each of the canto (no. 1), canto ripieno (no. 2), and alto (no. 3) parts. Adding these six singers to the two tenors and two basses gives a total of ten singers, matching the number reported in the invoice. Throughout this repertoire, vocal parts without singers' names at the top or those marked "ripieno" (i.e., parts containing only the nonsolo movements) may have been used by more than one person.

One final example, that of H 82 1d (1772), is particularly informative in this regard. Though eight singers are paid in the invoice (shown in Figure 3), there are only six extant parts (listed in Table 4). The autograph score D-B, Mus. ms. P 346, shows evidence of having been composed in two layers. Bach wrote out the first and last movements roughly contemporaneously on the same type of paper and with the same ink. At some later point, in preparation for this installation performance, he revised these movements, adding trumpets and timpani to the first and bassoons to the last, among other changes.[28] At this time, he also wrote out movements 2 through 5, though they

27. A brief comment on orthography: though Bach spells the name "Seidel," "Seydel," and "Seÿdel," almost certainly this is always the same individual. See Sanders, "C. P. E. Bach and Liturgical Music," 157. Far more confusing, perhaps, are the various "Hartmanns" and "Hollands," whose individual identities cannot be confirmed.

28. The trumpets are added to what would have originally been four blank staves at the top of the first movement. A similar situation can be observed in D-Bsa, SA 239, a later score for the *Magnificat*, H 772. In that case, however, the brass parts are composed into a fair copy score made by a copyist. It is certainly difficult to explain why there might have been four blank staves left at the top of the page, except to allow for this addition. Typically, either Bach would have left the bottom staves blank and written the new parts there, as we see with the bassoons in movement 11, or he would

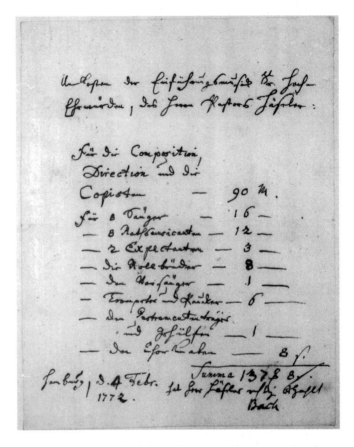

Fig. 3. EM Häseler, H 821d, autograph invoice, dated
Hamburg, February 4, 1772 (D-Hsa, Hs. 462, fol. 115).

Table 4. EM Häseler, H 821d, invoice and vocal parts, with sharing directions

Invoice (CPEB:B, no. 109)

"für 8 Sänger: 16 Marks"

Vocal parts	Name	Directions
1. Canto		
2. Alto		
3. Tenore	Michel	"the remaining [movements] are in Herr Wreden's part" (das daraus folgende steht in / Herr Wredens Stimme)
4. Tenore	Wreden	"the choral is in Herr Michel's music" (der Choral steht in Herr Michels Music)
5. Basso	Illert	
6. Basso	Hoffmann	"the chorale, and the remainder of the first part are in Herr Illert's part" (der Choral, und das übrige des ersten Theils / steht in Herr Illerts Stimme)

show varying degrees of compositional activity: the tenor aria movement 3 was borrowed wholesale from the *Magnificat*, H 772, whereas the soprano recitative movement 4 seems to have been composed right into the score.[29]

These two stages of compositional activity are reflected in the performing parts. The older layer is exclusively in the hand of the bassist Johann Andreas Hoffmann (Anon. 308), a copyist rarely seen in the Bach sources, whereas the newer layer is in the early hand of Michel and of Bach himself.[30] For the new movements 2 through 5, if the only copying necessary in a particular part was the chorale, then the "tacet" markings and the chorale were copied by Bach himself onto the same sheet of paper as the first movement (as in 2. Alto, 5. Basso, Oboes, Trumpets and Timpani). If more copying was necessary, it was done by Michel, often on a separate sheet. (See Figure 4, the alto part, where the first movement is in the hand of Hoffmann and the three tacet markings and the "volti" are in Bach's hand; on the verso, Bach has copied the chorale.)

The printed text booklet for the performance shows that five movements in the first half of the cantata—movements 6 through 10—are completely absent from the performing materials (see Table 5 for the list of movements).[31] Both the modern and eighteenth-century foliation and pagination of the performing parts are continuous, so we know that no material has been removed. It is likely that another work by Bach or another composer was performed here.[32]

---

have composed the new music directly into the appropriate parts, as seen in the third trumpet and timpani parts for H 821e.

29. The format and ruling of the score agree with the chronology suggested by the handwriting. In D-B, Mus. ms. P 346, pages 37–40 (first part of movt. 1): sixteen staves, each about 0.22 inch; pages 41–60 (rest of movt. 1, movts. 2–5): fifteen staves, each about 0.18 inch; pages 61–88 (movt. 11): fourteen staff lines, each about 0.18 inch.

30. Anon. 308 was recently identified as Johann Andreas Hoffmann by Moira Leanne Hill in "Der Sänger Johann Andreas Hoffmann als Notenkopist C. P. E. Bachs," BJ 102 (2016): 199–206. His hand appears in just three of Bach's works: H 776 (D-B, Mus. ms. P 337, and D-B, Am.B 85/I), H 821b (D-Bsa, SA 714), and H 821d (D-Bsa, SA 714). It also appears in copies of two Graun cantatas: D-B, Mus. ms. 8182 (3) and (4).

31. The print consulted is bound with the score in D-B, Mus. ms. 346.

32. One work Bach occasionally calls for in this manner is his double-choir *Heilig*, H 778. Its performance is always specifically indicated in both score and parts, as, for example, in the *Dank-Hymne der Freundschaft*, H 824e. More common for Bach when borrowing from another composer is to omit a movement in the score but copy it into the parts, as in *Einführungsmusik* Gerling, H 821h, where the first movement was borrowed verbatim, text and all, from a cantata by Christoph Förster. Most often, however, Bach tacitly copies the entire movement into both the score and parts, often tweaking things as he goes. This is the case in the first movement of H 821c, borrowed from a Georg Benda cantata, L 603.

Fig. 4. EM Häseler, H 821d, alto part in Michel's hand with Bach's emendations
(D-Bsa, SA 706, fol. 2r).

Table 5. EM Häseler, H 821d, list of movements

No.	Type*	Text incipit
1.	Chorus	Siehe, siehe, ich will den predigen
2.	Accomp. (T)	Durchdringe mich, erschüttre mein Gebein
3.	Aria (T)	Haleluja, haleluja! Welch ein Bund!
4.	Recit. (C)	Du kommst, du kommst! Du bist gekommen
5.	Chorale	Das ew'ge Licht geht da herein
6.	Recit.	Du predigst Gottes Heil der Welt
7a.	Aria?	Ich sehe dich auf Golgotha!
7b.	Chorus?	Da predigst du durch Blut und Wunden
7c.	Aria?	Ich sehe dich den dritten Tag
7d.	Chorus?	Da predigst du durch Sieg und Leben
7e.	Aria?	Ich sehe dich, dein Kleid ist Licht
7f.	Chorus?	Da predigst du durch Preis und Ehre
8.	Recit.	Heil und Gerechtigkeit
9.	Aria	Ich zittre; hilf mir, mein Erbarmer!
10.	Chorale	Tritt du mir zu, und mache leicht
11a.	Chorus	Gott, ich hebe meine Hände
11b.	Accomp. (T)	Preis ich deinen Vater frieden
11c.	Accomp. (B)	Aber darf ich auch erbeben
11d.	Chorus	Deine Güte, deine Treue
11e.	Accomp. (T)	Sanfte Vatergüte,
11f.	Accomp. (B)	Unter deinem goldnem Schilde
11g.	Chorus	Nimm für diese Segensgüter
12.	Chorus	[Repeat no. 1]

* The letter in brackets following the movement type indicates the solo voice designation, if appropriate. Entries followed by a question mark are inferences based on formatting in the text booklet.

It appears that to make up the first part of this cantata, Bach used the score and parts for an extant chorus (in this case, a generic biblical dictum, Psalm 40:10–11), appended four additional movements, and then performed yet another work. The second part is a through-composed setting of a "Song of Prayer" ("Gebet-Lied"), self-contained and possibly also representing older music. He still charged a significant sum (90 Marks) for composition, copying, and musical direction. Three notations in the parts in Bach's hand reflect the hasty—or at least time-sparing—preparation of this cantata in order to reduce both his and the copyists' work. Both the tenor part for Michel and the undesignated bass part (almost certainly for Hoffmann) instruct the user to read the chorale movement 5 from other singers' parts, those for [Carl Rudolph] Wreden and Illert, respectively. Even more interesting are Bach's two instructions to read "the remaining [movements]" (3. Tenore) or "the remainder of the first part" (6. Basso) from elsewhere, referring to the missing five movements in the first part.[33] To summarize, we have clear indications that one part was used by multiple singers both in the surviving part of the cantata (documented in instructions to read the chorale from another's part) and in the missing five movements (where the two tenors and two basses are instructed to read from one part).

* * *

Each of the ten performances considered here shows evidence of one part having been used by multiple singers. Furthermore, although Bach had eight salaried singers, it is clear that he often augmented this ensemble with additional voices, though not generally by more than two (for a total of ten).[34] Headings that refer to specific singers are much more common in tenor or bass parts than in soprano or alto parts. This may be because these singers were the most senior and highly paid members of Bach's standing ensemble. It seems that Bach preferred to provide each singer with his own part. That said, when Bach was in a hurry—as we see in H 821d—he often would assemble the parts more roughly from preexisting materials and even require the senior singers to share. Within soprano and alto parts, singers' names are most often found not as headings but rather as labels on specific movements, a notation that allowed multiple singers to perform from the same part. The part was simply passed to the appropriate singer for a given solo. Following his visit to Hamburg in 1772, Charles Burney quoted Bach as saying that he had come "fifty years too late."[35] According to Burney, Bach also advised him not to waste his time by actually attending a church service, a suggestion he disregarded. Burney could thus report that he "heard some very good music, of his [Bach's] composition, very ill performed, and to a congregation wholly inattentive."[36] Is it possible that Bach's use of one part for multiple singers reflects the apparent lack of interest by the congregation? Even if using one part per singer (rather than shared parts) permitted more effective rehearsals, evidently Bach was not willing to spend the time or money to provide those parts. Granted, this point is fairly speculative, since we know very little about how Bach conducted his rehearsals or what techniques he felt made them more or less successful. With regard to the quality

33. Jason B. Grant reaches the same conclusion—see CPEB:CW, 5/3.2, 170.

34. For the number of salaried singers, see Illert's report to the Hamburg Senate, transcribed in Sanders, "C. P. E. Bach and Liturgical Music," 104.

35. Charles Burney, *The Present State of Music in Germany, the Netherlands, and United Provinces*, 2nd ed. (London: Becket/Robson/Robinson, 1775), 2:246.

36. Ibid., 2:251.

of the upper voices especially, Sittard quotes from the *Musikalischer Correspondenz* of 1792: "Bach complained severely that he could not perform anything great and that all the good parts must be given to the two basses because the two choirboys seldom maintained their good soprano voices longer than two or three years and in various years were not serviceable. The tenors and altos are good people, but without capable voices."[37] We may thus see a possible connection between part sharing in the altos and sopranos (though not the tenors, who rarely shared) and Bach's assessment of quality. Again, it was perhaps the seniority of the tenors that spared them. Most often one singer performed from each part in Bach's own performances of his choral music, but occasionally multiple singers shared a part, either using it at the same time (e.g., in choruses and chorales) or passing it around (for solos, indicated by a name in the part). It must be emphasized, however, that these conclusions are based on a subset of performing materials and invoices; more study is required, especially in light of Jürgen Neubacher's findings about the musical establishment under Telemann.[38] The picture that emerges there broadens our perception of Bach as an ever-practical musical producer, skilled at adapting to the changing demands of diverse occasions and personnel.

37. "Schon der selige Bach klagte sehr darüber, daß er nichts großes aufführen könnte, und alles gute für diese zwei Stimmen geben müsse, weil die 2 Chorknaben selten über zwey oder drei Jahre ihre gute Discantstimme behielten und es denn in verschiedenen Jahren wieder daran fehlte. Die Tenor- und Altsänger sind gute brave Leute, aber ohne gefällige Stimme." Josef Sittard, *Geschichte des Musik- und Concertwesens in Hamburg vom 14. Jahrhundert bis auf die Gegenwart* (Altona: A. C. Reher, 1890), 53; translated in Sanders, "C. P. E. Bach and Liturgical Music," 100.

38. Neubacher, *G. P. Telemanns Hamburger Kirchenmusik.*

Recently Rediscovered Sources of Music of the Bach Family in the Breitkopf Archive

Christine Blanken

Through the eighteenth and early nineteenth centuries, Breitkopf in Leipzig was Germany's preeminent music dealer. Its sales catalogs published from 1762 to the end of the eighteenth century and the auction catalog of 1836 give us a vivid impression of music available on the market in printed form or as manuscripts.[1] The importance of the Breitkopf firm for the transmission of music of the Bach family has been thoroughly demonstrated; the last four decades of research on this topic have produced various studies, culminating in *Bach Perspectives 2: J. S. Bach, the Breitkopfs, and Eighteenth-Century Music Trade* (1996).[2] Yet despite the strong impact of these essays on our understanding of Breitkopf's manuscripts and their transmission, there remains considerable work to be carried out on this important music dealer.

Yoshitake Kobayashi was primarily responsible for establishing the method by which we are able to identify the Breitkopf provenance of a musical source. He demonstrated the handwriting characteristics of the Breitkopf firm's scribes and identified watermarks found in its sales copies.[3] He also described the firm's typical wrappers

---

1. Barry S. Brook, ed., *The Breitkopf Thematic Catalogues: The Six Parts and Sixteen Supplements 1762–1787* (New York: Dover, 1966); *Grosse Musikalien-Auction. Verzeichniss geschriebener und gedruckter Musikalien aller Gattungen, welche am 1. Juni 1836 und folgenden Tagen . . . von Breitkopf & Härtel in ihrem Geschäftslocale zu Leipzig gegen baare Zahlung . . . verkauft werden sollen* (Leipzig: Breitkopf & Härtel, 1836).

2. *Bach Perspectives 2*, ed. George. B. Stauffer (Lincoln: University of Nebraska Press, 1996).

3. Yoshitake Kobayashi, "Breitkopf Attributions and Research on the Bach Family," in Stauffer, *Bach Perspectives 2*, 53–63; and "On the Identification of Breitkopf's Manuscripts," in ibid., 107–21.

This chapter expands on results reported in my article "Ein wieder zugänglich gemachter Restbestand alter Musikalien der Bach-Familie im Verlagsarchiv Breitkopf & Härtel," BJ 99 (2013): 79–128 on recently discovered J. S. Bach sources. It also presents new information about Breitkopf sources stemming from Bach's sons, a subject that the earlier article treated only briefly.

and other markings, and, by unlocking the firm's characteristic numbering system, he provided the final clue that identifies a *Stammhandschrift*, the house copy from which others were made for sale. In addition to sources of works of J. S. Bach, Kobayashi identified many *Stammhandschriften* and sales copies of other composers in libraries worldwide. His identifiers, which have been widely accepted by scholars, have helped many other musicologists identify Breitkopf sources in their own areas of specialty.

Ernest May's study of the transmission of J. S. Bach's smaller organ chorales demonstrated that what traditionally had been called the "Kirnberger Collection" (D-B, Am. B. 72/72a) and believed to comprise works collected by Johann Philipp Kirnberger was in reality a music collection compiled by Breitkopf & Härtel.[4] As May's work demonstrates, various Breitkopf catalog entries show that the Bach organ chorales in the firm's library had been gathered over many years. May's work improved on a previous hypothesis (the so-called *Sammelmappe* theory) put forth by Hans Klotz, who proposed that Kirnberger, as Bach's former student, had access to manuscripts in the composer's personal collection housed in the St. Thomas school's "Componierstube."[5]

Also significant to Bach research was the recognition of Breitkopf's erroneous attributions of works to J. S. Bach. The mistaken attributions misled the editors of the Bach-Gesellschaft complete works and resulted in erroneous entries in Wolfgang Schmieder's *Bach-Werke-Verzeichnis* (BWV). A prominent example is the anonymously transmitted *St. Luke Passion* (olim BWV 246) from Bach's music library, copied in his own hand; other examples include the cantatas *Meine Seele rühmt und preist* (olim BWV 189) and *Wer sucht die Pracht* (olim BWV 221); I discovered the oldest source of the latter in 2013, but the actual composer remains unknown.[6]

A host of other problems concerning Bach sources in Breitkopf's catalogs still exists; many catalog entries refer either to lost sources or to sources that cannot be identified at all. One of the most intriguing of the unanswered questions is precisely who provided the music dealer with sources. Can some Breitkopf sources be traced back to the immediate family following the division of Bach's estate? If so, might some of

---

4. The title "Kirnberger Collection" goes back to Wilhelm Rust; see BG 40, xiii; it was used by Wolfgang Schmieder in the BWV, which refers to BWV 690–713a as "Choralbearbeitungen in Kirnbergers Sammlung" (1950) or "Choralbearbeitungen in der Kirnbergerschen Sammlung" (1990). See Ernest D. May, "Breitkopf's Role in the Transmission of J. S. Bach's Organ Chorales" (Ph.D. diss., Princeton University, 1974); and May, "Eine neue Quelle für J. S. Bachs einzeln überlieferte Orgelchoräle," BJ 60 (1974): 98–103.

5. "Die Sammelmappe befand sich nach Bachs Tode noch—oder wieder?—in den Bibliotheksschränken der 'Componierstube' der Thomasschule." See Hans Klotz, ed., *Die einzeln überlieferten Orgelchoräle*, KB, NBA 4/3 (Leipzig: VEB Deutscher Verlag für Musik, 1962), 13–18.

6. Blanken, "Ein wieder zugänglich gemachter Restbestand," 123.

them stem from items inherited by Bach's daughters? And what prints or manuscripts did the Breitkopf firm purchase from local Leipzig musicians, such as Carl Gotthelf Gerlach (1704–61), Johann Gottlieb Görner (1697–1778), and Johann Schneider (1702–88), to name only a few of the organists contemporary with the composer?[7]

A Forgotten Box from the Breitkopf & Härtel Archive

Most of Breitkopf's former holdings of Sebastian Bach's music—part of the firm's archive—are preserved in the Brussels Royal and Conservatory Libraries and were purchased (in large part) by Jean-François Fétis at an 1836 Leipzig auction.[8] Smaller portions of the firm's archive, in part purchased by the Leipzig organist Carl Ferdinand Becker (1804–77), are in the Leipzig Stadtbibliothek. The remainder is in the Bach-Archiv, Leipzig. Many other institutions also hold items from the dispersed Breitkopf archive. Prominent among them is a group of autograph Bach sources purchased by Otto Carl Friedrich von Voß (1755–1823), probably in the late eighteenth century, together with many manuscripts by other composers.[9] These sources are now in the Amalienbibliothek collection of the Staatsbibliothek zu Berlin. But as mentioned earlier, the Breitkopf catalogs from 1762 to 1836 indicate that considerably more music composed by Bach or his sons was available than can be accounted for in present-day music collections.[10]

When in 2013 I found a box of manuscripts dating from the early eighteenth century to the first third of the nineteenth, it was totally unexpected; all earlier inquiries about

7. From 1729 Gerlach was organist at the Leipzig Neukirche; he served there until his death and organized the *Figuralmusik* at this church. He may have been Bach's student. Görner was an organist at several Leipzig churches (1716, University Church; 1721, St. Nicolai; 1729, St. Thomas) and in 1723 became music director of the University Church. For the biography of Johann Schneider (1702–88), see the text paragraph beginning "Because Schneider is a common German last name" and notes 63 and 64.

8. See Ulrich Leisinger and Peter Wollny, *Die Bach-Quellen der Bibliotheken in Brüssel*, Leipziger Beiträge zur Bach-Forschung 2 (Hildesheim: Olms, 1997), 78–84.

9. Bettina Faulstich, *Die Musikaliensammlung der Familie von Voß. Ein Beitrag zur Berliner Musikgeschichte um 1800*, Catalogus musicus (Cassel: Bärenreiter, 1997), 521–30.

10. This is not to mention the sales copies identified in diverse libraries. On C. P. E. Bach, see Peter Wollny, ed., *Miscellaneous Keyboard Works II*, CPEB:CW, 1/8.2 (2005), 164–65 (for sources from the Prieger collection); Darrell Berg, ed., *Miscellaneous Sonatas from Prints I*, CPEB:CW, 1/5.1 (2007), 104–6 (for sources from the Grundmann collection, Beethoven-Haus Bonn); Christine Blanken, *Die Bach-Quellen in Wien und Alt-Österreich*, Leipziger Beiträge zur Bach-Forschung 10 (Hildesheim: Olms, 2011), 1:278–90 (for sources from the Hoboken collection and Prieger collection); and Daniel F. Boomhower, "C. P. E. Bach Sources at the Library of Congress," *Notes* 70, no. 4 (2014): 597–660 (for sources from the Prieger collection).

surviving remnants of the firm's archive—for example, those made by the editors of the *Neue Bach-Ausgabe* or by scholars from the Bach-Archiv Leipzig—had been answered negatively. This box contained thirty-five previously unknown sources comprising seventy compositions, most by J. S. Bach. They survived not only the auction of 1836 but also Breitkopf & Härtel's difficult times in the years before and after 1943.[11]

Why had no one taken notice of them previously? The firm's archive was cataloged for the first time only in 1962 when it came to the Sächsisches Staatsarchiv—Staatsarchiv Leipzig, an institution in the GDR era, in an internal card file.[12] When the archive was recataloged in 1990, all the archival material concerning the Bach-Gesellschaft edition was astonishingly overlooked.[13] Only a totally new cataloging in 2012–13 brought the old manuscript sources, the nineteenth-century sources, and other archival material from the BG to light.[14] For inexplicable reasons, the NBA did not access this important archival material, even though it had remained in place since the time of the archive's confiscation in 1962.[15]

This is only part of the story. The other is that the box was archived as part of the first complete edition but was most likely unknown to the editors of the BG itself. Only later was it filed among the records of the third annual volume of the BG, covering the Inventions and Sinfonias, BWV 772–801, probably because one manuscript in the box

11. See esp. Oskar von Hase, *Breitkopf & Härtel: Gedenkschrift und Arbeitsbericht*, 5th ed. enlarged by Hellmuth von Hase (Leipzig: Breitkopf & Härtel, 1968). Hellmuth von Hase, one of the firm's owners, describes the days during the bombardments of Leipzig in December 1943 and mentions some of the most important autograph manuscripts that he was able to save. See Rudolf Elvers, "Breitkopf & Härtels Verlagsarchiv," *Fontes artis musicae* 17, nos. 1–2 (1970): 24–28; *Die Musik in Geschichte und Gegenwart*, 2nd ed., s.v. "Breitkopf & Härtel," by Frank Reinisch; *New Grove Dictionary of Music and Musicians*, 2nd ed., s.v. "Breitkopf & Härtel," by Hans-Martin Plesske.

12. Personal communication from Dr. Thekla Kluttig, Sächsisches Staatsarchiv—Staatsarchiv Leipzig. See Thekla Kluttig, "Nur Briefe berühmter Komponisten? Archivgut von Leipziger Musikverlagen als Quelle für die Musikwissenschaften," *Die Musikforschung* 66, no. 4 (2013): 362–78 (esp. 366–72). I am indebted to Ms. Kluttig for bringing to my attention the new cataloging of the archival material of the BG and for allowing me to publish facsimiles of the sources.

13. Apart from one box pertaining to Ernst Naumann, ed., BG 40 (Orgelwerke, vol. 4, 1893) labeled "Bach, Johann Sebastian: Choralvorspiele und Choralvariationen für Orgel."

14. The holdings of the Breitkopf archive contain the editors' and publisher's material for the Bach Gesellschaft, including manuscript copies and nineteenth- and twentieth-century prints, as well as handwritten texts such as prefaces, *Revisionsberichte*, and so on that were used as *Vorlage*. The Bach-Archiv Leipzig has plans for a research project on this material.

15. Only a small portion containing late nineteenth-century source material for volume 42 of the Bach Gesellschaft, containing organ chorales, survived in the Bach-Archiv among remnants of Wilhelm Rust's estate.

contains pieces from that collection.[16] Even Wolfgang Schmieder, who had worked on the bwv during his time as archivist at Breitkopf & Härtel from 1933 to 1942 and published a catalog of the most valuable manuscript sources, never mentioned any of the sources from the Breitkopf archive listed in Table 1.[17]

The earliest and most valuable source is a manuscript copy of bwv 913 and 914 in the hand of Bach's first copyist, "Anon. Weimar 1" (see Figures 1–5). The scribe can probably be identified as Johann Martin Schubart (1690–1721), Bach's Mühlhausen and Weimar pupil who later served as Weimar court organist. Bach inserted the titles, most of the tempo indications and embellishments, and a few measures that Schubart left incomplete. Few of Bach's autograph copies provide fingerings, tempo indications, or organ registration, all of which are present here.[18] This manuscript copy, which Bach carefully revised, gives us rare insight into his manner of playing a toccata in the so-called Northern German *stylus phantasticus*, with its sudden changes in tempo and affect. The copy of bwv 913 shows tempo indications lacking in all other sources; thus it seems that Bach wanted to make sure that the performer understood how to play these sophisticated *stylus phantasticus* pieces.

Another important manuscript, a copy of the Toccata in C Major, bwv 564 (see Figure 6), was made by Bach's Leipzig organ colleague Carl Gotthelf Gerlach, who apparently copied it from an older, possibly autograph, manuscript from Bach's Weimar period.[19] It gives precise indications for changing hands ("destra" and "sinistra"), some fingerings, and embellishments in the first bar that are never played today. These and other readings were mostly already known; in fact, two other copies survive with the additional indications, but they have never served as the basis for a modern edition.[20] Because the copies date from the late eighteenth and early nineteenth centuries, their special markings have been disregarded as late additions. They must now be reconsidered by editors and performers alike as containing valuable insight into early eighteenth-century performance practice.

16. That catalog is D-LEsta 21081/7381, with a list of variant readings of bg 3, now preserved as D-LEsta, 21081/7385.

17. Wolfgang Schmieder, *Musikerhandschriften in drei Jahrhunderten: Ein Bilderquerschnitt durch die deutsche Musikgeschichte von Bach bis Reger* (Leipzig: Breitkopf & Härtel, 1939).

18. D-B, Mus. ms. Bach P 330, with Bach's transcription (bwv 596) of a Concerto in D Minor by Antonio Vivaldi, for example, provides organ stops. The *Clavierbüchlein* for Wilhelm Friedemann Bachs (US-NHub, Music Deposit 31) contains fingerings in a small study piece (bwv 994).

19. Indications for the Weimar provenance of the *Vorlage* include the typical wording of the title ("Toccata C♮ Pedaliter di Giovanni Sebastiano Bach") and the Italian spelling of the composer's name, typical of autograph headings from Bach's Weimar period.

20. Both D-B, Mus. ms. Bach P 1101 and 1103, copied by two unknown scribes and later purchased by Franz Hauser, show similar readings and may refer to the same lost (and probably autograph) manuscript. Ambrosius Kühnel copied D-B, Mus. ms. Bach P 1071 from Gerlach's copy at the Breitkopf firm.

Table 1. New sources of works of Johann Sebastian Bach from the Breitkopf archive (all in D-LEsta, 21081)

Eighteenth-century *Stammhandschriften* and sale copies			
Work	*Source type*	*Copyist*	*Call no.*
BWV 54 "Widerstehe doch der Sünde"	Sale copy after B-Br Ms. II 4196 (Fétis no. 2444)	Breitkopf copyist	7384
BWV 230 "Lobet den Herrn alle Heiden"	Sale copy; unknown model	Breitkopf copyist	7376
BWV 707 "Ich hab mein Sach Gott heimgestell"	*Stammhandschrift*	C. G. Gerlach	7369 no. 3
BWV 710 "Wir Christenleut" olim BWV 748 "Gott der Vater wohn uns bei" (J. G. Walther)	*Stammhandschrift*	J. L. Krebs	7370
olim BWV 221 anon., "Wer sucht die Pracht"	*Stammhandschrift*	C. G. Gerlach	7377
olim BWV 189 anon., "Meine Seele rühmt und preist"[1]	Probably *Stammhandschrift* wrapper only (Breitkopf)		7372 no. 7
BWV 772–801 (twenty-two pieces)	*Stammhandschrift*	Unidentified	7381[2]

Stichvorlagen and reference sources for Breitkopf's early editions of Bach's organ music[3]			
Work	*Source type*	*Copyist*	*Call no.*
BWV 542/2	*Stichvorlage*	Unidentified (first half of the eighteenth century)	7382
BWV 540/1		Unknown copyists	7474[4]
BWV 542/1	*Stichvorlage*	Ca. 1830/31	
BWV 550	*Stichvorlage*		
BWV 533	*Stichvorlage*		
BWV 572			
BWV 532	*Stichvorlage*	Unknown copyists	7475
BWV 539	*Stichvorlage*	Ca. 1830/31	
BWV 544			
BWV 545			
BWV 548			
BWV 553			

Table 1. Continued

Work	Source type	Copyist	Call no.
BWV 565	*Stichvorlage*		
BWV 569	*Stichvorlage*		
BWV 578			
BWV 740 (arrangement)[5]			
BWV Anh. 94			

Old manuscript sources not used for editions:			
Work	*Source type*	*Copyist*	*Call no.*
BWV 913		J. M. Schubart[6] / JSB	7371 no. 1
BWV 914			7371 no. 1
BWV 564 (fragment)		C. G. Gerlach	7369 no. 1
BWV 572 (fragment)		C. G. Gerlach	7369 no. 2
BWV 808/1		Breitkopf copyist[7]	7383 no. 2
BWV 903/2		Unidentified before 1800	7375 no. 1

1. Today ascribed to Melchior Hoffmann. See the overview of attributions in NBA I/41 KB (Andreas Glöckner, 2000), 120.

2. D-LEsta, 21081/7385 gives a list of variant readings between BG 3 (C. F. Becker, 1853) and the autograph score in D-B, Mus. ms. Bach P 610 (which presents three different hands: Wilhelm Rust and two others).

3. Breitkopf published several organ compositions by Bach in the early 1830s edited by Berlin music professor Adolph Bernhard Marx (1795–1866). For the editions and titles and the works edited, see NBA IV/5–6 KB (Dietrich Kilian, 1979), 1:286. The opera tenor and collector of Bach sources Franz Hauser (1794–1870) was one of the first to attempt a thematic catalog of Bach's works; his plan was not successful, but several handwritten catalogs from his estate, some with entries in his hand, have survived (D-B, Mus. ms. theor. K 419, K 419/10, K 420, K 435, K 437, K 461, K 463, and K 481).

4. The contents of 21081/7374 match two manuscript copies from the Deneke-Mendelssohn Collection in Oxford. As Dietrich Kilian pointed out in NBA IV/5-6, KB, p. 155, they were copied in Berlin. See GB-Ob, Ms. M. Deneke Mendelssohn c. 70 and c. 103; and Peter Ward Jones, "Zwei unbekannte Bach-Handschriften aus dem Besitz Felix Mendelssohn Bartholdys," in BJ 96 (2010): 283–86 (referring to c. 103, a collective manuscript, copied by Eduard Ritz and Fanny Mendelssohn between 1823 and 1825). Friendly communication from Nobuaki Ebata.

5. Arrangement correlates with J. N. Schelble's edition *VI varierte Choräle für die Orgel von J. S. Bach für das Pianoforte zu vier Händen eingerichtet* (Frankfurt: Dunst, 1831), BWV 740 = no. 3.

6. Together with the first print of the fugue BWV 914/4 (D-LEsta, 21081, 7371 no. 2), Breitkopf & Härtel, 1826. Schubart's initials were recently found in a manuscript in the hand of "Anon. Weimar 1" / "Anon. M 1," confirming the identification; see Peter Wollny, "Vom 'apparat der auserleßensten kirchen Stücke' zum 'Vorrath an Musicalien, von J. S. Bach und andern berühmten Musicis.' Quellenkundliche Ermittlungen zur frühen Thüringer Bach-Überlieferung und zu einigen Weimarer Schülern und Kollegen Bachs," BJ 101 (2015): 99–154, esp. 102 and 139.

7. The handwriting matches the scribe of the catalog in D-B, Mus. ms. theor. Kat 423, which gives an inventory of the organist Carl Christian Kegel's (1770–1843) Bach collection.

Fig. 1. Toccata in D Minor, BWV 913. Copyist Johann Martin Schubart,
formerly known as "Anon. Weimar 1," with Bach's autograph title
and entry "Allegro" (D-LEsta, 21081/7371 no. 1).

Fig. 2. Toccata in D Minor, BWV 913. Copyist Johann Martin Schubart, measures 14–15, with Bach's autograph embellishments and entry "adagio" (D-LEsta, 21081/7371 no. 1).

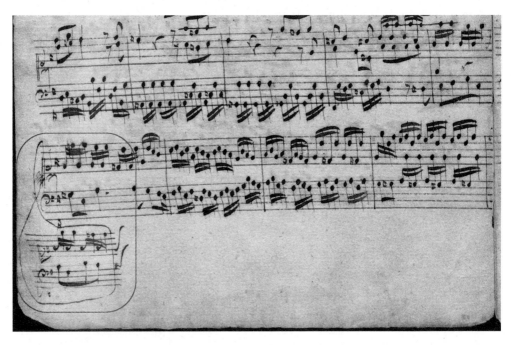

Fig. 3. Toccata in E Minor, BWV 914, measure 91b. Copyist Johann Martin Schubart, with Bach's autograph insertion of a missing half measure (D-LEsta, 21081/7371 no. 1).

Fig. 4. Toccata in E Minor, BWV 914, measure 139. Copyist Johann Martin Schubart, with Bach's autograph eighth notes inserted into the upper line and lower line, plus "Fine" mark (D-LEsta, 21081/7371 no. 1).

Fig. 5. Toccata in D Minor, bwv 913. Copyist Johann Martin Schubart, with Bach's autograph entries in measures 119–20 (see the tempo indications "Adagio" and "Allegro" and the word "Volti") (D-LEsta, 21081/7371 no. 1).

Fig. 6. Toccata in C Major, BWV 564. Copyist Carl Gotthelf Gerlach
(D-LEsta, 21081/7369 no. 1). *Vorlage* probably autograph.

Wilhelm Friedemann Bach: A Few Unique New Sources

Only one source for the Trio in B-flat Major, Fk 50(BR-WFB B 16), appears to transmit the original setting for two violins and basso continuo (Table 2).[21] Its title reads: "Trio / a / 2 Violini / e / Basso. // dal Sigr: F. W. Bach. / [Incipit]."[22] As is typical in manuscript copies written by the firm's professional scribes, this set of parts, written by Anon. J. S. Bach XV (according to Blechschmidt), might stem from a lost *Stammhandschrift*.[23] A source from the Itzig family transmits it as a work for flute and violin with adaptations to the range of the flute part, mainly in the form of octave transpositions.[24] Most likely a later version of a Halle composition made in Berlin, it contains numerous embellishments not found in the Breitkopf version.[25]

A letter of May 27, 1774, from Wilhelm Friedemann Bach to Johann Gottlob Immanuel Breitkopf (1719–94) shows not only that Bach was on good terms with

---

21. Wilhelm Friedemann Bach, *Kammermusik: Duette, Solo- und Triosonaten*, ed. Peter Wollny, *Gesammelte Werke* (Stuttgart: Carus, 2010), 3:ix, 112–19. Wollny cites Hugo Riemann's edition, *Collegium Musicum: Auswahl älterer Kammermusik für den praktischen Gebrauch*, vol. 45 (Leipzig: Breitkopf & Härtel, [1907]), as a substitute for the lost Breitkopf *Stammhandschrift* (D 5) and gives readings from the Riemann edition in small print in lieu of the lost autograph or Breitkopf sources. Riemann's edition, an arrangement for two violins and piano, gives no information about his source(s). Nevertheless, the pitches of the violins and the bass line of the piano are identical to those of the newly discovered Breitkopf parts in D-LEsta, 21081/7380 no. 1.

22. The parts can be dated approximately with the help of the watermark ([a] IGE; [b] [Wild Man with Tree], papermill Zittau/Mandau, Johann Georg Elssner I, ca. 1767–78).

23. "Catalogo dei Soli, Duetti, Trii e Concerti per il violino, il violino piccolo, e discordato, viola di bracchio, viola d'amore, violoncello piccolo e violoncello, e viola di gamba. Chi si trovano in manuscritto nella officina musica di Breitkopf in Lipsia. Parte IIda. 1762" (cat. Breitkopf 1762/2, col. 26, no. "II di F. W. Bach," from "VI. Sonate a due Violini et Basso, da diversi Autori. Racc. IV"); see Brook, *The Breitkopf Thematic Catalogues*, col. 58.

24. The work has been transmitted in parts from Sara Levy's collection, D-Bsa, SA 3645 (olim ZD 1703b) and copied by Anon. Itzig 9 (title page by Anon. Itzig 12 = F. Baumann); see Wolfram Enßlin, *Die Bach-Quellen der Sing-Akademie zu Berlin: Katalog*, 2 vols. (Olms: Hildesheim, 2006), 1:321. Its title reads: "SONATA in B. / a / Trè. / [Incipit] / Flauto Traverso / Violino / e / Basso Continuo / Dell' Sig[no]re W: Frd. Bach / à Halle."

25. Another, now lost source was located in the Kaiserin Augusta-Gymnasium in Berlin (Ferdinand Schultz, *Der ältere Notenschatz des Kaiserin Augusta-Gymnasiums*, Königliches Kaiserin Augusta-Gymnasium, Jahresbericht 31 [Berlin, 1900], 23: "3. Trios. . . . Bach, Wilhelm Friedemann [?]. Trio für 2 Violinen und Bass"). Presumably Riemann took this lost manuscript as a *Vorlage* for his edition in *Collegium Musicum* 45 (see note 21). Many readings of the Breitkopf source for this work do not match Riemann's edition—even excluding Riemann's many insertions (articulation marks, bows, ties, dynamics, meter changes, etc., in the second movement). The Andante of the Breitkopf source lacks some of the appoggiaturas found in the other manuscripts, and there are some pitch deviations.

Table 2. Breitkopf sources for works of W. F. Bach, all in D-LEsta

Eighteenth-century *Stammhandschriften* and sale copies			
Work	*Source type*	*Copyist*	*Call no.*
Fk 71 / br-wfb C 5 Sinfonia in B-flat major	*Stammhandschrift* (parts)	Unknown before 1762	21081/7388
Fk 50 / br-wfb B 16 Trio in B-flat major	Breitkopf sale copy (parts)	Breitkopf copyist ("Anon. J. S. Bach XV")	21081/7380 no. 1
Fk 32 / br-wfb A 89 Fugue in C minor	Breitkopf sale copy[1]	Breitkopf copyist	21081/7380 no. 2

1. This sales copy is listed only in the appendix of a later, undated Breitkopf catalog, Verzeichnis von Kirchenmusik, welche in richtigen und saubern Abschriften auf gutem Papier bey Breitkopf und Härtel in Leipzig zu haben sind (Leipzig, early nineteenth century) as "Bach, Friedem. Fuge in C♭."

the Breitkopf publishing house but also that he had played the trio with two Leipzig musicians. He writes: "During the previous war [the Seven Years' War, 1756–63], I gave your most honorable self a trio for two violins in B-flat, which I had tried out in your quarters with Mr. Schneider and the then Cantor of Merseburg. My score of this work is now lost."[26]

Bach had played the work in the publisher's house and residence, Zum Goldenen Bären, in Leipzig with Schneider and Penzel. These musicians can probably be identified as Johann Schneider (1702–88), the organist of St. Nicholas's, an accomplished violinist, and a member of the orchestra Grosses Concert from 1746 to 1748; and Christian Friedrich Penzel (1737–1801), a student at Leipzig University who was praised for his "Fertigkeiten auf dem Claviere" (accomplishments on the keyboard).[27] Penzel had been a St. Thomas's schoolboy from 1751 to 1756 and for two years had served as *Hofmeister* to the family of a "Rittmeister von Rackel" before becoming city cantor (*Stadtkantor*) and a schoolteacher (*Collega*) at Merseburg in 1765.[28] Penzel re-

26. "In währendem Kriege communicirte ich Ew. HochEdelgeb. ein Trio von zwey Violini aus dem B., welches auch damahls mit Herrn Schneiders und des ietzigen Merseburgischen Cantoris Begleitung in Dero Zimmer probirte. Die Partitur davon ist mir von Händen gekommen." The letter (in the Pierpont Morgan Library, Cary Collection, New York) is cited in Hans-Joachim Schulze, *Studien zur Bach-Überlieferung im 18. Jahrhundert* (Leipzig: Edition Peters, 1984), 22.

27. Schneider served in the Weimar court orchestra, was Bach's harpsichord pupil at Köthen, and was Johann Gottlieb Graun's violin pupil at Merseburg. The quote describing Penzel is from Johann Adam Hiller, *Wöchentliche Nachrichten und Anmerkungen, die Musik betreffend* (Hildesheim: Olms, 1970), 203–4.

28. Penzel's time at St. Thomas's began in 1751, not 1749, as some sources mention; see Richard Jones and Peter Wollny, "Penzel, Christian Friedrich," *Grove Music Online*, accessed 4 May 2015, http://www.oxfordmusiconline.com/subscriber/article/grove/music/21267.

mained in Leipzig until 1761, which can be considered the "terminus ante quem" of the musical encounter in Breitkopf's home. Moreover, since the catalog of 1762 (dated with "Leipziger Neujahrsmesse, 1762") offered the Trio in B-flat Major for sale, we can date the encounter to approximately 1760–61.[29]

Shortly before Bach wrote this letter, he had moved from Brunswick to Berlin, and his first organ concerts in the city had been enthusiastically received in the newspapers. He also must have wanted to sell his chamber music in Berlin, but he lacked manuscripts, including his autograph of the B-flat Major Trio. Soon after his arrival in Berlin he may also have become acquainted with the Itzig/Levy family, as he was instructing Sara Levy on the keyboard by 1775.[30] Four manuscripts produced by an Itzig family copyist include the Trio in D Major, Fk 47 (in two exemplars) and the Trio in B-flat Major, Fk 50; these illustrate the family's strong interest in Friedemann's chamber music, especially in settings with flute.[31] A set of parts for the Trio in D Major bears the library stamp "S. Levy"; the other shows a stamp with "B. Itzig" and thus belonged to Sara's older brother, Benjamin (1756–1831/33?). The 1783 catalog of Benjamin's music collection indicates that he too owned a copy of the B-flat Major Trio, Fk 50.[32] The source, now lost, may have corresponded to Sara Itzig's parts in D-Bsa, SA 3654.[33]

---

29. In that catalog the B-flat major trio is listed as part of "Raccolta IV" of six sonatas, together with trios by Johann Gottlieb Janitsch, Leopold Mozart, Georg Friedrich Handel, and Georg Czarth ("Tzart") and a C major trio by Johann Gottlieb Goldberg, but it is ascribed to J. S. Bach (olim BWV 1037). The C major trio is offered—under Goldberg's name—within the section of trios for flauto traverso, violin, and basso continuo of the same catalog, col. 13 (Brook, *The Breitkopf Thematic Catalogues*, col. 93).

30. Peter Wollny, *"Ein förmlicher Sebastian und Philipp Emanuel Bach-Kultus": Sara Levy und ihr musikalisches Wirken*, Beiträge zur Geschichte der Bach-Rezeption 2 (Wiesbaden: Breitkopf & Härtel, 2010), 23–25, 125.

31. An equally strong interest in works for viola by W. F. Bach and others is also reflected in her collection; on this point, see Mary Oleskiewicz, *Die Sammlung der Sing-Akademie zu Berlin Teil 4: Kammermusik und Klaviermusik* (Munich: K. G. Sauer, 2009), 43–44. The Bach trio manuscripts are D-B, Mus. ms. Bach St 477 and D-Bsa, SA 3644; both contain Fk 47 and are written by Anon. Itzig 9, following Yoshitake Kobayashi's "Schreiberkartei" des Johann-Sebastian-Bach-Instituts in Göttingen (now in Bach-Archiv Leipzig).

32. The trio is listed in Benjamin's catalog as a composition for two violins; see D-B, Mus. ms. theor. 583, p. 9.

33. Wollny, "Ein förmlicher Sebastian und Philipp Emanuel Bach-Kultus," 91 (for a list of Benjamin Itzig's Bach sources, see 91–95). Questionable in this respect is whether the Trio in D Major, Fk 47, like the Trio in B-flat Major, was also initially composed for two violins. Benjamin Itzig's parts show the following title: "SONATA in D♯ / a / Tre / [Incipit] / Violino o Flauto Trav: Primo / Violino o

These Berlin trio sources may reflect Friedemann Bach's presence in Berlin beginning in 1774 and his close association with the Itzig family shortly thereafter. Due to the trios' scoring, we may also take them to suggest that Friedemann mentored the Itzig family's amateur musicians by arranging or composing music for them. Likewise, the presence in them of written-out embellishments, lacking in the Breitkopf source, may be pedagogical.

Still more important is the only surviving source for the Sinfonia in B-flat Major, Fk 71 (br-wfb C 5), for two violins, viola, and basso (not figured) (see Figure 7 and Table 2). Because of his access to the Sing-Akademie collection, Martin Falck included it when he cataloged the works of Wilhelm Friedemann Bach. Zelter cataloged the sinfonia under ZD 1385 as part of a collective manuscript (or *Sammelband*) in score.[34] Falck's excerpts of this source, made before it disappeared, formed the basis of the work's publication in the complete works edition. Falck's commentary permitted the identification of the copyist as the well-known J. F. Hering.[35]

The oldest extant source for the four-part sinfonia is probably the recently discovered Breitkopf parts, which can be identified clearly as a *Stammhandschrift* by the numbers on the first page of the first violin part. Breitkopf's thematic catalog of 1762 mistakenly included the work as one of a group of six compositions by Carl Philipp Emanuel.[36] The 1764 catalog rectified the entry.[37] The header of the *Stammhandschrift*

Flauto Trav: Secondo. / Basso Continuo / Dell Sig[nore]. W. Fr. Bach / à Halle"; presumably the scribe omitted the setting's precise instrumentation. The autograph source (D-Bsa, SA 3650 [olim ZD 1703f]) is only a fragment and gives neither title nor scoring. Following the end of the Trio in D Major, Fk 47, the manuscript gives the complete first movement of the Trio in A Minor, Fk 49, and the beginning of its second movement. Even the setting of the Trio in A Minor, Fk 49, is by no means certain: the autograph heading in the source (D-Bsa, SA 3650) is somewhat difficult to read, and it is unclear whether or not Wilhelm Friedemann Bach himself wrote "Trio a 2 Flut: / e Cembalo" (Wollny, br-wfb B 15, 114) or rather "a 2 Violl. / e Cembalo" (Enßlin, br-wfb B 15, 323). Obviously, Falck was not sure about it either; he entered it in the catalog as the unfinished trio to "2 Viol. (od. Flöten?) und Baß"; see Martin Falck, *Wilhelm Friedemann Bach: Sein Leben und seine Werke, mit thematischem Verzeichnis seiner Kompositionen* (Leipzig: Kahnt, 1913), no. 49.

34. Containing Fk 67, 63, 68, 69, 71, and 79 within a collective manuscript of thirteen compositions. The manuscript had been lost since 1945. According to Falck/Wollny, other scribes were also involved (*Wilhelm Friedemann Bach: Orchestermusik III*, ed. Peter Wollny, *Gesammelte Werke* [Stuttgart: Carus, 2010], 6:90–91).

35. D-LEb, Falck-Nachlass; see Wollny, *Wilhelm Friedemann Bach: Orchestermusik III*, 6: 72–74.

36. *Catalogo delle Sinfonie che si trovano in manuscritto nella officina musica di Giovanni Gottlob Immanuel Breitkopf, in Lipsia, Parte 1ma. 1761* (cat. Breitkopf 1762/1), col. 2 (Brook, *The Breitkopf Thematic Catalogues*, col. 2).

37. Cat. Breitkopf 1764, 44 ("Bach, F. W. Organista in Hala. [*sic*] I. Sinfonia").

Fig. 7. Sinfonia in F Major, Fk 71 (br-wfb C 5) (lost since Falck's time).
Unknown copyist before 1762 (handwriting sample: violins 1 and 2,
viola, basso) (D-LEsta, 21081/7388).

(shown in the illustration of Fk 71 in Figure 7) originally read "d[i] S[ignore] Bach"; the numbers at the top right reflect the 1762 thematic catalog, where it is offered as number 6 of the "VI. Sinfonie del C. F. E. Bach." A later entry, which reads "Organist in Halla [*sic*]," corrects one of many errors found in the early Breitkopf catalogs. Furthermore, in the archive's "forgotten box," the sinfonia became mingled with parts from the Sinfonia in B-flat Major, Warb G 5/1, by Johann Christian Bach.[38]

Because Falck's excerpts from Sing-Akademie ZD 1385 and the Breitkopf *Stammhandschrift* show variant readings, above all with regard to embellishments, ties, and slurs, it is highly probable that the Sing-Akademie source was not copied from the *Stammhandschrift* or from other sales copies. In this respect, the manuscript transmission of the sinfonia Fk 71 resembles that of the trio Fk 50. Moreover, it is likely that the sinfonia was copied after a now-lost autograph source.

Carl Philipp Emanuel Bach: Early Attributions in the Breitkopf Catalogs

The early transmission of manuscripts of C. P. E. Bach's music copied in Leipzig, the town of his father and his musical upbringing, is for the most part unclear. Only a few individual manuscripts are known to derive from Leipzig, probably from the Collegium Musicum or from members of J. S. Bach's circle. Johann Friedrich Agricola copied C. P. E. Bach's Cembalo Concerto in A Minor, Wq 1 (from 1733), during Bach's Leipzig period, ca. 1739/40.[39] No such source exists for the early version of the second Leipzig cembalo concerto, Wq 2, composed in 1734. Of the altogether twenty-three trio sonatas he composed, five originated in Leipzig in 1731. The catalog of his estate mentions only those five sonatas, which he later reworked in 1747 in Berlin (Wq 143–47).[40] It is remarkable that only one trio (D minor, Wq 145), which is transmitted in its early Leipzig version in a single manuscript (for violin and obbligato keyboard,

---

38. The J. C. Bach sinfonias and the W. F. Bach sinfonia are now separately cataloged; see Staatsarchiv Leipzig, 21081/7372 (five sinfonias by or ascribed to J. C. Bach).

39. *Keyboard Concertos from Manuscript Sources I*, ed. Peter Wollny, CPEB:CW 3/9.1 (2010), 161. Today only the solo cembalo part from Wq 2 is extant; the other parts are lost. The later version, from 1746, is transmitted in manuscripts written by C. P. E. and J. S. Bach (PL-Kj, Mus. ms. Bach St 495). It is unclear whether the latter set of parts was copied for a performance (by a Collegium Musicum or in a more private performance?) ca. 1746/47, as J. S. Bach's involvement suggests. Generally speaking, it is impossible to ascertain the repertoire of the Leipzig Collegia Musica, for which the concertos originally might have been composed. As the above-mentioned source for Wq 2 suggests, Emanuel provided his father with music repertoire for the Collegia in the late 1730s and 1740s.

40. *Verzeichnis des musikalischen Nachlasses des verstorbenen Capellmeisters Carl Philipp Emanuel Bach* (Hamburg: G. F. Schniebes, 1790), hereafter cited as NV.

Table 3. Breitkopf sources for works of C. P. E. Bach, all in D-LEsta

Work	Source type	Copyist	Call no.
Wq 175 / H 650 Sinfonia in F major	*Stammhandschrift* (score)	"Leipzig 2" (according to Henzel)	21081/7378 no. 2
Wq 175 / H 650 Sinfonia in F major	Parts	Unknown ca. 1760	21081/7173
Wq 176 / H 651 Sinfonia in D major	*Stammhandschrift* (score)	Unknown ca. 1760	21081/7378 no. 3
Wq 177 / H 652 Sinfonia in E minor	*Stammhandschrift* (parts)	"Leipzig 1" ca. 1760	21081/7379 no. 1
Wq 158 / H 584 Trio in B-flat major (version for two violins)	*Stammhandschrift* (score)	Unknown (cf. scribe of Wq 149 in P 367)	21081/7378 no. 1
Wq 158 / H 584 Trio in B-flat major (version for two violins)	*Stammhandschrift* (parts)	Three unknown ca. 1760	21081/7379 no. 2
GraunWV D:XII:94 J. G. Graun, Sinfonia in C major	*Stammhandschrift* (score)	Unknown ca. 1760	21081/7378 no. 4

olim BWV 1036), does not survive in an original source from the Bach circle.[41] In addition to the trios, there are a few compositions for a solo instrument and basso of questionable authorship.[42]

In his autobiography of 1773, C. P. E. Bach mentioned "ein Paar Duzend Sinfonien" (a few dozen sinfonias), but the catalog of the estate (printed in 1790) offers only fifteen sinfonias by that date. The list, which begins with the year 1741, omits compositions from his Leipzig and Frankfurt periods.[43] Presumably, as indicated in his letter to the

41. D-LEm (Depositum in D-LEb), Mus. ms. 9, written by a copyist of Johann Nicolaus Mempell (1713–47), *Kantor* in Apolda (Thuringia). See Ulrich Leisinger and Peter Wollny, "'Altes Zeug von mir': Carl Philipp Emanuel Bachs kompositorisches Schaffen vor 1740," BJ 79 (1993): 127–202 (esp. 174–82). For original sources that survive from the Bach circle, see Christoph Wolff, *Trios I*, CPEB:CW 2/2.1 (2011), 176–77, 183 (appendix with olim BWV 1036).

42. See Leisinger and Wollny, "Carl Philipp Emanuel Bachs kompositorisches Schaffen," 192–96.

43. *Carl Burney's der Musik Doctors Tagebuch seiner Musikalischen Reisen* (Hamburg: Bode, 1773), 3:199, 207. See Burney's English version: "a great number of symphonies" (Charles Burney, *The Present State of Music in Germany, the Netherlands, and United Provinces* [London: T. Becket / Robson / Robinson, 1773], 264). See also NV, 43–44.

literary historian J. J. Eschenburg, Bach had destroyed most of his earlier compositions. The letter also mentions King George II's careful preservation of Georg Friedrich Handel's juvenilia in London: "The funniest thing of all is the gracious foresight of the king, by which Handel's youthful works were preserved to the extreme. I am not comparing myself at all with Handel, but I have recently burned more than a ream of old works, and I am happy that they no longer exist."[44]

The Breitkopf firm's earliest eighteenth-century catalogs (starting with the first catalog from 1762, which has incipits) advertise a small number of instrumental works purported to be by C. P. E. Bach, all of which Bach declared to be either spurious or unreliable. As he wrote in a letter of August 26, 1774, to the Göttingen music director Johann Nicolaus Forkel, "The manuscript things that Breitkopf sells under my name are partly not by me, and in any case they are old and incorrectly copied."[45] Clearly, Bach wanted Forkel to acquire manuscripts of his music directly from him, rather than from the Leipzig dealer: "What I am able to give away is at your disposal; this includes things that I only will give to you and no one else."[46] Whatever commercial reasons he had for making this statement, Bach was again eager to suppress old or badly copied versions of his music. What did he mean, then, by those compositions "partly not by me, and in any case . . . old and incorrectly copied"?

The nonthematic catalog of 1761 offers "VI. Sinfonie à 2 Violini, Viola e Basso, 1 c[on]. Corni, 2 c[on]. Ob. a 4 thl. 12 gl."[47] The following year's catalog of 1762 more clearly identifies these works with thematic incipits: it attributes the following sinfonias to "C. F. E. BACH, Musico di Camera di Ré di Pruss."[48]

1. F major, Wq 175
2. C major Anon. (GraunWV D:XII:94)[49]
3. G major, Wq 173

44. "Das Poßirlichste von allem ist die gnädige Vorsicht des Königes, wodurch Händels Jugendarbeiten bis aufs äußerste verwahrt warden. Ich vergleiche mich gar nicht mit Händeln, doch habe ich vor Kurzem ein Ries u. mehr alter Arbeiten von mir verbrannt und freue mich, daß sie nicht mehr sind." Letter to Johann Joachim Eschenburg, 21 January 1786, in CPEB:B, document no. 529.

45. "Die geschriebenen Sachen, die Breitkopf von mir verkauft, sind theils nicht von mir, wenigstens sind sie alt u. falsch geschrieben." Ibid., document no. 183.

46. "Was ich weggeben kann, steht zu Diensten, hierunter sind auch Sachen begriffen, die ich bloß Ihnen u. keinem andren gebe." Ibid.

47. *Verzeichniß Musicalischer Werke, allein zur Praxis, sowohl zum Singen, als für alle Instrumente, welche nicht durch den Druck bekannt gemacht worden; in ihre gehörige Classen ordentlich eingetheilet; welche in richtigen Abschriften bey Joh. Gottlob Immanuel Breitkopf, in Leipzig, um beystehende Preiße in Louis d'ors à 5 Thlr. zu bekommen sind. Erste Ausgabe, Leipzig, in der Michaelmesse 1761*, 45.

48. Brook, The Breitkopf Thematic Catalogues, col. 2.

49. Ascribed to "Graun" in another source (S-Skma, O-R). According to RISM ID no. 190023909,

4. C major, Wq 174

5. D major, Wq 176

6. B-flat major, W. F. Bach, Fk 71 (BR-WFB C 5)

Six of these sinfonias and four *Stammhandschriften* (nos. 1, 2, 5, and 6) are among the items in the forgotten box: (1) Wq 175 (see Figure 8); (2) a sinfonia ascribed to C. P. E. Bach (author unknown: possibly Graun?);[50] (5) Wq 176; and (6) the sinfonia Fk 71 by Wilhelm Friedemann Bach (see Tables 2 and 3). The four sources must all be of different provenance, for they share neither scribes nor watermarks.

The supplementary catalog from 1766 ("Racc[olta]. II.") assigns two more sinfonias "a 4 Voci" (F major, Wq / H *deest*, and G major, Wq *deest* / H 667) to "C. P. E. BACH, M[usico]. di C[amera]. in Berol[ina]."[51] Because neither sinfonia is listed in C. P. E. Bach's estate catalog, they can be safely regarded as spurious.[52] The *Stammhandschriften* of both sources have survived under shelf number D-B, Mus. ms. Bach St 225 (F major, attributed as "de Mons: Bach de Berlin") and St 228 (G major, attributed as "de Bach de Berlin"). Both manuscripts transmit the sinfonia in score form and were written either by a copyist working directly for Breitkopf or by a musician-copyist from whom Johann Gottlob Immanuel Breitkopf may have acquired the manuscripts. The same scribe is also present in a large number of manuscripts that transmitted orchestral music from Berlin. The handwriting and the watermark of those copies written by Breitkopf copyists match sources for two Graun sinfonias and Carl Heinrich Graun's opera *Silla* in the Stadtbibliothek in Leipzig. Christoph Henzel has named this anonymous copyist "Leipzig 1."[53]

---

it was copied originally without title/attribution by the Berlin copyist "Schlichting," who was also associated with Emanuel Bach. See GraunWV, 1:848.

50. See cat. Breitkopf 1766, col. 2 (Brook, *The Breitkopf Thematic Catalogues*, col. 202).

51. Ibid.

52. Ekkehard Krüger and Tobias Schwinger, eds., *Berlin Symphonies*, CPEB:CW, 3/1 (2008) in the appendix to the introduction by Stephen C. Fisher ("Lost, Doubtful and Spurious Symphonies"), xvii. Ernst Suchalla (*Die Orchestersinfonien Carl Philipp Emanuel Bachs nebst einem thematischen Verzeichnis seiner Orchesterwerke* [Ausburg: W. Blasaditsch, 1968], 127–34) argued that the Sinfonia in G Major, H 667 (Wq *deest*; transmitted in D-B, Mus. ms. Bach St 228), may be the sinfonia that Bach and his friend Count Ferdinand Philipp Lobkowitz (1724–84) had composed together in Berlin ("Sinfonie mit dem Fürsten von Lobkowitz, einen Takt um den andern, aus dem Stegreif verfertigt. B[erlin]. Mit Hörnern und Hoboen," NV, 65). Neither St 228 nor the Breitkopf catalog of 1766 transmits horns or oboes.

53. For a facsimile of the handwriting of "Leipzig 1," see GraunWV, 2:288 (source D-LEm, PM 5177). Other manuscripts written by copyist "Leipzig 1" are D-LEm, PM 5181 and 5182. These three sources also share their watermark with the Breitkopf source for Wq 177 (Silesian eagle; G / Cammerpappier; papermill from Giersdorf in Silesia). See Blanken, "Ein wieder zugänglich gemachter Restbestand," 125.

Another Henzel copyist ("Leipzig 2") is found in the forgotten box in one manuscript (D-LEsta 21081/7378 no. 2). This copyist transmitted two spurious sinfonias (listed in GrWV as D:XII:109 and Av:XII:57), which refer to the Breitkopf catalog from 1766.[54] These sources can be traced back to the catalog from 1766, column 2 (Brook, *The Breitkopf Thematic Catalogues*, col. 208), where in "Raccolta VIII" two groups of sinfonias are attributed to J. G. Graun. In the second group of sinfonias, four out of five compositions are either spurious or cannot be attributed with certainty to either of the Graun brothers:

1. G major GraunWV Av:XII:57 (J. G. Graun? F. Benda?) D-LEm, PM 4738 copyist "Leipzig 2"; provenance: Breitkopf
2. G major GraunWV D:XII:109 (J. G. Graun?) D-LEm, Becker II.12.2 copyist "Leipzig 2"; provenance: Breitkopf
3. C major GraunWV A:XII:1 D-LEm, PM 5183:3; provenance: J. C. Oschatz → Breitkopf
4. E-flat major GraunWV Av:XII:47 (J. G. Graun?) D-LEm, PM 5183; provenance: Breitkopf
5. A major GraunWV D:XII:111 (spurious) D-LEm, PM 5183; provenance: "J. B. L." → Breitkopf

There is good reason to assume that these manuscripts were used in concert societies in Leipzig. They may in part stem from the library of Johann Christian Oschatz, one of the town musicians, and at least one of the sources can be traced to Oschatz's library. In the two "Raccolte" with sinfonias allegedly by J. G. Graun, only one work's provenance, the sinfonia in C major GraunWV A:XII:1, can be traced: it belonged to Johann Christian Oschatz, a *Kunstgeiger* (and later *Stadtpfeifer*) in Leipzig from 1738 to his death on January 10, 1762. Oschatz played flute and oboe in Leipzig's Grosses Concert, as shown by the "Tabula Musicorum der Löbl[ichen] großen Concert=Gesellschafft 1746. [17]47. [17]48."[55]

54. D-LEm, PM 4738 and D-LEm, Becker II.12.2.

55. The Große Concert=Gesellschafft was a Leipzig concert society from which the present day Gewandhaus-Orchester stems. In the "Tabula Musicorum," an important source for a further study on the Leipzig orchestras, the town chronicler Johann Salomon Riemer gives a handwritten list of its members and their instruments for the years 1746–48. Most of them were town musicians, but, as Riemer carefully explains, church organists and students also participated in various roles. The list is preserved in the Stadtgeschichtliches Museum Leipzig and has been transcribed by Arnold Schering, *Johann Sebastian Bach und das Musikleben Leipzigs im 18. Jahrhundert*, Musikgeschichte Leipzigs (Leipzig: Kistner & Siegel, 1941), 3:263–64; cf. the facsimile in Claudius Böhm, "Ohne Universität kein Gewandhausorchester," in *600 Jahre Musik an der Universität Leipzig: Studien anlässlich des Jubiläums*, ed. Eszter Fontana (Wettin: Stekovics, 2010), 198. Ernst Ludwig Gerber provides additional

The fate of Oschatz's estate is unknown, but the Breitkopfs may have purchased parts of it from his widow.[56] A comparison of the two nonthematic catalogs of 1763 and early 1764 shows that the latter includes a significant number of new compositions for oboe and flute in different settings.[57] However, it has been possible to trace only one manuscript source that bears Oschatz's name: a trio by Georg Friedrich Handel for two oboes and basso in B-flat major, HWV 388.[58] The majority of chamber music from the early Breitkopf catalog seems to be lost, but it probably contained many Oschatz sources used by Leipzig ensembles.

The groups of sinfonia and trio manuscripts are both heterogeneous in terms of their provenance, scribes, and paper types. The sources for C. P. E. Bach's chamber works, especially in Berlin, are far more numerous than those of Friedemann Bach. It is thus more difficult to draw conclusions without a further comparison of individual readings—work that still remains to be done.

Five C. P. E. Bach trio sources under consideration here correspond to the Breit-kopf thematic catalog 1763, col 12, which groups six works under the heading "VI. Sonate a Flauto, Violino et Basso, del C. F. E. BACH, Mus. di Cam. di Ré di Prussia" (Table 4).[59]

The scribe, watermarks, and possessor entries of Wq 158 (D-Lesta 21081/7378) resemble those of the well-known group of trio sources in the Staatsbibliothek zu Berlin, bound together in D-B, Mus. ms. Bach P 367 (Table 4; see Figure 9).[60] This

---

details in his article "Hiller," in *Historisch-Biographisches Lexicon der Tonkünstler, welches Nachrichten von dem Leben und Werken musikalischer Schriftsteller, berühmter Componisten, Sänger, Meister auf Instrumenten, Dilettanten, Orgel- und Instrumentenmacher, enthält* (Leipzig: Breitkopf, 1790), 1, cols. 639–40.

56. On the fate of the estate, see Hans-Joachim Schulze, "Besitzstand und Vermögensverhältnisse von Leipziger Ratsmusikern zur Zeit Johann Sebastian Bachs," in *Beiträge zur Bachforschung* (Leipzig: Edition Peters, 1985), 4:33–46.

57. See *Verzeichniß Musikalischer Werke allein zur Praxis, sowohl zum Singen, als für alle Instrumente, welche nicht durch den Druck bekannt gemacht worden; in ihre gehörigen Classen ordentlich eingetheilet; welche in richtigen Abschriften* bey Bern. Christoph Breitkopf u. Sohn in Leipzig . . . zu bekommen sind, Zweyte Ausgabe (Leipzig: In der Neujahrsmesse, 1764).

58. D-B, Mus. ms. 9101/5.

59. *Catalogo de Soli, Duetti, Trii, e Concerti per il Flauto traverso, Flauto piccolo, Flauto d'amore, Flauto dolce, Flauto-Basso, Oboe, Oboe d'amore, Fagotto, Sampogne, Corno di Caccia, Tromba, Zinche e Tromboni. Che si trovano in Manuscritto nella officina musica di Breitkopf in Lipsia. Parte IIIza* (1763), col. 12 (Brook, *The Breitkopf Thematic Catalogues*, col. 92). Only a *Stammhandschrift* for the Trio in B-flat Major, Wq 158, from this group of six trios is still missing.

60. The parts in D-LEsta, 21081/7379, do not match the readings of the score to Wq 158, and they do not have the same scribes or watermarks. The scribe of Wq 149 in P 367 is the same as 21081/7378, no. 1. The watermark in P 367, fascicle 1–4 is (a) K; (b) P (from the papermill of Christian Gerhard

Fig. 8. Sinfonia in F Major, Wq 175. Copyist "Leipzig 2" (according to Henzel)
(D-LEsta, 21081/7378 no. 2).

score, like the trios in P 367, has been identified as a Breitkopf *Stammhandschrift*. The five trio sources were copied in Leipzig by four different scribes by or before 1763.[61] P 367 and 21081/7378 are marked by the same possessor's entry ("Schneider").

Because Schneider is a common German last name, we must exhibit caution when identifying the person who transmitted these sources. The Leipzig University en-

---

Keferstein in Penig/Saxonia, fl. 1741–75). The other compositions in P 367 (fascicle 5–12) do not match works listed in the Breitkopf catalogs/sources; see Darrell M. Berg, *Miscellaneous Sonatas from Prints I*, cpeb:cw, 1/5.1 (2007), 103 (source B 1).

61. We can associate the scribe of the trio Wq 163, Carl Friedrich Barth (1734–1813), formerly known as Anon. N 5 (Kobayashi) or "Doles-Schreiber," with J. S. Bach; Barth worked for the *Thomaskantor*

Table 4. Breitkopf trio sources for works of C. P. E. Bach

Work	Breitkopf catalog	Possessor	Call no.
Wq 163 / H 588 F major, fg/fl/b/cemb	Cat. Breitkopf 1763, col. 12, no. I	"Lucius"	P 367 (old number: "no. 1")
Wq 149 / H 573 C major, fl/vn/b	Cat. Breitkopf 1763, col. 12, no. II	"Schneider"	P 367 (old number: "no. 2")
Wq 151 / H 575 D major, fl/vn/b	Cat. Breitkopf 1763, col. 12, no. III		P 367 (old number: "no. 3")
Wq 148 / H 572 A minor, fl/vn/b	Cat. Breitkopf 1763, col. 12, no. IV		P 367 (old number: "no. 4")
Wq 158 / H 584 Trio in B-flat major, score, version for two violins	Cat. Breitkopf 1763, col. 12, no. V	"Schneider"	21081/7378 no. 1 (old number: "no. 5")

Fig. 9. Trio in B-flat Major, Wq 158. Unknown copyist, provenance "Schneider" (D-LEsta, 21081/7378 no. 1).

rollment included several students with this name, but so far none can be traced to Leipzig's concert life between 1750 and 1770.[62] One of the candidates, Johann Schneider (1702–88), was Bach's pupil at Köthen (1720); court organist and violinist at the Saalfeld court (from 1721); violinist at the Weimar court (from 1726); and organist of St. Nicholas's in Leipzig (beginning in 1729). He was also mentioned above in connection with the trio by W. F. Bach. Johann Schneider also played violin and, during the 1740s, organized the Grosses Concert.[63] We know little of his activity as a violinist in Leipzig's concert life; perhaps by the 1760s he no longer played violin, at which point he might have sold or given away the music sources.[64]

Johann Christian Bach and Leipzig Concert Life from 1764 until the Era of the Early Gewandhaus Concerts

The sources in Table 5 comprise relatively early sinfonias by the youngest Bach son. They feature watermarks of a Saxon origin that are typical of numerous Breitkopf sources, but they do not at all resemble other known Bach sources.[65] Their copyists

---

from 1746 until Bach's death. See M. Maul and P. Wollny, "Quellenkundliches zu Bach-Aufführungen in Köthen, Ronneburg und Leipzig zwischen 1720 und 1760," BJ 89 (2003): 97–141 (esp. 110–19). Barth copied much more C. P. E. Bach chamber music that was sold by Breitkopf, including sales copies of keyboard sonatas, now preserved in US-Wc. See Daniel F. Boomhower, "C. P. E. Bach Sources at the Library of Congress," in *Notes* 70, no. 4 (June 2014): 597–659 (esp. 620–23); and in D-BNba, Sammlung Grundmann, see *Miscellaneous Sonatas from Prints I*, ed. Darrell M. Berg, CPEB:CW, I/5.1 (2007), 104–5 (source B 6).

62. Georg Erler, *Die Immatrikulationen vom Wintersemester 1709 bis zum Sommersemester 1809*, Die jüngere Matrikel der Universität Leipzig, 1559–1809 (Leipzig: Giesecke & Devrient, 1909), 3:365–67.

63. Schering, *Musikgeschichte Leipzigs*, 263–64. Riemer's "Tabula Musicorum" (see note 55) mentions him as "Concertist auf dem Clavicemb[alo]" and on the second violin. Another prominent potential candidate, the composer (Johann Christian) Friedrich Schneider (1786–1853), must be ruled out as the possessor of the trio sources, since these *Stammhandschriften* must have been in Breitkopf's archive already in the early 1760s.

64. Johann Schneider's expert reports on newly built or renovated organs bear his name, but they are not by his own hand (e.g., Schneider's examination of the organ in Leipzig-Eutritzsch from 1736, Hauptstaatsarchiv Dresden, Ratslandesgericht, 9401, fol. 14v; Lynn Butler kindly provided copies of this source). Some records are signed by Schneider, but not more; we are lacking reliable handwriting samples with Latin characters. From 1766, an unrelated organist by the same name, Carl Heinrich Schneider (ca. 1735–90), substituted for Johann in his post at St. Nicholas; see Reinhard Vollhardt, *Geschichte der Cantoren und Organisten von den Städten im Königreich Sachsen*, Berlin 1899, facsimile ed. Hans-Joachim Schulze (Leipzig: Peters, 1978), 179.

65. See Yoshitake Kobayashi, "On the Identification of Breitkopf's Manuscripts," in Stauffer, *Bach Perspectives 2*, 112–13. Although the sets of parts in D-LEsta are *Stammhandschriften*, they partially match watermarks typically found in Breitkopf sales copies.

Table 5. Breitkopf *Stammhandschriften* for works of J. C. Bach (parts, all in D-LEsta)

Work	Breitkopf catalog	Copyist	Call no.
Warb C 15 Sinfonia in F major	Cat. Breitkopf 1766, suppl. I, p. 2	Three unknown	21081/7372 no. 1
Warb G 5/1 Sinfonia in B-flat "Zanaida" overture	Cat. Breitkopf 1773, suppl. VIII, p. 4	Three unknown (partly the same as in 7372/1)	21081/7372 no. 2
Warb C 17b Sinfonia in B-flat major	Cat. Breitkopf 1773, suppl. VIII, p. 4	Three unknown (partly the same as in 7372/1–2)	21081/7372 no. 3
Warb G 22/1 Sinfonia in D major "La Giulia" overture	Cat. Breitkopf 1766, suppl. I, p. 2	"Anon. Breitkopf 6"[1]	21081/7372 no. 4[2]
Warb YC 48 Sinfonia in E-flat major spurious[3]	Cat. Breitkopf 1767 suppl. II, p. 2	Unknown	21081/7372 no. 6

1. According to Y. Kobayashi, Schreiberkartei (card files) Johann-Sebastian-Bach-Institut Göttingen (now in D-LEb).
2. An extra bass part of Warb G 22/1 is transmitted in 7372 no. 5 (scribe: "J. S. Bach XXI," according to Blechschmidt); it was reused later as a cover for other manuscripts in the archive.
3. Also attributed to J. Haydn, s. Hob. III: Es.10.

and overall appearance also differ. Nevertheless, it is likely that eighteenth-century Leipzig ensembles used these performance parts.

Scholarship has paid little attention to the eighteenth-century Leipzig reception of the youngest Bach son. Few sources provide details concerning Leipzig performances of his works. Most of what we know about Leipzig concert life in the second half of the eighteenth century stems from the writings of Ernst Ludwig Gerber (1746–1819) and Johann Adam Hiller (1728–1804). The rest comes from (now lost) concert programs, auction catalogs of Hiller's and Johann Gottfried Schicht's personal music libraries, and Breitkopf's catalogs.

Musical sources that can be traced back to a Leipzig performance are extremely rare. One is Johann Christoph Farlau's copy of the performance parts for Johann Christian Bach's Harpsichord Concerto in F Minor, Warb C 73.[66] A student of Johann Christoph

66. D-LEb, Go. S. 40. The watermarks (a) large fleur-de-lis, surmounted by a coronet, with "IESV" below; (b) LW point to the paper mill of Johann Eucharius Siegfried Vodel (fl. 1742–62) in Niederlungwitz in Saxony and give an approximate date range. The information on the scribe follows

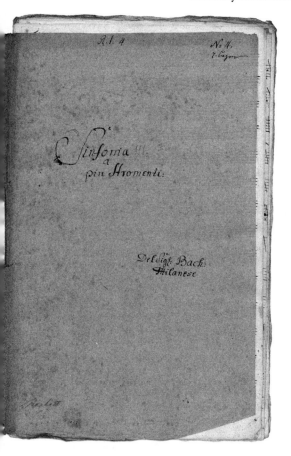

Fig. 10. "Del Sig: Bach: Milanese," Sinfonia in F Major, Warb C 15. Unknown copyists between 1764 and 1766 (D-LEsta, 21081/7372 no. 1).

Altnickol in Naumburg, Farlau (b. 1734–35) later studied in Jena (1756) and Leipzig (from 1767 until at least 1770) and collected a great deal of music by members of the Bach family. Among scholars, he is best known for transmitting the only source of the early version of the *St. Matthew Passion*, BWV 244b.[67] Farlau also copied instrumental music and may himself have participated as a player of the harpsichord in Leipzig's concert life during the 1760s: he prepared performing parts for harpsichord concertos

Peter Wollny, "Neuerkenntnisse zur Bach-Überlieferung in Mitteldeutschland," BJ 88 (2002): 36–47 (esp. 42–45). During his stay in Leipzig, Farlau worked for a lawyer; he has been traced in archival documents from September 1766 until October 1770.

67. Wollny, "Neuerkenntnisse," 42. According to Wollny, there is no documentary evidence for Farlau's stay after October 1770.

by (or ascribed to) Wilhelm Friedemann Bach (Concertos in D Major, br-wfb C 9, and G Minor, br-wfb C 17) and by Johann Christoph Friedrich Bach (Concerto in C Minor, br-jcfb C 46), as well as a lost concerto in an unknown key by Christoph Nichelmann, who was W. F. Bach's pupil in Leipzig and (ostensibly) C. P. E. Bach's pupil in Berlin.[68] He inscribed his monogram, JCF, on the title pages of these works, which probably indicates they were for personal use.

At the same time, another student in Leipzig with high musical ambitions was the later music historian Ernst Ludwig Gerber. In February 1768 Gerber copied out a harpsichord concerto by J. C. Bach (A major, Warb C 50), which he probably performed in Leipzig as the soloist.[69] Gerber's catalog shows that he owned a significant number of compositions for solo keyboard and orchestra, among them five works by (or attributed to) J. C. Bach.[70] Gerber—who himself performed as a student in several orchestras in Leipzig between 1765 and 1768—reported some details of the programs under Hiller's direction:

> Each concert consisted of two parts, between which a pause for relaxation was made. In the first part one began with a sinfonia, then followed 2) an aria, 3) a concerto, then 4) a *Divertissement* for several instruments, a quartet, solo, or a chorus from an opera. The second part resumed again with a sinfonia, then followed an aria, and in conclusion a *Parthie* for the entire orchestra. In each concerto the solo instruments changed. The arias, concertos, and sinfonias were rehearsed ahead of time on a designated day. All pieces for each concert, however, were selected by *Kapellmeister* Hiller, and the name of every participant in the concert was identified on a sheet of paper. There one found not only the names of the composers, singers, and players but also the texts of what was sung.
>
> In the years from 1765 to 1768, at which time I was a member, the orchestra comprised 16 violins, namely 8 firsts and 8 seconds, 3 violas, 2 violoncellos, 2 contrabasses, 2 flutes, 2 oboes, 2 bassoons, 2 horns, 1 lute, and 1 keyboard [the names of many but not all of the musicians follow here]. The excellence of all these virtuosos

68. D-Bsa, SA 243 (J. C. F. Bach, only the title cover is extant: the watermark points to a Thuringian provenance of the source); SA 253 (Nichelmann, only the title cover is extant); D-B, Mus. ms. Bach St 586 (W. F. Bach, br-wfb C 9).

69. B-Bc, 27134, fascicle 14, "Cembalo Concertato. di Chr. Bach / Londr:" (heading). Only the solo harpsichord part has survived. It bears the following date inscription: "E. L. Gerber d. 1 Febr. / 1768" (p. 7). See Leisinger and Wollny, *Die Bach-Quellen der Bibliotheken in Brüssel*, 498–99.

70. *Musikalische Werke sowohl theoretische als praktische: Dramatische Gedichte: Bildniße berühmter Tonkünstler und Prospekte und Abriße berühmter und merkwürdiger Orgeln: Gesammlet und angeschaft von: Ernst Ludwig Gerber Sondershausen 1791* (A-Wgm 1656/3). Five concertos in manuscript are mentioned there; the other four are numbered as "Concert I" through "Concert IV." The key and setting of the last one match Warb C 50 (p. 108). The two printed works mentioned (Riga: Hartknoch, 1776) are instead by J. C. F. Bach.

is demonstrated in part by the positions they previously held in princely orchestras and partly by the positions of honor and the reputation they had achieved afterward. The remainder of the orchestra was made up of young students, which Mr. Hiller had selected as the most useable from among those present, and also a few good members of the local town piper band, who played wind instruments.

Jedes Conzert bestand aus 2 Theilen, zwischen welchen eine Pause zur Erholung gemacht wurde. Im ersten Theile fieng man mit einer Sinfonie an, dann folgte 2) eine Arie, dieser 3) ein Conzert, hierauf 4) ein Divertissement für mehrere Instrumente, ein Quatro, Solo, oder ein Chor aus einer Oper. Der zweyte Theil hub wieder mit einer Sinfonie an, dann folgte eine Arie, und zum Beschluß eine Parthie für das ganze Orchester. In jedem Conzerte wechselten die conzertierenden Instrumente. Die Arien, Conzerts und Sinfonien wurden jedesmal an einem dazu bestimmten Tage vorher geprobt. Alle Stücke aber zu jedem Conzerte [wurden] vom Herrn Kapellmeister Hiller gewählt, und jedem Theilnehmer des Conzerts auf einem gedruckten Zettel bekannt gemacht. Man fand darauf nicht allein die Namen der Komponisten, der Sänger und Spieler, sondern auch die Texte von demjenigen, was gesungen wurde.

Das Orchester bestand in den Jahren 1765, 66, 67 und 68, zu welcher Zeit ich selbst als Mitglied dabey stand, aus 16 Violinen, nemlich 8 für die erste und soviel für die zweyte; 3 Bratschen, 2 Vionzells, 2 Contraviolons, 2 Flöten, 2 Oboen, 2 Fagotten, 2 Hörnern, 1 Laute und 1 Flügel (Here he gives names of the musicians and singers). Die Vortreflichkeit aller dieser Virtuosen beweisen theils die Aemter, in denen sie vorher bey Fürstl[ichen] Kapellen gestanden haben, theils die musikalischen Ehrenstellen, und der Ruf, zu denen sie nach der Zeit gelangt sind. Der übrige Theil dieses Orchesters bestand theils aus jungen Studierenden, welche Herr Hiller unter den Anwesenden, als die brauchbarsten, ausgewählt hatte, theils in einigen braven Mitgliedern des dasigen Stadtpfeiferchores, zu den blasenden Instrumenten.[71]

---

71. Gerber, "Hiller," cols. 640–41. Gerber lists the names of the professional players and singers of the Grosses Concert, following Riemer's "Tabula Musicorum" (1746–48) (cols. 639–40). They can be identified as follows: concertmaster, Johann Georg Häser (1729–1809); solo violinists, Carl Gottlieb Berger (ca. 1736–1812), in Leipzig, and Carl Gottlieb Göpfert (1733–98), at the time of writing concertmaster in Weimar; viola, Gottlob Friedrich Hertel (d. 1795), at the time of writing organist at the reformed church in Leipzig; violoncello, Johann Friedrich Berger junior (d. 1786); flutists, Johann George Tromlitz (1725–1805) and the lawyer Gottlieb Gottwald Hunger (1741–96), both still in Leipzig at the time of writing; oboist, Johann Gottlieb Herzog(?) (d. 1794), and bassoonist, Andreas Christoph Jonne (d. 1784), both town musicians; lute and viola da gamba, respectively, were played by two members of Graf Brühl's Kapelle, Johann Kropf(f)gans junior (1708-ca. 1771) and J. D. Müller; and pianists, Georg Simon Löhlein (1725–81), who later died as *Kapellmeister* in Danzig, and the above-named lawyer, Gottlieb Gottwald Hunger. Gerber names a gambist but does not include the instrument in his itemization of the instruments; it is unclear if this player was among the players of the "two" cellos he lists. He also omits the names of the ripieno violins and violists, all of the contrabassists, and the horn players.

After the Seven Years' War ended on February 15, 1763, with the Prussian occupation in Leipzig, the city's cultural life and its music distribution rebounded. Johann Adam Hiller conducted concerts in Leipzig at the inn Zu den drei Schwanen, the regular concert hall for performances by the Grosses Concert since its establishment in 1738. Breitkopf was heavily involved in these concerts: the firm supported their organization and the creation of programs and thereby profited from the city's flourishing concert life. Beginning in March 1764, Breitkopf's account books record occasional expenses for the printing of concert programs and librettos for the Grosses Concert.[72] The same records document expenses "für geschriebene und gedruckte Musikalien" (for written and printed music) that had been acquired by the concert society between the years 1764 and 1778, the last year it was active.[73]

A paucity of research has made it impossible to determine to what extent Breitkopf's catalogs reflected Leipzig's overall concert life. Furthermore, the firm's records were completely lost during World War II. It was not until the twentieth century that Hermann von Hase, a former Breitkopf owner who recorded the firm's history, and Arnold Schering, who wrote Leipzig's music history, cited significant amounts of information derived from programs, librettos, letters, and other lost records.[74] Such sources make it clear that Johann Adam Hiller exercised the greatest impact on Leipzig's concert life at the time. An excerpt from the 1805 auction catalog of Hiller's estate shows that he was probably the first in Leipzig to present Italian compositions by J. C. Bach.[75] In

72. Hermann von Hase, "Johann Adam Hiller und Breitkopfs," in *Zeitschrift für Musikwissenschaft* 2, no. 1 (Leipzig: Breitkopf & Härtel, 1919): 3–4. Hase lists thirty-nine concert programs in the season 1764/65; thirty-one in 1765/66; thirty-two in 1766/67; twenty-four in 1767/68; twenty-four in 1768/69; and so on. "[In] 1765 a short-lived ensemble, the Gelehrten-Konzert, was established at the university. Ten years later Hiller formed the Musikübende Gesellschaft, and it was this group that swiftly rose to prominence" (George B. Stauffer, "Leipzig," *Grove Music Online*, accessed 18 December 2015, http://www.oxfordmusiconline.com/subscriber/article/grove/music/16353).

73. Hermann von Hase ("Johann Adam Hiller und Breitkopfs," 6) cites the records without giving corresponding proof for the exact years.

74. On Schering's *Musikgeschichte Leipzigs*, see note 55.

75. [Hoffmeister & Kühnel], *Erste Fortsetzung des Catalogs geschriebener, meist seltener Musikalien, auch theoretischer Werke, welche im Bureau de Musique von Hoffmeister et Kühnel zu haben sind. NB. Grösstentheils aus J. A. Hiller's Nachlass* (Leipzig: Friedrich Schödel, [1805]). Hiller worked for J. G. I. Breitkopf translating books; he is traceable in the archive's records from 1761 to 1768: "Eine willkommenere und auch seinen Fähigkeiten entsprechendere Tätigkeit verschaffte ihm jedoch Breitkopf durch die Übertragung der Korrektur und Revision einer großen Anzahl von Musikalien, deren Druck die gewaltig aufblühende Notendruckerei übernommen hatte. Auch bei anderen musikalischen Arbeiten wurde Hillers Unterstützung in Anspruch genommen, so wurde er verschiedentlich mit der Bezifferung des Basses von Sonaten oder Trios betraut" (Hase, "Johann Adam Hiller und Breitkopfs," 1–2).

1785 Hiller edited the volume *Deutsche Arien und Duette von verschiedenen Componisten, in Concerten und am Claviere zu singen* (German arias and duets by various composers, to be sung in concerts and at the keyboard), which included two arias in German translation by (or attributed to) Bach.[76] Hiller's collection cannot be reconstructed with certainty because some of the musical sources named in the catalog cannot be identified; however, Table 6 shows that he owned compositions from every musical genre.

In 1764 the lost Breitkopf records mention the premiere of a "Sinfonia" by Johann Christian Bach at the Drei Schwanen-Concerts, where the composer is still referred to as "Signore Bach Milan."[77] Two years later, in 1766, the Breitkopf firm announced one of Bach's Milanese sinfonias for sale. Table 7 attempts to connect the various pieces of documentary evidence of the early reception of Bach's sinfonias in Leipzig.

The concert programs do not reveal which of Bach's sinfonias were performed. However, if we compare the two entries with the newly found sources, we see at least two matches. The two sources from the 1766 catalog read "del Sigl: Bach: *Milanese*" (emphasis added) and therefore must be the oldest ones, for the three later sources are attributed instead to "Signore Bach." Interestingly, all five sets of parts are *Stammhandschriften*. Their overall appearance (varying copyists, some not professional; various watermarks; divergent layouts) indicates that they first circulated in practical use before becoming part of the firm's archive.

Of additional interest is the Sinfonia in F Major, Warb C 15 (see Figure 10). Because the sinfonia was printed only in 1770, the Breitkopf manuscript source must have originated earlier, making it one of the manuscripts not copied from the print.[78] The Staatsbibliothek zu Berlin also transmits a group of sales copies of Johann Christian Bach's sinfonias. Here we find four additional sources bearing the Milano ascription that were offered as a set in the catalog from 1766 but that, in contrast to the sources in D-LEsta, were copied by a single—professional—scribe.[79] One of the four Berlin

76. RISM B/II, 152; see Ernest Warburton, ed., *The Collected Works of Johann Christian Bach*, vol. 48, pt. 2, sources and documents (New York: Garland, 1999), 405–6. Hiller in 1774 started a series of smaller pieces for keyboard and singing (*Sammlung kleiner Clavier- und Singstücke*). Together with the Breitkopf's edition a series of thirty small *Sammlungen* was published (RISM B/II, 347/2; see Warburton, *Collected Works*, vol. 48, pt. 2, 429); the fifth *Sammlung* (1774) contained the Andante from the Sinfonia in E-flat Major, Warb C 18, in keyboard reduction. The sinfonia had been published only in 1773 (RISM A/I B 238) and was thus sold via the Breitkopf auction catalog in 1773.

77. Cited in Schering, *Musikgeschichte Leipzigs*, 412.

78. Ernest Warburton, ed., *The Collected Works of Johann Christian Bach*, vol. 48, pt. 1, thematic catalog (New York: Garland, 1999), 90–91.

79. Cat. Breitkopf 1766, col. 2 (Brook, *The Breitkopf Thematic Catalogues*, col. 202); D-B, Mus. ms. Bach St 609 (Sinfonia in F Major, Warb C 15), St 610 (Sinfonia in E-flat Major, Warb C 11), St 613

Table 6. Hiller's personal collection of works by or attributed to J. C. Bach

Catalog entry	Work	Extant source / call no.
"Bach, J. C. Gloria in G. St[immen]"	Warb E 4	D-B, Mus. ms. Bach St 289[1]
"Gloria in G. P[artitur]" (p. 2)	Warb E 4	
"Bach etc. 4 Arie p. Sop." (p. 19)		
"Bach, Hasse, Naumann, 4 Arie p. Sopr. St." (p. 21)		
"Bach, Naumann, 3 ital. Arien und 1 Duett (deutsch) p. Sopr. P. St." (p. 21)		
"Bach, Jomelli, Sacchini, 3 Arie p. Sopr. P. St." (p. 21)		
"Bach, Naumann etc., 4 Arie p. Sop. P. St." (p. 21)		
"Bach, Graun, 4 Arie p. Sopr. P. St." (p. 21)		
"Anfossi, Bach, Bertoni, 3 Arie p. Sopr. St." (p. 22)		
"Bach, Sarti, 3 Scene. P. St." (p. 24)		
"Bach, Mislivezek, 2 Quartetti. P. St." (p. 24)		
"Bach etc., 3 Quintetti. P. St." (p. 24)		
"Bach, La Tempesta. Cantata. P. St." (p. 25)	Warb G 16[2]	
"Bach, J. C., Armina, Cantata à 3. St." (p. 26) [Rinaldo et Armida]	Warb G 20 (lost composition from 1778)	
"Bach, The favorite Songs in the Opera: L'Olimpiade. P." (p. 27)	Warb G 28 (RISM B/II, p. 176)	
"Bach, The favorite Songs in the Opera: Il Orione ed Adriano in Siria. P." (p. 27)	Warb G 4 (RISM B/BB 182) Warb G 6 (RISM B/BB 166)	
"Bach, J. C., 6 Sinf." (p. 29)		
"Bach, Galuppi, Platti, 3 Concerte" (p. 30) [keyboard concertos]		
"Bach, 5 Sonates p. Cembalo Viol. o Fl. e B[asso]" (p. 30)		
"Bach, J. Ch., 6 Canzonets a 2 V[oci]." (p. 36)	Warb H 12–17 (RISM B/BB 218) or H 18–23 (RISM B/BB 221)	

1. Parts (scribe: J. A. Hiller). There is another source in D-B, Mus. ms. Bach P 385 that has the same *Gloria* in score. It might have been written by a Leipzig copyist.
2. J. C. F. Bach also set this text to music; the auction catalog entry may have referred to his cantata (BR-JCFB G 25) instead.

sources transmits the same sinfonia: the Ouverture to *La Giulia*, Warb G 22/1. However, because the two concordant sources do not transmit the same readings, we can establish no connection whatsoever between them.[80] This one case in point can serve to demonstrate the general nature of Breitkopf source transmission.[81]

It is possible for a given composition to have more than one *Stammhandschrift*. In 1770 Huberty in Paris published a series of six sinfonias by J. C. Bach.[82] When Hiller announced this novelty, he provided incipits "so that one may see whether these sinfonies here are new, or whether one might already possess one or another of them."[83] He mentioned that two of them already had been transmitted in manuscripts in Leipzig: "The third [C major, Warb G 24/1] has been known here in manuscript already for a couple of years; the fourth [E-flat major, Warb C 11] is also already found in the Breitkopf catalog, and namely in the Supplem[ent]. I. sub tit[ulum] Bach no. V."[84] The two references offer still more proof that manuscripts of Bach's sinfonias frequently circulated during the 1760s in Leipzig.

We can only surmise how Bach's Milan compositions may have found their way to Leipzig. Perhaps Bach himself brought them to his hometown, which lay on one of the regular routes to the north leading to the Hamburg port. He could have passed through Leipzig on his way from Milan to London in May 1762. Although his mother,

---

(Ouverture to *Artaserse*, Warb G 1/1), and St 615 (Ouverture to *La Giulia*, Warb G 22), copied by "Anon. Breitkopf 5" (following Joachim Jaenecke, *Joseph und Michael Haydn: Autographe und Abschriften*, Staatsbibliothek Preußischer Kulturbesitz. Kataloge der Musikabteilung. Erste Reihe: Handschriften 4 [Munich: Henle, 1990]), which is "Anon. Breitkopf 44" following Kobayashi.

80. In fact, together with the single basso part (with figured bass), we have altogether three Breitkopf sources for this ouverture. By comparison with the sources in D-LEsta, the incomplete Berlin sources (the set of parts lacks the two violins) show deviating readings; there is no figured bass, but there are considerably more dynamics and articulation marks.

81. The two sources for the Trio in B-flat Major, Wq 158, by C. P. E. Bach give a similar impression: the score in D-LEsta 21081/7378, written out by nonprofessional scribes, deviates from the set of parts (D-LEsta 21081/7379); the parts show no figuration of the bass and deviate in slurring and appoggiaturas. These parts, full of mistakes, were used by Breitkopf neither as a *Stammhandschrift* nor as a sales copy.

82. *Six Simphonies A huit parties Composée Par Jean Bach* ... (Paris: Huberty, 1770), RISM BB 232a. One of them, the Sinfonia in E-flat Major, Warb YC 51, is presumed spurious by Warburton.

83. "Damit man sehen könne, ob diese Sinfonien an jedem Orte neu sind, oder ob man nicht eine oder die andere davon schon habe." Johann Adam Hiller, *Musikalische Nachrichten und Anmerkungen auf das Jahr 1770* (Leipzig: In Verlag der Zeitungs-Expedition, 1770), 24 ("Drittes Stück, 15th January 1770"). Hiller refers to cat. Breitkopf 1766, col. 2 (Brook, *The Breitkopf Thematic Catalogues*, col. 202).

84. "Die dritte ist hiesigen Orts in Manuscript schon seit ein paar Jahren bekannt; die vierte findet man auch schon im Breitkopfischen Catalogo, und zwar im Supplem. I. sub tit. Bach no. V." Ibid.

Table 7. J. C. Bach's sinfonias in Leipzig, in D-LEsta, 21081/7372

Work/ascription in D-LEsta, 21081/7372	Breitkopf cat. no.	Date of origin / first performance	Publisher/date	Hiller's Drei Schwanen-Concerts at Leipzig
Warb C 15 no. 1. Sinfonia F major "del Sigl: Bach Milanese"	Cat. 1766, col. 2 (Brook, *The Breitkopf Thematic Catalogues*, col. 202)	Milano, ?	Amsterdam (S. Markordt) 1770; RISM BB 235a	June 14, 1764: "Sinfonia dal Sign. Bach Milan"
Warb G 22/1 no. 4/5. Sinfonia D major Ouverture Pastiche *La Giulia* ("del Sig: Bach Milanese")	Cat. 1766, col. 2 (Brook, col. 202)	Milano, Carnival 1760	London (J. Welcker) 1766; RISM B/BB 252	July 16 1766: "Sinfonia del Sigr. Bach"
Warb YC 48 (spurious) no. 2. Sinfonia E-flat major	Cat. 1767, col. 2 (Brook, col. 258)			
Warb C 17b no. 3. Sinfonia B-flat major	Cat. 1773, col. 4 (Brook, col. 484)	London, 1767/68	Den Haag (B. Hummel) 1773; RISM B/BB 238	
Warb G 5/1 no. 6. Sinfonia B-flat major (Ouv. *Zanaida*)	Cat. 1773, col. 4 (Brook, col. 484)	London, May 7, 1763	Den Haag (B. Hummel) 1773; RISM B/BB 238	

Anna Magdalena, was no longer alive (she died in 1760), he may have wished to see his siblings again, or he may have wanted to establish further musical contacts in his hometown, such as with J. G. I. Breitkopf.[85] At any rate, the Breitkopf nonthematic catalog from early 1763 offers "Bach, Milanese VI. Sinf. à 8 Voci a 6 th[a]l[er]" as an "Anhang einiger neuer geschriebenen Musikalien" (appendix of some newly copied music).[86] The sinfonias were offered "nach der Ostermesse" (after the Easter fair) of 1763, making them the first offer of music by Johann Christian Bach in Leipzig.[87]

Hiller also owned a copied set of parts of Bach's *Gloria* in D Major, Warb E 4, composed in 1759–60. It was never printed in Bach's lifetime, nor was it ever distributed by the Breitkopf firm.[88] It is thus difficult to imagine how this *Gloria*, a major church composition, could reach Leipzig via Hiller and Schicht, except by way of the (now lost) autograph or the composer himself. The autographs of Bach's other major Italian church compositions were transmitted in different ways, but none of them seem to have found their way to Leipzig. The Grosses Concert programs show that Bach's works were performed in Leipzig several times. Since most of the concert programs have been lost, we must depend upon the firm's own written history and Schering's volumes in the series Musikgeschichte Leipzigs for additional information about those performances. The Breitkopf *Stammhandschriften* for Bach's sinfonias give the impression that the sources frequently were used as performance parts, after which Breitkopf offered them for sale. The music dealer probably acquired these parts—written by several nonprofessional copyists—directly from the musicians themselves.

Johann Gottfried Schicht (1753–1823), a later *Thomaskantor*, also collected music by J. C. Bach. An accomplished performer of solo keyboard music, the twenty-three-year-old Schicht came to Leipzig University in 1776 to study law. He performed in Hiller's Grosses Concert until the concerts ended on March 29, 1778. A program dated

85. Of J. C. Bach's twelve siblings, only five were still alive in 1762: Gottfried Heinrich (1724–63); Elisabeth Juliana Friederica ("Liesgen") (1726–81), who married Altnickol in Naumburg but lived again in Leipzig after her husband's death in 1759; Johann Christoph Friedrich (1732–95) in Bückeburg; and Johanna Carolina (1737–81) and Regina Susanna (1742–1809), both in Leipzig.

86. *Verzeichniß Musikalischer Bücher sowohl zur Theorie als Praxis, und für alle Instrumente, in ihre gehörige Classen ordentlich eingetheilt; welche bei Bernhard Christoph Breitkopf und Sohn in Leipzig . . . zu bekommen sind, Dritte Ausgabe, Leipzig, nach der Ostermesse 1763*, 88.

87. Whether the sinfonias in the thematic catalog of 1766 (Brook, *The Breitkopf Thematic Catalogues*, col. 202) match the six sinfonias from the nonthematic catalog of 1763 is uncertain. The works have not yet been identified.

88. D-B, Mus. ms. Bach St 289.

January 22, 1778, names Schicht as the keyboard soloist in a concerto.[89] This role is affirmed by Schicht's autobiography:

> Already in the first years of my academic career, I was chosen as a performer of keyboard [*Flügel*] concertos in the Dreyschwanen-Concerts. Because this ceased and *Kapellmeister* Hiller introduced me to *Kapellmeister* Naumann, who installed a similar institution [series of concerts] in Apel's house, now Thomas's house, I thus became responsible for both concerto solos on the harpsichord and on the organ.[90] A similar thing took place at the Gewandhaus concert hall, where from 1781 to 1785 I was also simultaneously appointed as a first violinist.[91]

> Schon in den ersten Jahren meiner akademischen Laufbahn wählte man mich zum Konzertspieler auf dem Flügel in dem Dreyschwanen=Konzerte. Da dieses nun einging und der Kapellm[eister]. Hiller, an den ich vom Kapellm. Naumann nachdrücklich empfohlen war, ein ähnliches Institut im Apelschen, jetzt Thomäischen Hause errichtete; so übertrug er mir ebenfalls das Konzert= und Orgelspielen. Ein Gleiches geschah auf dem Saale des Gewandhauses, von 1781 bis 1785, wo ich auch zugleich bey der ersten Violine angestellt war.[92]

From his autobiography we learn that Schicht served as a first violinist from 1781 to 1785 in the Gewandhaus concerts, which he conducted from 1785 until 1810. From this point in time he became the *Thomaskantor*, a position he retained until his death in 1823.

Schicht's estate catalog of 1832 offers a vivid impression of the earlier stages of his life, particularly with regard to his involvement in Leipzig's concert life. It shows that

---

89. The other posts Schicht held are not mentioned here because they don't concern the J. C. Bach sources in D-LEsta.

90. The Dresden *Kapellmeister* Johann Gottlieb Naumann (1741–1801) kept very close contact with his teacher Hiller; see Andreas Glöckner, "Ein unbekannter Besuch Joseph Haydns auf der Leipziger Thomasschule," BJ 101 (2015): 247–56 (esp. 250–51). Documentation as to whether Naumann also conducted concerts in Leipzig has yet to surface; if he did, these concerts may have taken place in the late 1760s or early 1770s, in between his travels to Italy. Thomas's house is presently the Königshaus, located in the Leipzig marketplace (Markt 17 / Petersstraße 13). The concert hall was located in the rear house of this famous Leipzig building.

91. The concerts moved to the newly built concert hall in the second floor of the Gewandhaus (presently Universitätsstraße/Gewandgäßchen) in 1781.

92. Article "Schicht (Johann Gottfried)" in Ernst Ludwig Gerber, *Neues historisch-biographisches Lexikon der Tonkünstler, welches Nachrichten von dem Leben und den Werken musikalischer Schriftsteller, berühmter Komponisten, Sänger, Meister auf Instrumenten, kunstvoller Dilettanten, Musikverleger, auch Orgel- und Instrumentenmacher, älterer und neuerer Zeit, aus allen Nationen enthält* (Leipzig: Breitkopf & Härtel, 1814), 4, cols. 58–59.

Table 8. Schicht's personal collection of works by or attributed to J. C. Bach

Entry	Work	Extant source
"Bach, J. C. Gloria in G major, Part. 48 1/2 Bog. Stimmen 83 Bog[en]." (p. 4, no. 96)	Warb E 4[1]	
"J. C. Bach, Bach Milanese. 12 Concerte p. le Clavecin. 106 B[o]g[en]." (p. 29, no. 905) [probably prints or copied after the prints op. 1, op. 7, or op. 13, which contain altogether three series of six concerts; see Warb C 49–54, 55–60, and 62–67]		
"Bach, J. C., 6 Sonaten, Op. 18. 6 Sonaten. Op. 15" (p. 32, no. 942); both opp. are for keyboard [probably prints: RISM B/BB 343 and B 358]	Warb A 18–A 21	
"Bach, C. F. E., Bach, Milano, Abel, Holzbauer, Schwindel, diver. Sinfonies p. l'Orchestre" (p. 35, no. 1021)		
"Haydn, J., Bach Mil., Ude, Corzetti, Campioni, Hoffmann L. Ditters, Trios p. 2 Violons e Basso" (p. 36, no. 1030)		
"Bach, J., Bertoni, Bianchi, Boroni, Galuppi, 7 Duette [from operas] Part. und Stimmen 90 Bg." (p. 48, no. 1260)		
"Andreozzi, Anfossi, Bach, G. Ch., Benda, Cannabich, Caruso, Gazzaniga, Haydn, Hasse, 16 Arien [for bass] in Part[itur]. 80 Bg." (p. 48, no. 1273); excerpts from operas:[2]		D-LEm, Becker III.15.31/1–2
"Contrasto assai più degno" from the opera *Temistocle*	Warb G 8/6	D-LEm, Becker III.15.31/1, copyist Schicht
Rec. "Eccoti in altra sorte" and aria "Non m'alletta quell riso fallace" from *Temistocle*	Warb G 8/7a–b	D-LEm, Becker III.15.31/2, anon. copyist
"Bach, Benda, Bertoja, Bianchi, Boroni, Borghi, Campioni, Caruso, 24 Arien [for Soprano], theils in Stimmen und theils in Part" (p. 49, no. 1284); excerpts from (pastiche) operas:		D-WRgs, Goethe Notensammlung 32/349
"Chiari fonti" [originally inserted in Gluck's opera *Orfeo ed Euridice*]	Warb G 29/3	D-WRgs, Goethe Notensammlung 32/349(1)
"Accorda, amico, il fanto" [originally inserted into Gluck's opera *Orfeo ed Euridice*]	Warb G 29/5	D-WRgs, Goethe Notensammlung 32/349(2)
"Si scorderà l'amante" from the opera *Temistocle*	Warb G 8/8	D-WRgs, Goethe Notensammlung 32/349(3)

Table 8. Continued

Entry	Work	Extant source
"Infelice, in van m'affanno" from the opera *La Clemenza di Scipione*	Warb G 10/17b	D-WRgs, Goethe Notensammlung 32/349(4)
Recitative "Mi scordo i torti miei" and aria "Dolci aurette"	Warb LG 3	D-WRgs, Goethe Notensammlung 32/349(5)
"Se mai turbo il tuo riposo" from the opera *Allessandro nell'Indie*	Warb G 3/6	D-WRgs, Goethe Notensammlung 32/349(6)

1. Cf. Hiller's estate catalog; see p. 50 and footnote 81.
2. Explicit entry: "ex Bibl. Schicht Nr. 1273" (and perhaps Warb G 8/7a–b); no reference to Schicht's catalog.

he owned a significant amount of music by J. C. Bach, namely, twelve harpsichord concertos, an unknown number of sinfonias and trios, a *Gloria* in G major (the same one that Hiller had also possessed), and several opera arias. The catalog also makes clear Schicht's strong interest in Johann Christian Bach's music and other contemporary music (Table 8).[93] Unfortunately, many of these items are listed as groups of numerous works and thus cannot be easily identified.

The auction catalogs of the two influential leaders of the Grosses Concert and the Gewandhaus concerts, Hiller and Schicht—together with the new sources that have come to light—offer some insight into the repertoire of these orchestras (and perhaps other concert societies as well) in Leipzig following the Seven Years' War.[94] Further evaluation of these sources, Breitkopf's manuscripts, and their scribes will shed still

93. *Versteigerungs-Katalog der von dem verstorbenen Herrn J. G. Schicht, Cantor an der Thomasschule zu Leipzig hinterlassenen Musikaliensammlung, welche als Anhang der Bücherauction . . . dem Meistbietenden gegen baare Zahlung überlassen werden soll* (Leipzig, [1832]).

94. A third Leipzig auction catalog contains additional manuscripts with music by J. C. Bach: mainly operas, excerpts from operas, cantatas, keyboard music (solos and concertos), and one sinfonia. However, their provenances are unclear; see [Hoffmeister & Kühnel], *Catalog geschriebener, meist seltener Musikalischen und theoretischer Werke, welche im Bureau de Musique in Leipzig im Fürstenhause zu haben sind* (Leipzig, 1802). A handwritten entry (in the examplar D-B, Mus. Ab 645) reads: "Nachlass eines Goldschlägers [Christoph Friedrich] Werndt in Leipzig, der mit Musicalien gehandelt" (Georg Poelchau).

more light on Leipzig's reception of the music of Johann Christian Bach.[95] Furthermore, these sources will also provide insights into the reception of the youngest Bach son's music in Protestant Germany. With Leipzig as the epicenter of music distribution in the second half of the eighteenth century, a further investigation of the transmission of J. C. Bach's music in Germany must begin in Leipzig.

95. The various catalogs from the St. Thomas school library list sources with music by J. C. Bach, among them four keyboard concertos (three handwritten and one printed) and two arias. See Andreas Glöckner, *Die ältere Notenbibliothek der Thomasschule zu Leipzig: Verzeichnis eines weitgehend verschollenen Bestands*, Leipziger Beiträge zur Bach-Forschung 11 (Hildesheim: Olms, 2011), 64. Many of the musical sources that document the school's involvement in Leipzig's concert life have yet to be traced.

CONTRIBUTORS

CHRISTINE BLANKEN studied in Göttingen and Vienna. She was awarded her doctorate from the University of Göttingen in 1999, at which time she became research assistant at the Johann Sebastian Bach-Institut Göttingen, working on the Göttinger Bach-Katalog. In 2005 she moved to the Bach-Archiv Leipzig, where she currently leads a research team. Her activities include the Bach-Repertorium (editions of Bach family documents and music, and especially the two versions of C. P. E. Bach's *Magnificat* and his *Bürgercapitainsmusiken* for CPEB:CW); the revised *Neue Bach Ausgabe* (organ chorales); Bach digital; and Bach family music reception. She is currently researching Bach's cantata librettist Christoph Birkmann (whom she identified in 2013–14) and Bach's circle of student musicians. She has been active as a church organist since 1990.

EVAN CORTENS holds a PhD in musicology from Cornell University with a focus on eighteenth-century German music. His dissertation examined the cultural and historical context of the sacred works by Christoph Graupner, a contemporary of J. S. Bach. His articles have appeared in *Bach: The Journal of the Riemenschneider Bach Institute* and *Haydn: The Journal of the Haydn Society of North America*, and his edition of Johann Samuel Schroeter's *Six Keyboard Concertos, op. 3* was published by A-R Editions in 2013.

ROBERT L. MARSHALL is Sachar Professor Emeritus of Music at Brandeis University. He is the coauthor, with Traute M. Marshall, of *Exploring the World of J. S. Bach: A Traveler's Guide* (2016); the author of *The Compositional Process of J. S. Bach* (1972; winner, Otto Kinkeldey Award) and *The Music of Johann Sebastian Bach: The Sources, the Style, the Significance* (1989; winner, ASCAP-Deems Taylor Award); the editor of *Eighteenth-Century Keyboard Music* (2nd ed., 2003); and the coeditor of *Variations on the Canon: Essays on Music from Bach to Boulez in Honor of Charles Rosen* (2008). His writings on Bach and Mozart have appeared in the *Bach-Jahrbuch, Bach Perspectives, BACH: Journal of the Riemenschneider Bach Institute*, the *Journal of the American Musicological Society*, the *Musical Quarterly, Commentary*, the *New York Review of Books*, and the *New York Times*.

MARY OLESKIEWICZ, a prize-winning flutist and scholar, is internationally active as a performer, speaker, and master teacher. Her numerous musicological essays, critical editions, and commercial recordings focus on the music of J. S. and C. P. E. Bach, J. J. Quantz, and Frederick the Great and on music at the Berlin court. She has been a contributing editor to *C. P. E. Bach: The Complete Works* and has published critical first editions for AR Editions, Breitkopf & Härtel, and Steglein. She has held research fellowships from the Alexander von Humboldt Foundation and the DAAD and currently serves on the Alumni Council of the American Friends of the Alexander von Humboldt Foundation. A professor of music at the University of Massachusetts Boston, she has also taught historical performance at Queen's College and at the University of the Arts (Berlin). She performs with numerous historical instrument ensembles; her solo recordings have appeared on the Naxos and Hungaroton Classic labels; for more about her, visit www.MaryOleskiewicz.com.

DAVID SCHULENBERG is the author of *The Keyboard Music of J. S. Bach*, books on W. F. and C. P. E. Bach, and the textbook and anthology *Music of the Baroque*, now in its third edition. He has also edited keyboard sonatas and concertos by C. P. E. Bach and is a contributor to the new Breitkopf & Härtel edition of the organ works of J. S. Bach. A performer on harpsichord and other early keyboard instruments, he has recorded chamber music of C. P. E. Bach, Quantz, and Frederick the Great on the Albany Records, Naxos, and Hungaroton labels. He is a professor of music at Wagner College in New York City and is also a faculty member in the Historical Performance Program at the Juilliard School. Selections from his writings, editions, and recordings are online at faculty.wagner.edu/david-schulenberg/.

GENERAL INDEX

chords, 64, 102; and Silbermann pianos, 28;
sinfonias of, 22, 149n38, 157, 163, 165–67,
170; symphonic style of (in keyboard music),
64, 101–2; trios of, 170
Bach, Johann Christoph Friedrich ("Bückeburg Bach"), 1n2, 13, 16–17, 160, 160n70,
167n85
Bach, Johann Gottfried Bernhard, 1n2, 15–16
Bach, Johann Nicolaus, 74n170
Bach, Johann Sebastian, 2; aesthetic legacy of,
9, 11–12, 17–18, 21, 23; autograph sources
of, 4, 4nn12–13, 134–36, 136n19–20,
138n2, 139–42; and *Brandenburg Concertos*
dedication, 43–44; Breitkopf sources for the
music of, 133–37t; Collegium Musicum,
149, 149n39; concertos by, 149n39; and
counterpoint exercises, 5–6; estate of, 74,
74n170; inventions by, 95, 97, 135; keyboard instruments owned by, 62, 66n143,
74, 74n170; keyboard technique of, 89–90,
90n19; and mistaken attributions, 133; and
performance practice, 136, 136n18, *139–41,
143*; and Silbermann's pianos, 24, 68–69,
73–74; and St. Thomas cantorate, 5; transmission of organ chorales by, 133, 135n15;
visits to Berlin and Potsdam, 24–25, 42–44,
68–69, 74; and Weimar period, 4n13, 136,
136n19, *139*; and "well-regulated church
music," 21
Bach, Maria Barbara, 8, 13, 15
Bach, Regina Susanna, 167n85
Bach, Veit, 22
Bach, Wilhelm Friedemann, 8; and counterpoint exercises, 5–6; and Forkel, 69; Halle
period of, 3–6, 144, 147n33; Itzig family and, 146–47; Kirnberger and, 3, 3n8,
7, 50n81; marriage of, 8–9; new musical
sources for works by, 144–49; opera by, 7–8;
reputation and career of, 2–12 (passim), 15–
17, 21, 25, 61n125; and sale of his father's
manuscripts, 3–4, 6; and Shudi harpsichords,
53, 57, 61, 64–**66**; travels by, 6, 43n60. *See
also* Anna Amalia, Princess: as patron and
admirer of Friedemann Bach
Bach, Wilhelm Friedrich Ernst, 17, 25n1
Bach-Archiv (Leipzig), 134, 135, 135nn14–15
Bach-Gesellschaft edition, 133, 135, 135nn14–
15
Barth, Carl Friedrich, 155n61

Bartoschek, Gerd, 34n29, 35n36
basso continuo: notation of, 74, 74n172, 104;
and obbligato parts, 95n31
batteries, 84
Bebung, 74, 87, 87n10, **88**, 109n55
Becker, Carl Ferdinand, 134, 153, 169t
Beethoven, Ludwig van, 84, 99, 99n37, 102
Behrens, Stefan, 50nn82–83, 50n85, 51n86,
51n88, 78t
Benda, Franz, 26n3, 30, 30n16, 41, 153
Berg, Darrell, 84n3, 108n52
Berger, Carl Gottlieb, 161n71
Berger, Johann Friedrich, Jr. 161n71
Berlin: Carnival in, 29, 48, 75t; *Hofkapelle* of,
duties, 18, 29, 30–31, 41, 44, 56–57, 73;
Hofkapelle of, personnel, 20, 29, 73, 73n166;
Hofkonzerte in, 27, 29, 30, 47–49; house con-
certs in, 52n89; newspaper reports on music
in, 45, 47, 47n78, 68–69, 146; Russian invasion of, 13; and Seven-Years' War, 12–13.
See also *Hofoper* (Berlin); Sing-Akademie zu
Berlin
Berlin Stadtschloss, 43–49; Amalia organ at
(*see* Marx, Ernst: Amalia organ of 1755);
Comoediensaal in, 48–49; dramatic spectacles
in, 28, 48; *Hofkonzerte* in, 27, 29, 47; keyboard instruments of, 35n37, 36–37, 45–46,
49–51, 68, 71, 77t–78t, 82t; as location of
king's music soirées, 26, 45; music catalogs
of, 72n165; music rooms of, 43–46, 50–51,
61, 71; as residence of Frederick II, 43–45,
56, 75t; as residence of Margrave Christian
Ludwig of Brandenburg-Schwedt, 35–36,
36n38, 43–44; as residence of other royal
family members, 43–47, 49–50, 75t
biblical texts, 2, 21, 129
Bielfeld, Jakob Friedrich von, 32–33
Blanken, Christine, 56n102
Blasiuskirche (Mühlhausen), 15n37
Blondel, Jacques-François, 26n5
Bogenflügel (also *Bogenklavier*): debut of, at
Prussian court, 24, 47–48, 62; Emanuel
Bach's opinion of, 63; Emanuel Bach's so-
nata for, 88, 88n14; Kirnberger and, 63n130;
purchase of, at Prussian court, 62–63, 76t,
81t
Böhmer, Johann, 67n147, 76t
Breitkopf, Johann Gottlob Immanuel, 152;
correspondence of, with C. P. E. Bach, 14,

INDEX OF WORKS

A page numbers in *italics* refers to an illustration, a page number in **bold** refers to a musical example, and a page number followed by a *t* refers to a table.

Index of Works

Bach, Wilhelm Friedemann:
ORCHESTRAL WORKS (*continued*)
Fk 68 / WFB-BR C 3: Sinfonia in G Major, 147n34;
Fk 69 / WFB-BR C4: Sinfonia in G Major, 147n34;
Fk 71 / WFB-BR C 5: Sinfonia in B-flat Major, 145t, 147, 147n34, *148–49*, 152
PEDAGOGICAL STUDIES: BR-WFB I 1, No. 21a–b: Counterpoint exercises, **6**

Benda, Georg
VOCAL WORK: L 603 (*see also under* Bach, Carl Philipp Emanuel, H 821c): *Ich will den Namen des Herrn preisen* (Cantata), 127n32

Corelli, Arcangelo
CHAMBER WORK: Op. 5: Sonatas for Violin and Basso Continuo, 33

Förster, Christoph
VOCAL WORK: *Ehre sei Gott in der Höhe* (cantata), 127n32

Frederick II, King of Prussia, called "the Great"
CHAMBER WORK: Sp. 21: Sonata for Flute and Basso Continuo in A Minor, 91n21
ORCHESTRAL WORK: Sinfonia No. 3 in D Major, 101, 101n44

Goldberg, Johann Gottlieb
CHAMBER WORK: Trio Sonata for 2 Violins and Basso Continuo in D Minor, 146n29 (formerly attributed to J. S. Bach; BWV olim 1037)

Graun, Carl Heinrich
VOCAL WORKS
GraunWV B:I:6: *Rodelinda* (opera), 48;
GraunWV B:I:8:54: "Tu vuoi ch'io viva, o care" (duet from opera *Artaserse*), 97, 97n35, **98**;
GraunWV B:I:27: *Silla* (opera), 152;
GraunWV Bv:IX:7: *Das Licht scheinet in der Finsternis* (cantata), 127n30;
GraunWV Bv:IX:14: *Ich nahe mich zu deiner Krippen* (cantata), 127n30

Graun, Johann Gottlieb
ORCHESTRAL WORKS
GraunWV A:XII: Sinfonias, 153;
GraunWV A:XII:1: Sinfonia in C Major, 153;
GraunWV Av:XII:47: Sinfonia in E-flat Major, 153;
GraunWV Av:XII:57: Sinfonia in G Major, 153;
GraunWV D:XII:94: Sinfonia in C Major, 150t, 151–52, 152n49;
GraunWV D:XII:109: Sinfonia in G Major, 153;
GraunWV D:XII:111 (attribution uncertain): Sinfonia in A Major, 153

Handel, Georg Friderick
VOCAL WORKS
HWV 56: *Messiah*, 14;
HWV 56: "Ich weiß, daß mein Erlöser lebt" (aria from *Messiah*), 14;
HWV 56: Hallelujah Chorus (from *Messiah*), 14
CHAMBER WORK: HWV 388: Trio for 2 Oboes and Basso Continuo in B-flat Major, 154

Bach Perspectives
is a publication of the
American Bach Society,
dedicated to promoting the study
and performance of the music of
Johann Sebastian Bach.
Membership information is available online at
www.americanbachsociety.org.

THE BACH PERSPECTIVES SERIES

The University of Illinois Press
is a founding member of the
Association of American University Presses.

———————————————————

Composed in 10/14 Janson Text
by Jim Proefrock
at the University of Illinois Press
Manufactured by Sheridan Books, Inc.

University of Illinois Press
1325 South Oak Street
Champaign, IL 61820-6903
www.press.uillinois.edu